Critical Muslim 48

Saliha

Editor: Ziauddin Sardar

Deputy Editors: Robin Yassin-Kasab, C Scott Jordan, Zafar Malik,

Senior Editors: Aamer Hussein, Hassan Mahamdallie, Ebrahim Moosa

Reviews Editor: Shamim Miah

Poetry and Fiction Editor: Naomi Foyle

Publisher: Michael Dwyer

Managing Editor (Hurst Publishers): Daisy Leitch

Cover Design: Rob Pinney based on an original design by Fatima Jamadar

Associate Editors: Tahir Abbas, Alev Adil, Abdelwahab El-Affendi, Naomi Foyle, Marilyn Hacker, Nader Hashemi, Jeremy Henzell-Thomas, Leyla Jagiella, Vinay Lal, Iftikhar Malik, Peter Mandaville, Boyd Tonkin, Medina Whiteman

International Advisory Board: Karen Armstrong, Christopher de Bellaigue, William Dalrymple, Syed Nomanul Haq, Anwar Ibrahim, Robert Irwin, Bruce Lawrence, Ashis Nandy, Ruth Padel, Bhikhu Parekh, Barnaby Rogerson, Malise Ruthven

Critical Muslim is published quarterly by C. Hurst & Co. (Publishers) Ltd. on behalf of and in conjunction with Critical Muslim Ltd. and the Muslim Institute, London.

All editorial correspondence to Muslim Institute, Canopi, 7-14 Great Dover Street, London, SE1 4YR
E-mail: editorial@criticalmuslim.com

The editors do not necessarily agree with the opinions expressed by the contributors. We reserve the right to make such editorial changes as may be necessary to make submissions to *Critical Muslim* suitable for publication.

© Copyright 2023 *Critical Muslim* and the individual contributors.

C. Hurst & Co (Publishers) Ltd., New Wing, Somerset House, Strand, London, WC2R 1LA

ISBN:9781805260684 ISSN: 2048-8475

To subscribe or place an order by credit/debit card or cheque (pounds sterling only) please contact Kathleen May at the Hurst address above or e-mail kathleen@hurstpub.co.uk

A one-year subscription, inclusive of postage (four issues), costs £60 (UK), £90 (Europe) and £100 (rest of the world), this includes full access to the Critical Muslim series and archive online. Digital only subscription is £3.30 per month.

The right of Ziauddin Sardar and the Contributors to be identified as the authors of this publication is asserted by them in accordance with the Copyright, Designs and Patents Act, 1988.

A Cataloguing-in-Publication data record for this book is available from the British Library

Cover art: 'Saliha 1' by Zafar Abbas Malik

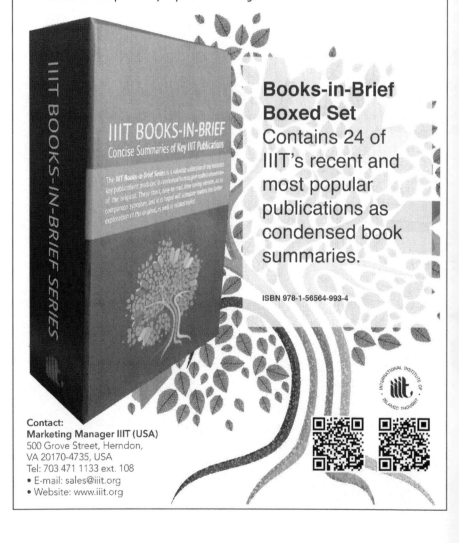

Critical Muslim

Subscribe to Critical Muslim

Now in its twelfth year in print, *Critical Muslim* is also available online. Users can access the site for just £3.30 per month – or for those with a print subscription it is included as part of the package. In return, you'll get access to everything in the series (including our entire archive), and a clean, accessible reading experience for desktop computers and handheld devices — entirely free of advertising.

Full subscription

The print edition of *Critical Muslim* is published quarterly in January, April, July and October. As a subscriber to the print edition, you'll receive new issues directly to your door, as well as full access to our digital archive.

United Kingdom £60/year
Europe £90/year
Rest of the World £100/year

Digital Only

Immediate online access to *Critical Muslim*

Browse the full *Critical Muslim* archive

Cancel any time

£3.30 per month

CONTENTS

SALIHA

Saliha n. The virtuous, the righteous, the pious, the one who does good deeds. 'And give good tidings to those who believe and do righteous deeds that they will have gardens (in Paradise) beneath which rivers flow' (the *Quran* 2: 25).

ET CETERA

SALIHA

INTRODUCTION: TRANSLATIONS AND OTHER VIRTUES

Robin Yassin-Kassab

Positive communication is a virtue by itself, aiming as it does to overcome barriers between people and thereby to increase understanding. Such communication has been the life work (so far!) of Scottish-Sudanese writer Leila Aboulela, whose first novel was called *The Translator*. It's an apt title not only for that book but, with a bit of metaphorical leeway, for Aboulela's entire oeuvre, and no doubt for Aboulela herself too. The two recurring themes linking her series of successful novels and story collections are translation – in the widest sense of the word – and conversion, which is another kind of transition between conditions. And the conversion – character development tending towards the divine – is made possible by the translation, a most virtuous form of communication.

Sammar, the first novel's heroine, is quite literally a translator from Arabic to English. A Sudanese woman living alone in Aberdeen after the death of her husband Tarig, she translates texts for Aberdeen University, and specifically for Rae Isles, lecturer in postcolonial politics. Sammar is a widow and a disoriented single parent – she's left her young son in Khartoum to be cared for by her aunt and mother-in-law Mahasen. She suffers depression, migraine, and the harshness of the Scottish weather – 'a world dim with inevitable rain'. Only her faith keeps her just about even.

Gradually, though, she falls in love with Rae. For a stretch, the text is reminiscent of a classic epistolary novel, though the letters are replaced by nightly phone calls. There is an exchange of perspectives and a meeting of minds. But the course of love does not run smooth. 'Mixed couples just don't look right, they irritate everyone,' opines Sammar's Pakistani-origin friend Yasmin. Sammar's problem with the relationship is less prejudiced, more humane, but deeper. She can only marry a Muslim, and Rae, though knowledgeable about and respectful of Islam, isn't one. For Sammar, this obstruction isn't a matter of social coercion. She lives in Scotland, not Sudan, and could ignore Sudanese social rules if she chose to. But Islam is important to her, and it's important that she marries a Muslim. Therefore she wants Rae to convert.

Rae, meanwhile, has helped her to find a translation job in Egypt. This will allow her to visit her son and aunt in Sudan. Before she leaves, she brings the tensions over the conversion issue to a head, but unsuccessfully.

The novel's next section unfolds in Khartoum. Sammar reconnects with home and her son, but Mahasen turns on her, blaming her for Tarig's death. In this strained atmosphere Sammar does some soul-searching, then prays that Rae will convert for his own sake, not for hers. Before too long, she receives the news that Ray has indeed said the *shahada*. Soon he arrives in Khartoum, and the couple arrange their marriage.

The novel is a comedy in the classical sense that the conflict in the story ends in positive resolution, and specifically in a happy marriage. Indeed, this is high-quality rom-com territory, and if Muslim women were more of a target audience for Hollywood, *The Translator* would have been adapted for the big screen long ago.

But the novel is very different to a run-of-the-mill rom-com. The answered prayer as a plot device is something not seen in the contemporary novel, except here, nor — as far as I know — in Hollywood movies.

In interviews, Aboulela has cited *Jane Eyre* as an important influence. Charlotte Bronte's novel is another comedy in the classical sense (though obviously not in terms of jokes) because the key conflict — Jane can't marry Mr. Rochester because he's already married — is resolved, and the marriage between the heroine and her beloved becomes possible. Yet the process of resolution is much gentler in *The Translator*. Bronte's Mr. Rochester is blinded in the fire which conveniently kills his wife (he is symbolically castrated, as psychoanalytic critics love to point out). He must be disabled, reduced, and in some way tamed, before he becomes a suitable husband. Rae's conversion, on the other hand, results from a process of growth. He gains in virtue, and Sammar is rewarded for virtuously holding to her religious values. They proceed, we imagine as we reach the final page, into a virtuous marriage.

Let's look again at how translation works here. What are the gaps – of language, culture and feeling – that need to be bridged?

First there is the cultural distance felt by migrants. Sammar is alienated not only by the weather in Scotland, but by the people too, people shaped in a very different context to her own. They are 'private people ... made private by cold'.

Beyond that, there is the strangeness felt between a first-generation immigrant like Sammar and second and third-generation immigrants. Sammar is more of an expatriate than an immigrant – she is rooted in the particularities of her Sudanese home. But Yasmin – that friend of Pakistani origin – defines herself, and all other brown and black people, in opposition to the majority white society around her. 'She had a habit of making general statements starting with "we", where "we" meant the whole of the Third World and its people. So she would say, "We are not like them", or "We have close family ties, not like them".'

The widest gap is that between the Islamic world and the secular west. Sammar not only translates Arabic to English but also Islam and Muslim culture (at least African-Arab Muslim culture) to Rae, and thereby to the western reader. But beyond Sammar's work, the novel itself, in its most complex move, translates Scottish/western culture as perceived by a non-western Muslim back to the western reader.

An example is Sammar's reading of a get-well card sent to Rae by his daughter: '"Get well soon, Dad," the card said and it had a picture of a bandaged bear. Sammar found the wording strange without "I wish" or "I pray", it was an order, and she wondered if the child was taught to believe that her father's health was in his hands, under his command.'

This last form of translation may constitute a productive estrangement for the western reader because cultural habits seen from a new perspective come into focus more clearly, no longer taken for granted but freshly interrogated. In this respect, the reading experience may be analogous to travelling – you see home with new eyes and learn as much about it as you do about the foreign land you're traveling through.

The second novel in this jeweled chain is *Minaret*. Moving back and forward in time as well as space, it's more formally ambitious than the first. And it presents a conversion narrative of a different sort. Here the

new Muslim isn't an ex-secular Christian but a secular, 'cultural' Muslim
who begins to take religion more seriously in exile.

Her conversion is preceded by transitions across class and culture. Najwa
is born 'an aristocrat on my mother's side with a long history of acres of
land and support for the British and hotels in the capital and bank accounts
abroad.' Her father is of more modest background, but his position as an
advisor to the Sudanese president elevates him above his peers. The family
have servants, including an Ethiopian refugee.

Najwa is torn from her comfortable milieu – the university with its
spoilt upper class and Communist middle class students, and the American
Club disco playing the Bee Gees and Bob Marley – when a coup upsets the
Sudanese power structure. Her father is arrested, charged with corruption,
and later executed.

The family flees to England, specifically to Arab west London, where its
unraveling continues. Najwa's mother sickens and dies. Her twin brother
Omar descends into drug addiction, and then to prison. So Najwa lives
alone in a small flat in Maida Vale. Steadily downwardly mobile, she
eventually finds work as a housemaid to a Sudanese-Egyptian family. All
her previous privilege has drained away. Her employer knows nothing of
Najwa's gilded life in Khartoum, and certainly doesn't consider her an
equal: 'She will always see my hijab, my dependence on the salary she gives
me, my skin colour, which is a shade darker than hers.'

Najwa pursues an unsatisfying extra-marital relationship with Anwar,
one of the Communist students from Khartoum University now studying
in London. Despite or perhaps because of his proclaimed progressive
values, Anwar fails to protect her from the unwanted attentions of his flat
mates, and mocks both her elite background and her attachment to Sudan's
Muslim culture.

One day she realises that Ramadan has started without her noticing. The
loss she feels then is a catalyst generating a deeper engagement with Islam.
She attends the Regent's Park Mosque and the women's group which
coalesces around the religious teacher Um Waleed.

Here Aboulela offers the reader unusual access to Muslim women's
spaces. 'Around us the mood is silky, tousled, non-linear; there is tinkling
laughter, colours, that mixture of sensitivity and waywardness which the
absence of men highlights.' She describes the women's pleasure in seeing

each other out of hijab, the extra levels of intimacy and knowledge this unlocks: 'It is as if the hijab is a uniform, the official, outdoor version of us. Without it, our nature is exposed.'

This commitment to outdoor conformity would usually be presented negatively by a western novelist – and by most non-western novelists too, working as they do within a secular tradition in which the struggle of the individual against the demands of society is a key thematic frame. Here, however, the public limitation imposed by the hijab is something to be celebrated. It is seen from the perspective of women who choose to wear the hijab, not as dehumanising but as life affirming.

Najwa's growing traditionalism – though her life is in no way traditional – is also presented sympathetically. She wishes her brother had been punished the first time he took drugs with one hundred lashes, according to sharia. 'I do wish it in a bitter, useless way because it would have put him off, protected him from himself.'

When she falls in love with Tamer, her employer's son, she makes the following jarring statement: 'I would like to be his family's concubine, like something out of the Arabian Nights, with lifelong security and a sense of belonging. But I must settle for freedom in this modern time.'

A lot is contained in this declaration, both a provocative, unashamed traditionalism and a self-aware, ironic recognition that the fantasy cannot be realised. The irony is underlined by use of the English, Orientalist title *the Arabian Nights* rather than the Arabic *A Thousand Nights and a Night*.

She disputes with her boyfriend Anwar, who not only sees Islamic faith as a mental weakness, but also argues that it is 'not benign': 'Look at what happened in Sudan, look at human rights, look at freedom of speech and look at terrorism. But that was exactly where I got lost. I did not want to look at these big things because they overwhelmed me. I wanted me, my feelings and dreams, my fear of illness, old age and ugliness…'

This, of course, is straightforward realism – for most Muslims, Islam isn't a political problem but something inextricable from life itself. Yet this treatment of the topic is also remarkably unusual. In the works of novelists from Muslim-majority countries as much as from the non-Muslim west, Islam is generally either ignored or employed as an antagonist. The hero must overcome the obstacles strewn in his path by Islam in order to achieve resolution.

Aboulela's writing rescues Islam from this straitjacket. And while it is certainly Islam-positive, it (fortunately) isn't proselytising. She writes novels, not pamphlets posing as novels. All the action and the ideas expressed on the page are driven first by character.

In *Minaret*, Najwa turns away from Anwar towards Tamer, who is religious like her. The reader thinks he can glimpse the happy resolution to come. But unlike the first novel, the conclusion here is not at all comedic. It's more of a question than an answer. Tamer is too young for Najwa, and too far above her socially. Rather than kick against these realities and strike out for individual fulfillment — as the heroines of most novels would — Najwa accepts her lot.

It's an intriguing and in one sense deeply unsatisfying ending, but one which engages the reader still more deeply with the troubled heroine, who continues to struggle with her desires, and with her past. By her own lights she has done the right thing. Personally, I'm not sure I agree, but I respect her perspective as I would respect that of an actual flesh and blood person. I feel that Najwa is out there still, somewhere in west London, struggling towards happiness and probably not quite finding it, but holding to the guiding rope of prayer and Muslim community as she travels.

Minaret might be my personal favourite of these books. The only thing I don't like about it is the cover (of my paperback copy, at least) which depicts a veiled woman revealing beautiful eyes. More or less the same cover can be found on dozens of novels written by Muslims or set in Muslim contexts. But *Minaret* is very distinctly different from most of those.

The next book, *Lyrics Alley*, is the first of Aboulela's historical novels. The focus moves back to 1950s Sudan, the radio age. Cotton tycoon Mahmoud Abuzeid spends his life crossing between his two wives. One is Sudanese. She lives in a traditional *hoash* and supposedly represents 'decay and ignorance … the stagnant past'. The other is Egyptian. She lives in an Italian-decorated salon, and is younger, educated, 'modern', outward looking – supposedly.

This novel isn't in any way about the immigrant experience, but it follows the emerging Aboulela thematic pattern: worlds which are foreign to each other are brought into close cohabitation, and are in need then of translation, of a translator, so that they may better understand each other: 'They belonged to different sides of the saraya, to different sides of him.

He was the only one to negotiate between these two worlds, to glide between them, to come back and forth at will.'

The story follows Abuzeid family politics against a backdrop of the geo-politics of northeast Africa between World War Two and the Free Officers' revolution in Egypt. British imperial power is waning, Egypt and Sudan are moving in separate directions, and Sudan is on the brink of independence. Change is in the air in general, and is dramatised specifically in the life of Mahmoud's son Nur. Paralysed in a swimming accident, all Nur's plans are suddenly stymied and his hopes dashed. He crashes deep into depression, but then, guided by Badr, an Egyptian teacher and a man of religion, he is able to understand his disability as a trial rather than a curse.

Nur's conversion is one of attitude or perspective as much as religion. He realises that he has been 'blessed with literacy', and embarks on a new life as a poet whose lines become lyrics in popular songs. For Nur, 'The words on the page are a mirror. They reflect his secrets and his beauty.'

Next comes *The Kindness of Enemies*, a dual narrative juxtaposing Scotland in 2010 and the Caucasus in the mid-nineteenth century, and making good use of the parallels and contrasts between the two timeframes. The book's hero is Imam Shamil, and its heroine is Princess Anna Elinichna of Georgia – both actual historical figures.

Shamil, who leads the Caucasian Muslim resistance against encroaching Russians, abducts Anna. He hopes to exchange her for hostages held by the Czar, but also wishes to restore Georgia to independence and to place Anna on its throne. As Anna, despite her captivity, comes to respect Shamil and his way of life, there are hints at potential Muslim-Christian cooperation against imperialism.

Like the Algerian Emir AbdulQader al-Jazairi – considered a founding figure of human rights discourse – Imam Shamil practiced jihad before the word was debased by its current proclaimers. These nineteenth century men understood jihad in the classical sense, as an ethical, rules-based warfare prosecuted in self-defence. They observed the Islamic moral imperatives: prisoners were treated as guests, non-combatants and surrendered troops were not to be harmed, and the physical jihad would only bear spiritual fruit if it were coupled to an inner self struggle. They were genuinely virtuous leaders. As such, their stories should be heard more often, by Muslims and non-Muslims alike.

This novel's main twenty-first century protagonist, in any case, is Natasha Hussein, an academic at Aberdeen University. Natasha's research project is 'how did this historical change in the very definition of jihad come about?' Hers is perhaps the most western of voices among Aboulela's major characters. Daughter of a mainly absent Sudanese father and a recently dead Georgian-Russian mother, she calls herself 'a failed hybrid', and writes reports for the police on her potentially radicalised Muslim students. Her situation echoes in some way that of Shamil's son Jamaleldin, taken hostage and turned into the Czar's godson, so a Russified Chechen, a Christianised Muslim. In another way, it hints at the plight of contemporary Muslim communities fallen into the gaps between cultures – because after 9/11 and 7/7, 'Many Muslims in Britain wished that no one knew they were Muslim' – and then points more generally to the predicament of second generation immigrants who 'grew up reptiles plotting to silence their parents' voices, to muffle their poor accents, their miseries, their shuffling feet, their lives of toil and bafflement, their dated ideas of the British Empire, their gratitude because they remembered all too clearly the dead-ends they had left behind.'

Natasha's development through the novel, as she studies Shamil and interacts with some of his descendants, and when she returns to Sudan after her father's death, may be understood as a very subtle and gradual process of conversion, which only begins to turn towards the religious in the final pages.

The next book, *Bird Summons*, is the most stylistically ambitious of Aboulela's novels. It returns to the human source material of the first two: that is, immigrant Muslim women in the west. The story is framed around an excursion of the Aberdeen-based 'Arabic-speaking Muslim Women's Group' to visit the tomb of the convert Lady Evelyn Cobbold, or Zainab, a real person who lived from 1867 to 1963. Arguments over the nature of the trip mean that in the end only three women actually set out. These are Salma, an Egyptian massage therapist married to a Scottish convert; Moni, Sudanese, mother to a disabled son; and Iman, a young and beautiful refugee from Syria, whose third marriage has just collapsed.

Using free indirect style, the narrative shifts smoothly and continuously between these three perspectives. Each woman has a dilemma to work out, and the journey from their familiar urban lives into the wild countryside jolts them into spiritual motion. Salma is tempted by her suddenly reappeared first love, and by an imagined alternative life in Egypt. Moni is torn between her husband, who wants her to join him in the Gulf, and her son, who needs the care he receives in Scotland. Iman struggles with self-esteem and independence, as well as her difficult relationship with the hijab.

The novel contains a great deal of magic too. A lot of the action happens in a forest. Like Shakespeare's forest of Arden, this is an arboreal realm of fluidity and change. The normal rules do not apply here, and the story is flooded by a lively symbolism, by dream scenes and Ovidian transformations. The hoopoe bird (of Farid ud-Din Attar's *The Conference of the Birds*) is a very present character, a cross-cultural spiritual guide as comfortable with Scottish fables as with Sufi lore.

Is *Bird Summons* the most 'female' of the books? It's certainly the one in which men are least present, or in which they are significant only as presences in the minds of the women. It's also a novel of middle age – though one of the focalising women is still young. It deals with the disappointments and constrictions of lives seemingly set in place, and with regret concerning doors closed and paths not taken. Like all of Aboulela's stories, it's a tale of spiritual regeneration. The plot structure it adopts is 'death and rebirth', following not only the renewal of its three major characters but hinting also at a spiritual renaissance shared even by the Scottish landscape: 'They had come to a country where people had stopped praying and not realised that they were the ones brought here to pray. They did not realise that they were a continuation, needed to fill a vacuum, awaited by the ancient forests and masses of rocks.'

This new perspective elides the distance between Scotland and Sudan, between the West and Islam. For the trees and the rocks, translation isn't necessary.

Now we arrive at Aboulela's most recent book: *River Spirit*. This is the most straightforward of her historical novels, and perhaps the most skillfully crafted too. It certainly makes compulsive reading. There are no time shifts between present and past, though there are regular shifts of perspective between a large cast of focalising characters whose stories are told sometimes in first, sometimes in third person. And there is also General Gordon – the actual historical figure – whose chapters are written in the second person, thus: 'You can be a catalyst. Your very presence on this soil will stop the Mahdi in his tracks.'

In the late nineteenth century, Sudan was ruled by Egypt, but the rulers of Egypt were actually Albanians, and they in turn were ruled by an uneasy alliance of the Ottoman and British empires. In this complex colonial context, a man claiming to be the Mahdi sparks a kind of revolution, then a civil war. On one side stand people like Azhar-educated Yassin, a lover of modernity who embodies the political pragmatism of those who benefit from the status quo. On the other side are people alienated from the status quo for reasons more economic than ideological: 'There were taxes we couldn't pay, land we farmed only to yield enough to keep us alive and the rest went to them, boys stolen to prop up their armies, girls taken for their harems.'

The last two phrases may seem to suggest that the Mahdi's uprising sought to end slavery, but the reality was much more complex. The Baggarra tribe in Kordofan are described as 'free-spirited cattle nomads whose livelihood was threatened by Gordon's insistence to end the slave trade'. In other words, some Sudanese resented British interference because it upset a long-standing and lucrative slaving economy. (This is a fault line that the reader knows will sour Sudan's future. The descendants of these Baggarra nomads would in many cases fill the ranks of the Janjaweed during the Darfur genocide in the 1990s. These flames are being rekindled once again by the warring militias in Sudan today.)

The established Aboulela themes are less clearly apparent in *River Spirit*, but still there is a (problematic) translator of a sort, the Scottish artist Charles, who paints General Gordon in two very different ways, and who purchases a black woman in the market to use as a model. The woman in question — Akuany, who becomes Zamzam — fiercely resists this representation.

Akuany's story points to the difficult cultural 'conversions' forced by slavery and empire. When, during her childhood, her village is raided, Akuany loses her home and family as well as her native tongue (Chollo). She is renamed to suit the culture of her exile. At a later stage, she finds herself in a Turkish official's harem, where the concubines aim to become pregnant, to be 'um al-walad', mother of the master's child, and thus to win their freedom. This was a common means of social mobility: '… in every Sudanese family there is a branch that trailed back to a manumitted woman who went through agony to deliver a free child.' Like Najwa, the unwillingly deracinated immigrant of *Minaret*, Akuany envies the traditional female role which is denied her. 'This was how a free woman looked and spoke,' she thinks, 'after growing up safe in a father's house and moving to that of a trustworthy husband. All through life protected and held firm. A virgin on her wedding night, chaste afterward, luxuriant in her modesty, never been whipped, never been violated.'

It would be a mistake, however, to assume that Aboulela is recommending the traditional role in any simple way. In the novel's prologue she describes Rabiha of the Kinana tribe (another historical figure) running all night, despite a snake-bitten foot, to warn the Mahdi of an enemy attack. 'With each last breath,' Aboulela writes, 'she is a rebel, striving to become more than an obedient wife.' So traditional and non-traditional perspectives compete in these novels as they do in life, and that's because Leila Aboulela is no more a dogmatist than she is a pamphleteer. The thoughts and feelings which concern her are not primarily her own, but those of her characters. Her writing is always rooted in character, and through character in the sensuous detail of life, particularly in Muslim sensory experiences – what it feels like to fast and to break a fast, to pray with others, to wear hijab – as well as in the sensory experiences of women. Here there's nothing prim or prudish in her approach.

Aboulela has been praised for writing 'halal' fiction – and certainly these are novels which Muslims will enjoy reading – but her greater achievement has been to represent Muslim women in some of their great diversity, people like my own sisters and cousins, a huge demographic which is almost never portrayed in fiction, except in stereotypical terms. Aboulela describes these women to others, gives them voice, and offers them fictions which are a mirror to themselves.

To test this out I gave a copy of *The Translator* to my sister Rula. English for Rula is a second language, so at first she read slowly. At a certain point in the reading, however, she increased her pace. 'I've never read a book like this before,' she said. 'The main character is just like me!'

She's a virtuous character, my sister. She is patient, modest, compassionate, loving, pious, open-minded, and tolerant. I think she brings out the best in me. And where, on our human level, do we find virtue, except in character, and in the relationships between characters?

Several of the essays in this *Virtues* issue of *Critical Muslim*, like Aboulela's novels, are driven by character. First among them is our editor Ziauddin Sardar's tribute to his wife Saliha, his description of their long and fruitful marriage, and his lament for Saliha's recent death.

The name 'Saliha' comes from the Arabic, meaning 'she who performs good and virtuous deeds', and this Saliha was indeed generously endowed with *'akhlaq*, the "character traits" that define a virtuous person. These virtues are spelled out in the Qur'an: humility, sincerity, patience, modesty, prudence, forgiveness, courage, love, and justice. She did not acquire these virtues. They were infused within her by the Grace of God; and enhanced by her upbringing, by the traditional setting of her family background, and by her own conscientious personality.'

Theirs was simultaneously an 'arranged' and a 'love' marriage. The relationship was intimate and idiosyncratic, intensely personal, and at the same time it involved an entire family: 'marriage in our tradition is a social act because it is not personal and individual, it never involves just two people, each alone with their own angst and dreams. Marriage is much too important to be left to the precarious dreams and delusions of a would-be bride and groom.'

Within this framework, there were strong elements of romance: 'I was always married to Saliha. Even before I was married. Even before I was born.'

It's a very powerful and moving piece of writing, both an elegy and a celebration, which traces their connection from the times when Zia, as a child, would carry Saliha on his shoulders, to the wedding night, when Saliha handed Zia a copy of 'Intermediate Biology' (there's a great deal of humour here too). The narrative continues through their shared life, first in Jeddah, then London, as children are born, friends are made, projects are begun, and books are written.

Saliha, Zia writes, was 'the invisible but ever present co-author of all my works'. The 'behind every great man is a great woman' line is often delivered as a cliché, whether it's true or not. In this case, it was certainly true, and noticeable, as I can attest. I didn't really know Saliha, but I attended a few *Critical Muslim* editorial meetings in her home. As Zia jumped about, laughing, complaining, and provoking those present, Saliha oiled the social wheels with encouraging smiles as much as cups of tea, and with the occasional cutting comment too. The two characters balanced and complemented each other. And Zia reports very accurately when he writes: 'those who were privileged enough to meet Saliha instantly noticed the calm, the grace, and the inner and outer beauty that emanated from her.'

In its mature years their relationship settled into 'joyful sets of choreographed routines', but was in the end violently interrupted by Saliha's sudden illness and death. The narration of this episode is full of the kind of raw human emotion recognisable to anyone who has experienced profound loss. Finally, the essay describes Saliha's absence, and also her perpetual presence. Because Zia experienced Saliha's presence after her death.

The late Sinéad O'Connor experienced absent presences too. As a child undergoing terrible abuse at her mother's hands, she once saw Jesus, and another time the Holy Spirit manifested as a 'small, white, very misty cloud'. Scornful materialists will put such experiences down to the tricks played by traumatised brains, but as Naomi Foyle's essay points out, 'consciousness studies remain resistant to materialist reductionism.'

Foyle describes Sinéad O'Connor/ Shuhada' Sadaqat as 'a wounded healer who succumbed to her wounds,' as well as 'a riveting artist, a powerful voice of protest, a modest and private benefactor to many, a proud single mother, and a courageous role model who spoke openly about her many physical and mental health difficulties.'

What's unusual in this essay is its attention to the singer as 'a punk liberation theologist'. This is an entirely logical treatment of Sinéad's tortured, generous life, but not one I've seen written anywhere before. Sinéad bore witness to the abuses of the Catholic Church, and paid a great price for it. But still she took Christianity very seriously, and engaged deeply with Rastafarianism, and in the end converted to Islam, taking on the name Shuhada', meaning 'martyrs' or 'witnesses'. Throughout her life, she kicked against corrupt religiosity while working to 'rescue God from religion'.

Aamer Hussein's essay, on the other hand, describes a woman – Muhammadi Begum, 'the first woman of letters in Urdu literature' – who worked to rescue other women from lives confined to the women's quarters. For her, 'virtue, in the sense of an honourable, upright existence' encompassed 'the values of a traditional household while moving beyond its boundaries'.

And Ebrahim Moosa's essay focuses on the virtuous character most often referred to by Muslims – the Prophet Muhammad, whose 'open secret was his embodiment of virtue.' Moosa finds a certain lack of virtue in contemporary Muslims, even as their praise of the Prophet passes the borders of logic. 'Often expectations soar,' he writes, 'when believers lack in work, labour, and aspiration. His twenty-first century devotees expect him and his teachings to answer every question from the solution to poverty to quantum mechanics and physics. Few pay attention to the history and humanity of the Prophet Muhammad. His true virtue lies in him being a mortal with high standards.'

Are these high standards culturally determined, or are they universal amongst all humans, even amongst the higher mammals? Colin Tudge, in his essay "The Bedrock Virtues", asks 'what qualities *in fact* are widely recognised as "virtues". From there we might reverse engineer and seek to discover what those virtues have in common, and get some further insight into what virtue actually *is*.' Following this reverse engineering, Tudge finds that 'among the plethora of candidates, just three are outstanding. They are: compassion, humility and the sense of Oneness. All three are at the core of all the great religions and of many traditional, "indigenous" religions too.'

Jeremy Henzell-Thomas continues the search for common ground. His essay here, "Virtuous Words" launches an etymological investigation of 'virtue' alongside a survey of Greek, Roman, Christian and Islamic approaches to the concept. He finds that moderation – etymologically as well as conceptually connected to modesty – is a key Islamic virtue.

This returns us to the notion of balance, of crucial importance in the Islamic tradition – the Muslims, after all, are 'a middle people' – and also a crucial factor in successful human relationships. Zia describes his relationship with Saliha thus: 'She provided a counterbalance to my obvious shortcomings. I tend to be a little – some will say quite a lot – arrogant. But Saliha was totally selfless; humility positively shone in her. My patience is rather limited. In contrast, she seemed to have patience in abundance.'

May we all increase in virtue. May we all find other humans to balance our vices and to create in partnership a virtuous whole. And may our cultures, in dialogue with other cultures, arrive at a virtuous common ground.

PERFORMATIVE TEACHINGS OF THE PROPHET MUḤAMMAD

Ebrahim Moosa

In the Muslim imaginary, both in the popular version and the learned genre, the Prophet Muhammad is remembered as the paragon of virtue. Panegyrics and praise poetry, theological treatises, and cosmological theories assign to him the eternal status of prophethood. As a famous prophetic report (*hadith*) puts it: 'I was already a prophet when Adam was between water and clay.' In other words, for Muslims, the Prophet Muhammad had a cosmic existence that preceded Adam's actuality in the world.

Yet, few can dispute that Muḥammad, the son of ʿAbdullāh, the messenger of God whose hands shaped a world-making people among the Arabs in the seventh century, led by example and character. Only a person of character whose determination was steeled by a divinely inspired proclamation could manage to successfully will the transformation of his society from polytheism to monotheism, from injustice to justice, and from an inward-looking people to an *umma* who set their eyes on the world beyond their region. Only a leader who could inspire people by example could initiate an impulse, followed by continuous momentum whose effects were felt far beyond its rugged borders. Within a century the Umayyad dynasty vied with pre-existing civilisations and empires for worldly pre-eminence as well as salvation in the hereafter. The Prophet Muhammad's transformative impulse was at the time felt in cultures near and far, and with the passing of fourteen centuries, no continent is left untouched by the presence of Islam. The Prophet Muhammad's open secret was his embodiment of virtue. In the words of the Qur'an the Prophet Muhammad is a moral archetype, 'an excellent exemplar' (*uswa ḥasana*) (33:21) and the bearer of a 'a strong character' (*khuluq* ʿaẓīm) (91:4). Āʿisha, his wife, when asked about his character, famously and promptly said, 'his character was the embodiment of the Qur'an.'

Specialised writings on the Prophet's virtues constitute a genre of literature that is hard to summarise and difficult to quantify. But they amount in the tens of thousands and in every conceivable language Muslims use.

Vocabularies of Virtue in Islam

What does it mean that the Prophet is the embodiment of the Qur'an? The Qur'an consists of accounts of past communities of faith as well as those who rejected faith. It portrays the horrors of the Day of Judgement when humankind will flee each other, each seeking their own path from perdition. It previews the heavenly gifts for those who recognised God in the world and followed divine commandments. It talks about prophets and angels, articulations of God's will and actions with peoples over time in broad brushstrokes and at times with fine detail. God's retribution and reward are two motifs, but it contains many more stories of God's beneficence and unlimited mercy to humanity. All of this is a prelude for the reader of the Qur'an and a follower of the Prophet Muhammad to become a member of the 'party of God' (ḥizbullāh). Admission to the 'party of God' requires the moral subject internalise good conduct and virtue.

It is no exaggeration to say that the call to virtue is repeatedly made in the Qur'an, in the reports of the Prophet Muhammad, and in the myriads of writings of Muslims, especially the traditions of practice of sufism and a range of popular religious practices. The Prophet Muhammad's virtue is captured in poetry, art, architecture, music, song, even the rhythmic dance of the dervishes, leave alone the extraordinary and abundant intellectual, scholarly, edificatory, and historical writings, detailing his virtues and their impact on the human soul in innumerable languages of the world.

Vocabularies abound to articulate the notion of virtue in all Muslim core languages of practice and reflection. Most popular is the ṣ-l-ḥ root word used in the Qur'an for the male who does good, ṣāliḥ or the female, ṣāliḥa who performs good and virtuous deeds. This root word and its variants occur around 182 times in the Qur'an. Often the translation 'pious' or for ṣāliḥ and 'pious deeds' for ṣāliḥat do not capture the full impact of the expression. The ṣ-l-ḥ Arabic root is rich in its performative mode, as a verb or noun, for it accomplishes things through acts and deeds. The variants of this word are plenty which include making peace, ṣulḥ, the one who makes things good and reformed, *muṣliḥ,* and hence reforming and mending the world is called *iṣlāḥ,* just as an individual also mends their ways from heedlessness to conscientiousness. 'Those who perform *ṣāliḥāt,* virtuous or wholesome deeds from among men and women, and have faith, shall enter paradise and will not be wronged one fleck.' (4: 124). Many verses reinforce this same teaching that wholesome and virtues deeds are indeed those that are favoured by God.

Another key vocabulary is the word *iḥsān,* derived from the Arabic root *ḥ-s-n* for beauty. When *ḥ-s-n* is used in *iḥsān,* it means to perform beautifully and excellently. Often this concept is used in conjunction with 'faith' *(īmān),* with 'surrender' *(islām),* with God-consciousness *(taqwā)* and with the performance of wholesome or virtuous deeds *(al-ʿamal al-ṣāliḥ)* in many verses of the Qur'an. But the crux of *iḥsān* is captured in a portion of the report of Jibril (Gabriel) who appears to the Prophet as a visitor who asks a series of questions. Among the questions asked: 'What is *iḥsān?*' To which the Prophet replies: 'That you worship God as if you see God. And if you are not able to see God, know that God sees you.'

The pinnacle of beauty and bliss in Islam is to be in the presence of the Divine. Devoutly worshipping God is only a prelude to the perfection of beauty. The crowning perfection of sublime beauty will only be possible in the hereafter when humans will be gifted to behold the visage of the Divine. Thus, to be virtuous means to internalise the beatific attributes of God in one's soul and body. Worshiping God *as-if* one sees the Divine is a means to gain that deep and intimate consciousness of God in one's life.

The Stage

If Muslims salute and emulate the character of the Prophet, then their adversaries in faith and the political enemies of the Prophet of Islam, from ancient to modern times, all regularly assault his character. If any human being has been judged, misunderstood and whose character has been subject to mischief, and I daresay a subject of great envy because his followers adore him so, then it is the Prophet of Islam.

Critics and devotees, champions and detractors make one common and fatal error: they either judge the man unfairly or, expect him to be a man who should resonate with their times, especially in modern time. Just as his seventh-century impatient Meccan foes expected him to provide them with a one-shot manufactured book of revelation, so too do people today expect him to meet their sometimes-unreasonable expectations. Often expectations soar when believers lack in work, labour, and aspiration. His twenty-first century devotees expect him and his teachings to answer every question from the solution to poverty to quantum mechanics and physics. Few pay attention to the history and humanity of the Prophet Muhammad. His true virtue lies in him being a mortal with high standards. We ought to point out that his character and virtues preceded his experience with the ineffable and miraculous revelations he announced to the world. Revelations which no doubt infused the world, and inspired the ever-expanding community of Muslims for over fourteen hundred years.

The Arabian Prophet was a magnificent being who never hid his vulnerabilities. Scared and overwhelmed by his first revelations around 610—given his encounter with a supernatural being in the cave of Ḥirā— who asked him to recite like the poets and soothsayers of his culture. After that experience he hastened to his trusted friend, partner, and wife Khadīja. To her he confessed his distress and confusion following that experience. It turns out that the figure was an angel who asked him to 'recite' like persons of wisdom, virtue and character were expected to do. In other words, they were expected to say something profound. What involuntarily came out of his mouth was: 'Recite! Recite in the name of thy Lord who created....'

Perplexed by this experience, he detailed his encounter to Khadija. With her help he consulted other folks who consoled him and explained that his experience was a sign. Indeed, it was an encounter with a divine emissary, the archangel Gabriel, as tradition taught. Khadīja validated his experiences, comforting him, shrouding him, and cradling his perplexed body and soul. She did so in the most delicate and subtle manner as recounted in some of the most touching accounts in the traditions. She reassured him that the image that haunted him for some time was indeed an angel - a source of enrichment and divine comfort. He had no reason to fear. It is an extraordinary account of an Arab man in a patriarchal society who so effortlessly relies on his wife's wisdom, in what becomes the decisive and life-altering moments in the life of Muhammad, the son of Abdullāh, who will from that moment be known to his followers and the world as Muhammad Rasūlullah, Muhammad the Messenger of Allah. Khadija not only consoled him, but became the first to testify to his truthfulness and to accept his proclamation and mission. For all intents and purposes, she was the first mortal to anoint him as God's Chosen One, al-Muṣṭafā. By the Prophet's own words, her passing during his last years in Makka was an irreparable loss. Later wives of the Prophet were deeply envious of the reverence and dedication to her memory he continued to show in his life.

The Prophet is later reminded in passages of the Qur'an of these events in cryptic form:

> 'O you enwrapped one in robes
> Keep vigil the night, except a little
> (a half of it, or diminish a little, or add a little)
> And chant the Qur'an very distinctly
> Behold, we shall cast upon you a weighty word.' (73: 1-5)

Further revelations say:

> 'O you shrouded in your mantle
> Arise and warn!
> Your Lord magnify
> Your clothes purify
> And defilement flee!' (74: 1-5)

The Context

If one cannot understand the Prophet Muḥammad as a seventh century man in the urban-rural setting of Makka and Medina, then much is lost. Two aspects of his persona are interwoven. One must be able to hold together in one articulation the soaring, elevating and brilliant prophetic imagination of his revelations, on the one hand, and the everyday events, basic and elementary ethical and moral practices that reveal the Messenger's true character, on the other. Failing to keep those threads of context, supernatural divine speech, everyday advice and mundane practices as a seamless unity, then the extraordinary character and virtue of the Prophet will escape you. Practices and behavior patterns are literally welded into the terrain, culture, and experiences of Arabia. If you miss that, you miss everything. If you are looking for a modern man in the teachings of a seventh-century Prophet, you are frustrating yourself and completely upending the Muslim experience. For Muslims experienced the Prophet differently in every age without distorting the record.

Think about his reality and how he himself had to adapt to change. For nearly a decade after announcing prophecy in Makka he was married to a single wife, Khadija. At her death, his closest and dearest friend Abu Bakr entreated him to bestow upon his family the honour of family ties, and proposed that the Prophet marry Āʾisha, at the time a very young daughter of his friend. Custom and friendship demanded that he comply. The marriage was not consummated till Āʾisha reached her teens. This marriage has created great consternation and controversy among moderns, but especially Islam and Muslims' modern religious foes cast all kinds of aspersions. The modern faithful are also unable to grasp the different eras in history in which experiences were very different. Intriguingly not a single of the Prophet's Makkan political foes thought such a marriage to be a violation of the morals of the time. Recall they left no stone unturned to harass and besmirch him. As his stature as a political figure grew in Medina, the Prophet needed to consolidate political affiliations with the various tribes and clans under his banner now as Messenger of God. Marriages with women, almost all of them widows or divorcees, allowed him to consolidate such kinship ties. These social relations helped to tie his prophetic and political roles into a differentiated, but singular authority. Such practices of political marriages were *de rigueur*. If he did not act according to the social norms at the time, it would have been viewed as odd and possibly chalked up as a political deficit.

He had only one slave, but early in his prophetic ministry he freed him. Violating sacred rules such as deliberately breaking your fast or breaking an oath involved penalties, and often one of the options was to free a slave. Yet he did not outlaw slavery in a society enmeshed in a slave economy, as most of the world was at the time. But he pointed to what was a better practice and option. Women were by all accounts given better rights and duties under Islam compared to the pre-Islamic dispensation, but marriage equality was not a priority. Marriage bonds together with stipulated rights and duties could be transacted, but male authority had a greater role in the moral economy of the marriage consistent with the norms of patriarchy. Changes in these and other social and moral practices were malleable and alterable by the changing moral economies and political theologies Muslim societies and communities adopted over time. What were acceptable practices in Arabia were viewed differently in later times and were easily replaced with newer practices. Hence, the Prophet expected and required his community to cultivate thought and understanding (*fiqh* and *tafaqquh*) for the purposes of their evolving needs.

Even the lives of prophets were not without tenderness and the human touch. At times he had to adopt a different standard for himself and his closest family. When his daughter Fatima, who felt overburdened by domestic chores, asked her father to assign her a slave, he declined her request. Most people of average means owned slaves at the time. If he felt at times that he could not hold his society to the higher standard he personally aspired to, given that such change might cause social upheaval, the Prophet had no hesitation in holding himself and his immediate family to a higher standard. Most likely, he denied Fatima the help of a slave for this reason.

Again, he and other persons of means and social standing often married more than one wife. But when his son-in-law and cousin Ali expressed a wish to marry another wife alongside Fatima, the Prophet's emotions as a father who cared for his daughter's emotional wellbeing tenderly surfaced. 'Fatima is part of me,' he agonisingly announced. 'What hurts her, hurts me,' he added. 'Ali got the hint and abandoned his plans to marry a second wife.

Narratives

Beautiful narratives of realist and believable proportions are recounted in the prophetic traditions, the hadith literature, a rich resource often neglected. Hadith reports are perhaps the best resource for the anthropology of early Islam and the shape of the psychology of the early Muslim community, providing glimpses of the mindset of the Prophet's closest friends and family. Failing to give attention to these narratives, I believe, is to lose a sense of proportion of how the Prophet interacted with his community. But more importantly, we miss a sense of the two-way interaction between the Prophet and his people. I agree with the scholar Ali A. Mian on the need to enlarge what he called the 'ethnographic imagination' to better study and understand the person of the Prophet.

Hadith collector and scholar Muḥammad bin Ismāʿīl al-Bukhārī (d.870) provides an account of a very routine interaction between the Prophet and

'Ali, the cousin of the Prophet married to Fatima. It appears that the Prophet was trying to wake 'Ali and Fatima to perform the optional early morning prayers. These prayers are called *tahajjud*, to keep a vigil at night, before morning breaks. This is how Bukhārī narrates it, with some editing for clarity.

> 'Ali b. Abi Talib, may God be pleased with him, said: 'The Messenger of Allah, came to me and Fatima, may God be pleased with her, at night and woke us both for prayers.' He ['Ali] said: The Prophet then went back [to his home] and then prayed for a long portion of the night.' He ['Ali] said: 'He did not hear us being awake.' ... 'So he [the Prophet] returned to us and woke us again.' The Prophet then said: 'Rise you two and pray.' 'I sat up,' 'Ali said, 'and rubbed my eyes, and I said [to the Prophet]: 'We, by Allah, will not pray except what God had decreed for us. Nevertheless, our souls are in the hands of Allah. If Allah willed to make us rise, we would have risen!' 'Ali said: 'The Prophet, on whom be peace, then turned back, and on turning back was hitting his thigh and repeating the phrase: *'And humans are contentious in most things'.'* (18:54). Another report states the Prophet repeated, the phrase 'Ali used: 'We will not pray except what God had decreed for us.' 'We will not pray except what God had decreed for us.

This is such an unusually beautiful and touching account. It shows the Prophet's care and inspiring nature. He urges his immediate family to perform additional devotions. Part of his reasoning is perhaps that his family should adhere to a higher standard. But 'Ali's free-spirited nature is also on display here and so is their human and natural interaction. Whatever 'Ali's personal reasons might have been for not doing the optional prayers on that night, he had a witty reply for the Prophet while rubbing his eyes. 'We, by Allah, will not pray except what God had decreed for us,' he said. Even the Prophet might have been amused by this quick-witted reply, for he slapped his thigh and repeated 'Ali's words. You almost visualise how the Prophet both surprised and amused at 'Ali's reply is engaged in thought about what just transpired and spontaneously the words of the Qur'an *'And humans are contentious in most things'* came to his mind. I think this is a moment of irony, not judgment, following the repartee with his son-in-law. In fact, I almost get the feeling the Prophet is impressed with 'Ali's reply and hence slapped his thigh and repeated the answer he received, and possibly did so with a smile on his lips.

The Source

Biographers and especially experts in prophetic reports (*muḥaddithūn*) have a very human and humane grasp of the temperament and psychology of the Prophet, and most do so without exaggerating his virtues. To his credit, the legendary collector of hadith, al-Bukhari – who provides a treasure of reports most highly revered by Sunni Muslims after the Qur'an – in his authoritative collection, dedicates a *Book on the Merits and Virtues of the Prophet*. It brims with subtleties and insights on how the Messenger of Islam presented himself to the world and how he was observed by others. Browsing through Bukhari's *Book of Virtues*, one notices how the collector painstakingly plots for ethical and historical continuity between pre-Islam and Islam. Very early in the *Book of Virtues* Bukhari shares the following report.

> The Prophet said: 'People are akin to mines: the best of them in pre-Islam are also the best in Islam. But more so when they dedicate themselves to gain moral insight. You will find the best people among them to strongly dislike seeking leadership.'

Several elements shine through this wisdom-filled simile.

First, think of the rich imagery involved in the wording of the Prophet in describing humans to be the repositories of something precious like mines and quarries. Extraordinary eloquence was indeed among the many virtues of the Prophet, as many accounts attest. Not only is the high standard of eloquence evident in his speech, but his revelation, the Qur'an, is the epitome and inimitable (*iʿjāz*) standard in style and presentation. Eloquence among the Arabs was viewed as a gift from the unseen world. The ability to express ideas clearly with an economy of words was a highly valued trait by the Arabs. A short and pithy expression is both memorable and easy to recall from memory. For this reason, tradition remembers the Prophet Muhammad as being gifted with an 'all-comprehensive diction' (*jawāmiʿ al-kalim*).

Second, ponder the words used in the simile: humans are like 'quarries' or 'mines.' These sources of essential minerals or valuable stones and metals are permanent features on the earth's surface. Ibn Ḥajar al-ʿAsqalānī (d.1449), possibly the most noted commentator and authority on the *Sound Book of Bukhari*, displays a capacious comprehension of the imagery of 'quarries' or 'mines.' In his reading, this analogy means humans are analogous to being 'different sources' of richness and value, just as mines offer a variety of precious minerals and metals. Like we value sources of material wealth, similarly human beings too are valued for their diverse talents, gifts, and abilities. The Prophet Muhammad does not only assume humans are different in his teaching, but indeed he valued the fact that difference was strength. What is essential about humans is their character and the inherent goodness evident in all people, all things being equal: these qualities are viewed as a fortune in and of itself, qualities that a new faith values and appreciates. But the take home wisdom is that even devotees of a polytheistic faith are carriers of character. Islam and the Prophet rather valued the good things that already existed in people and human society and worked with those resources to make a new community.

Third, it is known from the history of Islam that those people who excelled in their pre-Islamic way of life were the human capital the Prophet sought out at every opportunity. He often yearned and hoped that such talented people would become part of his faith community. At an early and rather dark and challenging period of Islam in Makka, the Prophet prayed asking God to strengthen his community with one of two highly noted people in the city. One was Abū al-Ḥakam, who later attained infamy as Abū Jahal, 'Father of Ignorance,' since he made no secret of his loathing of Islam and the Prophet. The other was 'Umar Ibn al-Khaṭṭāb who at first was equally villainous towards the first Muslims, but later converted and occupied a distinguished place in Muslim history. The Prophet understood the good in people to be transferable. Virtue and the good, the Prophet taught, is not a monopoly of Muslims. Like wisdom, wherever you find the good, you are encouraged to espouse it.

Fourth is the condition under which the gift of good character is forever nourished: if humans cultivate thinking, understanding and insight, captured in the simple and frequently used Arabic word *fiqh*. The report, says: *idhā faqihū or faquhū*, 'when people gain understanding.' *Fiqh* is possibly the most glibly used word in Islamic discourse but often the most poorly understood concept. It immediately evokes the notion of applied Islamic law, which is clearly one use. At a fundamental and more significant level, *fiqh* even as a set of derivative rules entails reasoning and effort (*al-raʾy wa 'l-ijtihād*). Understanding involves 'inquiry and reflection,' says the lexicographer and theologian, Mīr Sayyid Sharīf al-Jurjānī (d. 1414).

The implication is that persons with good character and virtue cannot merely rest on their laurels or parade their good character topped with superficial piety. The Prophet aspired for a community gifted with rich and diverse integral human endowments, but these should be continuously nourished with thinking, inquiry, and reflection. Early Muslims grasped the importance of thinking, reflection, and interpretation. In the tenth century, the poet Abū Ṭayyib al-Mutanabbī (d. 965) mocked those Muslims who followed religion in unthinking ways. Aware that some traditions encourage men to pluck or trim their lip hairs as a sign of cultural distinction, others viewed it almost as an article of faith. Mutanabbi, in lines dripping in unrelenting sarcasm, criticised that attitude:

> Is the sole purpose of religion that you pluck your moustaches?
> What a sorry community (*umma*) whose display of ignorance embolden other
> peoples to mock them.

Sceptics might say nothing has changed, but that is an aside. The moral of the story is this: without intellectual vigilance, even the best talented human community can flounder. Persons with superb character and integrity can easily become dupes and fools, if thinking is not cultivated. The precondition in the prophetic report is crucial: not only is Islam in search of people with virtue and character, but the same people should also be capable of thinking. Otherwise, they become naïve and holy fools, a liability to humanity. Islam, German philosopher and cultural critic, Friedrich Nietzsche (1884-1900), concluded in *The Anti-Christ*, savoured the senses and celebrated nobility since 'it owed its origins to manly instincts, because it said Yes to life even in the rare and exquisite treasures of Moorish life!' From the teaching of the Prophet discussed here, it is evident that the Arabian Prophet taught his community to be intelligent and noble at the same time. Just as he expected that they should be world-affirming but equally in awe of accountability in the afterlife, all in one single seamless teaching.

Fifth, virtues and the character of people do not change from the pre-Islamic period to the Islamic era, the Prophet taught. The adoption of Islam rather changes their life purpose and the meaning and end of their lives. For at its core, virtue is synonymous to dignity and nobility of character truly affirmed by Islam. The prophetic analogy of humans being precious sources is apt. Once precious metals or stones like diamonds are extracted from the depths of the earth, their qualities do not change. Rather the lustre of precious stones and metals only increase with further refinement and polishing. So too is the case with virtue. The Prophet of Islam recognised the excellent qualities in people even though they worshipped a deity that was antithetical to his invitation to a monotheistic God. It is an extraordinary trait of the Prophet Muhammad to see past the false ideology the Makkans pursued, but he never gave up on them as human beings, as persons of excellence and nobility of character. Nobility in character in turn attracts and stresses the virtues of generosity, chastity, restraint, and other valued qualities. Together these serve as a bulwark against negative qualities such as miserliness, corruption, and injustice. Muslims call excellent and valuable qualities 'beautiful character or morality – *maḥāsin al-akhlāq*'.

Sixth, there is humility in the coils of virtue, with the result that people of character shy away from promiscuous and ambitious plots to seize leadership at any cost. The reason the virtuous are reluctant, explains ʿAsqalānī, is due to their acute sense of the burden of responsibility and the challenges they would encounter as leaders especially when enforcing justice and mobilising people to counter oppression and injustice. Persons of intelligence and faith, added ʿAsqalānī, grasp and shudder at the burden of responsibility. Often ambitious persons, minus talent and humility vie to attain authority and leadership without serving the greater purpose of the well-being of the umma as their primary task. Most times leadership is a parade of mega-egotistical proportions, where self-gratification takes priority over the improvement of the conditions of the people who are being ruled.

If one word summarises both the essence of the teachings of the Qurʾan and the life, practice, and teachings of the Prophet of Islam, then it is the need to pursue good deeds, in short, virtues. Virtues are embedded in the soul which become manifest in the heart, mind, and body. Virtues can come naturally just as they can be acquired, inculcated, and internalised. It comes with practice. Virtue and wisdom are very intimate. A famous prophetic tradition teaches: 'Oh people! Do not give wisdom to those who are undeserving, for then you oppress wisdom. Do not deny wisdom to the deserving, for then you will oppress them'. It is a delicate balance to navigate the path of virtue. But its achievement is infinitely rewarding.

SALIHA

Ziauddin Sardar
Illustrated by Zafar Malik

1.

'Meri jaan'.

That's what I called her. When she was anxious or concerned about something: *meri jaan*, my life, my love. I would put my arms around her. She was not a natural hugger. Her first reaction would be to hold back. But once I clasped and held her firmly, she would calm down; her worries would melt away. We would become one. A single life.

Usually, she was Begum. It was, as I was eventually to discover, part of her name. Her birth certificate has her name as 'Saliha Begum'. It is an honorific given to Muslim women of high social or cultural standing in South Asia. Sometimes it is just added to the first name without a solid reason. In Saliha's family there are many Begums. Her mother and aunts are Begums. But by the time she got married, and had Sardar added to her name, Begum had been dropped. Her first passport, issued in Multan, Pakistan, on 27 December 1977, has Saliha Basit (her father's name) written underneath her photograph in blue ink, with Sardar added in black, as though an afterthought. But I called her Begum: she was my Begum, my queen, my wife, my beloved, who elevated my position, gave honour and dignity to my life.

My nephews and nieces, and some younger members of our extended family, called her 'Dulhan' – Bride. When we were getting married, my nephew, Atif, who was two years old, asked: who is the woman sitting on the podium, wrapped in red garments. She is the Dulhan, he was told. He, and other children present at the wedding, started to call her Dulhan. The appellation stuck.

But she was appropriately named, and was always Saliha – the virtuous one. It is a Qur'anic term that also means righteous, pious and just. In its different forms, the word occurs a hundred times in ninety-eight verses of the Qur'an. Saliha personified righteousness. She was, according to the Qur'an, one who 'does righteous deeds and has faith' (16:97). For her, wealth and consumerism were nothing more than 'allurements of the life of this world'. She was interested in 'the things that endure' (18: 46).

'Things that endure' were the virtues that were deeply engrained in her. She embodied what in Muslim history and circles is called *akhlaq*, the 'character traits' that define a virtuous person. These virtues are spelled out in the Qur'an: humility, sincerity, patience, modesty, prudence, forgiveness, courage, love, and justice. She did not acquire these virtues. They were infused within her by the Grace of God, and enhanced by her upbringing, by the traditional setting of her family background, and by her own conscientious personality. She provided a counterbalance to my obvious shortcomings. I tend to be a little – some will say quite a lot – arrogant. But Saliha was totally selfless; humility positively shone in her. My patience is rather limited. In contrast, she seemed to have patience in abundance. Her humility combined with her modesty. But modesty for her was not about hijab or how you dress. (Hardly any women in her family wore the hijab). The outward manifestation of modesty was limited to her *dupputas*, which she wore like a shawl, covering her head and shoulders. Being a traditional woman, she did not really like to hug. There was always an initial reluctance even to hug her husband. 'You can just as well love me from some distance', she would say. Modesty was about how you lived, and she lived frugally, hated any kind of waste, shunned extravagance, and never, never overindulged herself. Moderation defined her lifestyle. I can be harsh, particularly when dealing with annoying folks. She was as gentle as a dove, and never had a bad word for anyone.

She was not an intellectual. But she symbolised the rare and unfashionable virtue of prudence, the cerebral virtue that connected and gave meaning to all her other virtues. For Saliha, it was not good enough to know what is the right thing to do. She *felt* what was the right thing to do, what was the right way to do it, and when she should do it. She had an inner moral compass that not only enabled her to reflect, judge and act, but to do all this within the framework of traditional Islamic ethics and morality. I tend to emphasise reasoning at the expense of feeling, and, as such, am an abridged individual. Saliha was a holistic, integrated person who could think and feel what was the right thing to do and did it without reserve. She had a living awareness of reality beyond her material existence.

Every now and then, she got angry. She was always pining for children. She was unhappy that I wasn't always there when she needed me. But most of all she was livid about the discrimination she saw around her, the ever-present injustices of the world. She would get frustrated when she could not articulate her feelings. In frustration, she would exclaim: 'Is there no limit to the greed of some people?'. 'Why can't the refugees be treated like human beings?'. 'When will the suffering of the Palestinians end?'. The questions were often thrown in my direction, and she expected a satisfactory answer. 'But Begum', I would plead, 'it's not my fault that the refugees are being treated so badly.' 'I am not responsible for the war in Ukraine!' 'I am not responsible for the actions of the Israelis.' Of course, the replies were never satisfactory. Her standard retort would be: *'loog insan naheen han'* – people are not human. *'Ham main insan bana hay'* – we have to become human. Her anger was often directed towards me. But I knew that her inner disposition was always oriented to a greater good. She saw justice as our obligation to all others. Everyone had value independent of our own interests. They had to be treated with equality, compassion, and love, and embraced as though they were an integral part of us. They were *us*.

Despite her anger at the injustices she saw all around her, those who were privileged enough to meet Saliha instantly noticed the calm, the grace, and the inner and outer beauty that emanated from her.

2.

I first met Saliha, my mother once told me, when I was seven.

In those days, most of my extended family lived in Bahawalnagar, a town just east of the Sutlej river, the longest of the five rivers that flow through the crossroads of Punjab – the land of the five waters. Saliha's parents lived with their parents, and other members of the large family, in a two-bedroom house in the centre of the town, towards the end of the Railway Bazaar, the main street. The family had arrived in Bahawalnagar after partition, and the traumas of the perilous migration – during which members of family faced riots, attacks, were lost, presumed dead, and found – were fresh and deep.

Upon his arrival in Pakistan, Saliha's father, Abdul Basit Khan, immediately enrolled in the Air Force. He served for twelve years, and then resigned because of 'beard issues'. He joined the local police department but could not tolerate the corruption he saw all around him and left after a couple of years. Finally, he became Secretary of the Union Council to the District of Bahawalnagar. Her mother, Zubaida Begum, became the principal of a nearby primary school, where she remained until her retirement. Basit and Zubaida married in their late teens, as traditional families tended to do, and in some cases still do.

They lived in the house of Abdul Raziq Khan – known to all as Nana, Grandfather, although sometimes I called him Dada – who was a noted pre-partition judge in Punjab. His elder brother, Abdul Khaliq Khan, served as a minister to the Nawab of Hyderabad. And, his maternal uncle, Maloof Khan, was an internationally famous hunter. But all that was in 'India'; the illustrious family history became irrelevant in Pakistan. Abdul Raziq Khan had trained as a *hakim* – an Islamic physician and doctor, who, as the Arabic term suggests, is also a wise and learned person. So, he opened his surgery in Railway Bazaar and started practicing. Eventually he became a celebrated 'Hakim Sahib' of Bahawalnagar. Saliha was born in Hakim Sahib's house on 29 January 1958. She was the eldest and the only daughter of Abdul Basit Khan and Zubaida Begum, who had four sons after her: Abdul Majid Khan, Abdul Wajid Khan, Abdul Qadar Khan, and Abdul Mumin Khan.

I lived with my parents in Dipalpur, an ancient town about eighty miles north of Bahawalnagar. It was the first place my father thought he could replant himself after his long and perilous journey from India. We shared our modest dwelling with my mother's youngest brother, Shahid. When the news of Saliha's birth reached Dipalpur, the whole family, which by now also included my sister, Huma, then three years old, got on a bus to see the newly born. It was perhaps one of the most dangerous journeys of my life. It took about five hours, on a narrow, single lane bumping road, where horrendous accidents were not unknown. The bus driver, under the influence of whatever he incessantly chewed (a mildly intoxicating tobacco, or hashish, I later learned), drove at great speed with little care. When we entered the bus, he pointed to a warning calligraphed on the inside: 'Remember God! And pray. Before they pray on your grave'. I sat, with my young uncle Shahid and the other children, in the front of the bus, shouting at the bus driver to avoid approaching potholes and on-coming traffic. The passengers let out a loud sigh of relief on reaching the destination, and, indeed, prayed in unison, thanking God for their safe arrival.

As soon as we entered Hakim Sahib's house, the entire visiting family rushed to kiss and embrace the baby – almost suffocating her in the process. She was passed like a valued parcel from person to person. As one of the youngest, I was last in the queue. She was carefully handed to me, with my mother watching over me to ensure that I did not, unconsciously or enthusiastically, mishandle or drop her.

Over the next year, we travelled a few times to Bahawalnagar. I used to play with Saliha and carry her on my shoulders, my mother says. Then, my parents and I moved to Sahiwal (known in those days as Montgomery). Soon afterwards, we migrated to Hackney, London. And I did not see Saliha for almost twenty years.

In Bahawalnagar, the extended family tried to establish its roots. But making a new life in a new place was not easy and sent family members hiving off in all directions scrambling to find jobs and opportunity. Some moved to Lahore, some to Karachi. Saliha's parents stayed in Bahawalnagar, where she went to school. Later, she moved to Lahore to attend the Government Model College for Girls, Model Town. The family was rather poor and could not afford to pay her fees. So, on 12 October 1974, she wrote a letter to the Principal of the College:

> Madam – I am the student of 11 years in the Government Model College for Girls under your kind control. The income of my father is very small, and he has to support a large family. The prices of every commodity these days is abnormally high, and it is very difficult for him to make both ends meet. I may add for your kind attention that I belong to teachers family and many members of the family are attached with the education department.
> I, therefore, request you kindly to grant me fee concession.
> I shall be highly thankful to your kindness.
> Yours obediently,
> Saliha Basit

I don't know whether the 'fee concession' was granted. But I do know that the family was facing hardship, and, with the dispersal of family members all over Pakistan, and with my own family's migration to London, there was another concern. The bonds of family that were the matrix of their lives seemed to be weakening. To some extent, my mother, Hamida, and Saliha's mother, Zubaida, had anticipated this. The sisters were uprooted from all the normality they had known. They had suffered the trauma of partition, which had by now become an integral part of their selves. Now they faced the drifting apart of loved family members. So the sisters hatched a plan, before partition, just after they married, to reverse the global forces that were shattering their tradition – not so much ritual and practices to which both were devoted, but the essence that shaped their identity, the core values and ideas that told them who they really were and how they could relate to the changing world around them. They agreed that their first-born children, if they were a boy and a girl, would marry each other. This way, they could preserve the family bonds, even when different members of the family were located in different parts of the world, and pass on to their offspring the solidity and support the sisters had once known.

The sisters were resilient and tenacious. They had a particular notion of family: an institution to share and ease the burdens, to support and encourage, and to provide a safety net that does not permit people to fall through the cracks. For them, family were your counsellors, helpers, diversions, a source of company and society that does not judge and reject however much it may comment, nag, harangue and in infinite variety surround you with unending streams of opinion for your own good, whether it's a good you agree with or not. And they were determined to implement their plan and promise. But neither ever mentioned their cherished scheme to the offspring concerned.

The time came when the arrangement so long planned had to be put in place. Saliha graduated from the Government Model College for Girls with a degree in psychology. I grew up to manhood to become that new creation, a British Asian. I was taken on a purposeful visit to Pakistan in 1976 and presented with the proposal. But I was told she had said 'yes'. I thought: traditional families can be quite manipulating. It was quite possible that she murmured 'no' but her no was interpreted as perhaps, maybe, and then yes. If she had remained silent when the question was asked, that too would be interpreted as yes. So, there was no option for a no.

And in any case, I was not keen to marry a cousin. We were worlds apart. She did not know me. I hardly knew her. So I did not see Saliha, and said 'no'. I later learned that in fact she had said yes. But after hearing that I said no, she changed her mind and said no too. But 'no' was conspicuously absent from the vocabulary of the two sisters.

I had in fact fallen in love during my visit to Pakistan. But in a different way to a different person. I discovered Munni Begum, the peerless diva of

Pakistani music. I was mesmerised by her on my first encounter. I saw her as the Aunty next door who would pop in at just the right time to sing the exact *ghazal* that expressed my thoughts or feelings.

Meanwhile, my mother and the other Aunty in my life attempted to build a consensus. There was a lot of to-and-fro during the next year. The two sisters were well versed in the art form of nudging their children in the direction they desired. The art involves subtle manoeuvring, reiterating of tragic and triumphant segments of family history, and constant reminders (that have stayed with me ever since) of the important virtue of looking after the less fortunate members of the extended family. I was told that marriage in our tradition is a social act because it is not personal and individual; it never involves just two people, each alone with their own angst and dreams. Marriage is much too important to be left to the precarious dreams and delusions of a would-be bride and groom. However, because a marriage involves the extended family, this does not mean it is not personal. Stop thinking in discrete boxes, my mother said, separating and partitioning, as you are missing the point. Extended families and their collective actions do not eradicate the individuality of each member. On the contrary, they place an emphasis on the idiosyncrasies, the personhood of each member. An extended family is, par excellence, the safe and secure environment in which to stake your ground for being exactly who you are, and to be accepted as such. One is an abstract unit of a social abstraction. Instant love is an illusion; love grows as a couple bond, grow as a unit, to make a life together. No soul, let alone a twenty-six-year old, I thought, can survive such an onslaught.

Inevitably, I returned to Pakistan in 1977. My arrival in Karachi was already being seen as an affirmative action. The entire extended family settled in Karachi accompanied me to Bahawalnagar. *Charpais* – traditional woven beds – were laid out outside Hakim Sahib's house for the visiting men to sleep on. I spent a sleepless night on a *charpai* fighting off a battalion of mosquitoes.

The following morning, I got up to go to the toilet. It was a small closet on a corner of the veranda. I entered, accompanied by a *lota* – a round brass vessel that resembles a tea pot – and sat awkwardly on two small pillars. The end product dropped onto a container underneath. Not accustomed to squatting, it was not an easy manoeuvre to perform. As I was trying unsuccessfully to balance myself, a hand emerged from underneath the pillars and pulled the container away. I was shocked. Froze. Cleaned myself quickly, using the *lota* water, as best as I could. And came out on to the veranda to rapturous laughter.

I had entered the closet while it was being cleaned. Apparently, the cleaner had made the usual announcement at the beginning of the process, but I was unaware. Amongst the gathering on the veranda was Saliha, carrying a *balti* of water. There was a sublime smile on her face. There was also a grace and beauty that astonished me. I was mesmerised. 'Oay,' I shouted to attract her attention. 'Do you think I would make a reasonable husband?' 'Probably', she shouted back, 'but not for me'. Then she threw the *balti* of water over me!

I was always married to Saliha. Even before I was married. Even before I was born.

3.

Hakim Sahib was well known, and people were keen to attend the wedding of his granddaughter. So, invited or not, virtually half of the then population of Bahawalnagar was there. A 'Mehndi' ceremony was held. The women of the household decorated the bride with henna. It was all done with consummate skill: all varieties of patterns and flora and fauna were created on the hands and feet of the bride. The wedding itself was a modest affair. I had to wear a *shalwar kurta* suit, an Afghan *topi* on my head, and garlands of tinsel and flowers around my neck. She wore the traditional red wedding dress, adorned with jewellery. Not that I saw her. While I was outside in a tent, she was in a room inside the house. A young local Mullah arrived with a huge register. He asked me three times whether I accepted Saliha Basit as my wife. I replied '*Jee Haan*' (Yes Sir) every time. Then, he went inside the house and asked Saliha if she accepted Ziauddin Sardar as her husband. She took her time to reply, then whispered '*Jee Haan.*' The Mullah was not sure, or did not hear. 'Can't hear you', he said. She shouted: 'JEE HAAN! JEE HAAN! JEE HAAN.' Her voice reverberated so even those outside in the tent could hear it.

The Mullah filled in the marriage certificate:

Nikah Nama
Form No 2.
Muslim Family Law Ordinance 1961, Bahawalnagar.
Groom's age: 27.
Bride's age: 20.
Dowry: 20,000 rupees, currency of the time.
Date: 29 Dhu'l-Hijjah 1397; 11 December 1977.
Fees paid for registration: 20 rupees.
Name of the representative of the bride.
Names of the eight witnesses.

When it came to the witnesses, numerous people rushed in to sign. It was obvious that some of them were complete strangers. So there was a commotion when the family members, neighbours and acquaintances had to be sorted from other eager witnesses. When the document was signed, the Mullah tore the form from the register and handed it to Hakim Sahib. But he did a poor job; the first column of the form was left attached to the register.

The registration was followed by a sumptuous feast. A number of family members came forward to read wedding poems (*Saraas*) written for the occasion, with the names and virtues of the bride and groom sprinkled generously throughout. At around three o'clock in the morning, I was allowed in the bridal chamber, after paying – bribing? – the women who were guarding the bride.

This is how I described what happened next in *Balti Britain*.

Once inside the room, I could not move. I stood there behind the door looking at Saliha.... Slowly, the noise and the buzz around the house subsided. Someone had put a *ghazal* on a tape recorder; clearly, I could clearly hear Munni Begum singing:

> *I am drinking with my eyes,*
> *Let not this atmosphere change.*
> *Do not lower your gaze*
> *For this night may fade away.*

I managed to walk a few steps and sat beside her.

> *There's still some night left*
> *Do not remove your veil.*
> *Your faltering and falling drunk*
> *May regain his balance.*

She removed her *duppata*, placed her arms around my waist and embraced me.

> *Owner of my life*
> *Put your hands on my heart*
> *I fear that the joy of your arrival*
> *would stop my heart from beating.*

She leaned forward, grabbed a book that was lying under the cushion and handed it to me. I read the title: *Intermediate Biology*.

Many, many years later, I discovered that Saliha kept a diary. The entry for the wedding day, in Urdu, reads:

11 December 1977: 'On 11 December 1977 we got married and my life took a new turn. This was the most beautiful day of my life because I acquired the person I desired. In every way, Zia is ideal for me. Even though we have not seen each other for 19 years. But Zia is not a stranger to me in any way. He understands everything I say and do. Perhaps, he too desires me as much as I desire him. There is not enough time for me to write down his qualities. But I like everything he says. He has a very warm and shining personality, but he spends lot of time thinking of naughty things to do. He loves children; he is frequently seen carrying a child. He is passionate about helping the poor, the labourers and the sick. He seeks to help them as much as he can'.

Wedding over, we went to Karachi. After making arrangements for her UK visa, I had to return to London. I was enormously miserable about leaving her behind. I did not know how long it would take her to get her visa and join me in London. She was even sadder. On 29 January 1978, her birthday, she wrote in her diary:

Zia, who is dearer to me than my life, left for London on the six o'clock flight in the morning. I longed for him all day; I wanted to hear his voice. To hear him call: 'Begum, Begum!'. I wanted to smell his particular odour...

And again, on 4 February 1978: 'I am waiting for his letter. He must have written to me as soon as he got back'.

Saliha was granted 'leave to remain' and joined her husband. But by the time she arrived in London, I had left for Jeddah where I was then working.

11 June 1978: Today, my life took a new turn. I left Pakistan and all my relatives and arrived in London. There were people at the airport to collect me. But not the one for whom I left everyone and everything behind. I missed him terribly today.

The following day, 12 June 1978: 'This is my second day in London. Only I know how I managed to pass the night without Zia. I am so close, yet so far. When will this separation end?'

The next day, 13 June 1978: 'I have all I need here. Everyone loves me. But despite it all, I want to sit quietly, and not speak to anyone. I just don't want anyone or anything in my thoughts but Zia'.

She stayed with my parents in our council house in Warwick Avenue. I wrote to her regularly, encouraging her to improve her English, and perhaps learn to cook. She came to London with virtually nothing. But she did bring four books: *Lazeez Khanna* (Delicious Food) by Rabia Saeed in Urdu, *Quranic Advice*, Arabic text with English translation by Marmaduke Pickthall and Urdu translation by Maulana Faateh Mohammed Jallendhri, a copy of Sura Yaseen without translation that always remained by her bedside along with a small pocket-size booklet of *duas* (prayers).

Lazeez Khanna had a couple of well-thumbed pages. My mother must have told her about my fondness for *karelas*. That is why, I figure, when picked up, *Lazeez Khanna* would automatically open on page 240, with a recipe for bitter gourd with meat:

Karela Ghost
Ingredients: Meat half *ser*. Ghee one-and-half *chhataank*. Karelas one *pao*. Cloves one *tola*. Cardamom one *tola*. Onion one *chhataank*. Ginger eight *tola*. Dry coriander one *tola*. Red pepper 1.5 *tola*. Turmeric 2.5 *maasha*.

Method: Fry meat in *ghee* till it turns red. Then add onion and stir. After a little while, add water, salt, coriander and ginger, keep stringing, and cook till the meat is nice and tender. Add water if necessary. Peel the karallas, sprinkle with salt and turmeric, and put them aside in a warm place. After a while, rub them with your hands to get their bitterness out. Then rub them with yogurt and leave them aside for two to three hours. After this time, wash them with water, fry them in ghee, and mix with the meat. When they are well done, pour the gram masala. Finally, take them out of the *choola* (fireplace) and enjoy!

Lazeez Khanna uses traditional ancient South Asian units of measure which made little sense to me. The measures begin with rice: 8 grains of rice equal 1 Ratti, 8 Ratti equal 1 Masha, 12 Masha equal 1 Tola, 5 Tola equal one Chhataank, and finally, 16 Chhataank equal one Ser (kilogram). They made complete sense to Saliha: it was all done by hand, a pinch here, two or three pinches there, and then a handful! It all came out perfectly every time. And it was all instinct. There was an intimate connection between the hands that cooked and the hands that ate. Observing her cook made me think that our culture is not a random collection of arbitrary habits. It emerges from naturally directed instincts and is an amalgam of expressions of our instincts. Hence, the common themes across cultures, the virtues that bind us all – family, ritual, love, friendship, loyalty. For Saliha, instinct was a penchant for learning. And she learned a lot from the books she brought with her.

Apart from *karela ghost*, Saliha learned to cook *biryani* and *palou*. But her Ancient Shammi Kabaabs became legendary. The recipe is too long and complicated (and, in any case, presents a translation challenge that I cannot possibly meet) to include here. But *Lazeez Khanna* explains that just because they are called 'ancient' does not mean they are not contemporary. And *Shammi* does not suggest Sham, meaning Syria. They are not Syrian in origin. 'It is just that the method used to make them was developed in the royal household of Arab, Iranian, and Indian Muslim kings'; and to this day, it is the best method to make them'. Needless to say, they require much preparation.

When it came to *Quranic Advice*, she never got past the first page. Advice from Part 1, Chapter 1:

> 'And do good, surely Allah loves those who do good'.
> 'Surely Allah loves those who turn to Him in repentance and loves those who keep clean'.
> 'Allah loves the steadfast'.
> 'Allah loves the equitable'.
> 'Surely Allah loves those who put their trust in Him'.

But she took all the advice to heart.

4.

We got married – again.

Saliha was without me for about three months. I managed to escape Jeddah and return to London in early August 1978. My father had already made an appointment for us. So we went to Westminster Town Hall for a 'civil marriage' – 'pursuant to the Marriage Act 1949!' It was not much of an affair; only my parents, brother and sister were in attendance. But it was the first time I actually looked closely at Saliha's Pakistani passport, which we had to present to the Registrar. It stated:

Colour of eyes: black
Colour of hair: black
Visible distinguishing mark: mole right side of chin.

I looked, again and again, for the said mole. It wasn't there. Anywhere.

A couple of months later, I went back to my job at the Hajj Research Centre, King Abdul Aziz University, in Jeddah. Saliha came with me. We shared a flat with my life-long friend Zafar Malik, who also worked at the Hajj Research Centre, and his wife, Sameena. The two women became the best of friends. Jeddah life was austere; there wasn't much to do, and nowhere particular to go after work. The four us were transformed into conjoined twins, sharing our lives, frustrations and joys together. The Maliks' first child, Saad, was a source of diversion, and we took turns to look after and play with him. For us, Saad was like our own son. Occasionally, we went for evening walks on the promenade and had dinner with our colleagues at weekends – which were on Thursdays and Fridays – and, out of sheer boredom, sometimes watched Egyptian films and soap operas on a grainy black and white television.

While life was just about bearable for me and Zafar, for the women it was intolerable. They couldn't go out on their own and were cooped up all day in our small two-bedroom flat. Worse, they had to be wrapped up in black *abayas*, faces and hair covered, looking like ghostly figures from an Edgar Allen Poe story. Saliha longed for the freedom she enjoyed in Pakistan. 'Why do we have to wear black shrouds', she asked. 'Why can't we be simply modestly dressed?'. This is Saudi Arabia, the birth place of Islam, I told her. They want women to suffer as much as possible. This is why the *abayas* are black because black is the worst colour to wear in scorching sun and flaming heat. The best colour to wear is white. That is why Saudi men *always* wear white *thawbs*.

The situation become more complicated when Saliha became pregnant. I did not want my child to be born in Saudi Arabia. So I had to take her back to London. That meant negotiating two exit visas – *khurooj*, as they are called. Not a simple task in the 1970s! But Saudi Arabia does offer something unique: the opportunity to perform the hajj. I wanted Saliha to become a hajjan, someone who has performed the hajj. Fortunately, the 1978 hajj was in November and we were able to perform the hajj together. I like to think that my eldest daughter, Maha, is also a hajjan as Saliha was carrying her during our pilgrimage.

Perhaps 'together' is not the right word. I performed the hajj as a research exercise: Zafar and I walked from Jeddah to Mecca, along with a rowdy donkey, tracing the old caravan route – as described in *Mecca: The Sacred City*. Saliha and Sameena went with my Hajj Research Centre colleagues. It was, as the hajj is meant to be, a devotional activity, requiring much effort, and a great deal of prayer and supplication. A genuinely humbling affair. But for us it was also a very joyous occasion, with a great deal of laughter.

Saliha returned to London soon after hajj. We were separated again. I wanted my first child to be female, and somehow I managed to convince myself that I was going to have a daughter. I sent postcards from Jeddah with one line messages: 'Beautiful Saliha – Write to me every week. I am restless without you', or 'to the two young girls in my life'. Always signed: 'only yours'. She replied with letters in Urdu, describing her pain at being separated yet again.

The separation was just as agonising for me in Jeddah, where I was experiencing every type of bureaucratic nightmare imaginable to a mortal, making sure I had an exit visa to return to London in time for the birth. In anticipation of leaving Saudi Arabia – 'desert purgatory' as I used to call it – for good, I also started freelancing for the science journal *Nature*. Most of my free hours, however, were spent on reading and writing, which were not only a good use of my time but also served to ease my frustrations at Jeddah life and the agony of enforced segregation. Islamic classics were my chosen reading. I read Rumi's *Masnavi* a number of times, but seldom understood what he was getting at. It was only after I had truly experienced the angst of separation I understood that:

A true lover is proved such by his pain of heart
No sickness is there like sickness of heart.
The lover's ailment is different from all ailments;

Love is the astrolabe of God's mysteries.

'Sickness of heart' is also a main theme of much of Urdu poetry. And none other than Aunty Munni Begum expressed it best. I indulged my passion for *ghazals* by constantly listening to her. When she sings, 'complications at every step, confusion for every soul' — *'har qadam zehmatian, har nafs uljhanain'* — she is actually talking to me! I wondered at her mystical habit of popping up at fateful junctures of our lives!

My repeated hounding of the university bureaucracy eventually paid off. I returned to London a week or so before the anticipated delivery date. We waited anxiously. She was late. Saliha was amused, as were my parents, that I was convinced it is a girl. But one day I just could not wait any longer. *'Challo'*, I suggested to my wife, let's go to the hospital. She was reluctant. 'It's not time yet', she said. 'We will go when I am good and ready'. She was ten days overdue. Ready or not, we were going to the hospital. She agreed to go, and I gently guided her towards St Mary's Hospital, Paddington, which was then located only five minutes' walk from my parents' flat. (In 1986, it relocated to its current position in Praed Street).

It was eight in the evening. By the time we reached the hospital gate, her contractions had started. She was immediately admitted to the labour ward. I asked the doctor on duty to let me stay with my wife. She agreed. Then I pushed a little: 'I would like to deliver the baby'. She looked at me in astonishment. The conversation that followed, I vaguely recall, went as follows.

'I am the father. I want to deliver my child'.
'We are obstetricians. Delivering babies is what *we* do'.
'As a father, I have a right'.
'You have the right to stand at a distance and watch'.
'Not good enough. I want to be involved in the actual delivery'.
'No, no. You know nothing about delivering babies'.
'I *do*. I am science journalist'.
'Who do you write for?'.
'For *Nature*. The most foremost science journal in the world'.

The golden word had been uttered. *Nature*. The young obstetrician was also a budding researcher who was having problems getting her papers published. So we reached a compromise: I will help with the publication of her paper, she will allow me to handle the baby just after the second stage of birth. (She never contacted me, and the promise remained unfulfilled).

So it happened. I stood outside the booth watching the delivery. Then I was allowed inside and permitted to carry the baby just before the arrival of the placenta. As I had wished and always thought, it was a girl. This was when I made my first blunder, a categorical mistake for which Saliha never forgave me. An error of fatherly love. I kept hold of the baby. While she lay on the hospital bed, exhausted, with her arms stretched out for her child to be handed to her to hold and caress, I kept the baby in my arms. She had to be wrenched from me and handed to her mother.

She brought us great joy, and changed the dynamics of family life. I wasn't going to be separated from both my wife and my daughter. A few months later, I quit my job at the Hajj Research Centre, and brought all the money I had saved while working in Jeddah in a carrier bag (we were not allowed to open a bank account) to London. It was enough to buy a house. We moved out from our parent's place and moved into a modest dwelling in Colindale. It was to become our permanent home.

Life was hard. I managed to get a job as Deputy Editor of *Arabia: Islamic World Review* (now defunct), but it only lasted a few months. I got sacked for co-authoring an editorial that painted the then Saudi monarch, King Fahd bin Abdulaziz bin Saud, in a less than favourable light. I started working for *New Scientist*, but the income was never enough. Moreover, to Saliha's irritation, I was frequently on assignment in the Middle East. Or on a research trip. Or attending a conference. At home, our lives revolved around Maha, Munni Begum, and our cat, Lucy. I took Maha with me whenever and wherever I could. My nickname for her was '*Dunya*', my world; and she was the axis of my world; she *is* the axis of my world.

Our financial situation improved when I joined London Weekend Television (LWT) as a reporter. Conventional 16mm film was being replaced with video, and my reports where shot on tapes (then referred to as ENG, Electronic New Gathering). The rough footage had to be edited. So almost every week, I would go down, tapes in hand, to the editing suites to have my reports edited and ready for transmission. The editor assigned to me was called Arun Kalarya. Our love of film, Indian culture, and the fact that we spoke to each other in Urdu/Hindi/Punjabi, was the superglue that bonded our friendship. It just so happened that Arun also lived in Colindale – just a few streets away from our house. So we met frequently, not just at work but also at our homes. Arun's wife, Indu, and Saliha connected instantly. They were of the same age, had the same effervescent personalities, and behaved like sisters cemented together at birth. Indu was Saliha's confidant: my shortcomings as a husband (which were many, and emerging), were relayed to Indu in hushed tones. In times of trouble, Indu would be in our house within minutes.

An established tradition in our family requires that some of our closest friends must be Hindu/Jain. My father's best friend was Mr Mittal, who lived close to us when we lived in Hackney. Every Saturday morning he would come to our house, the two friends would talk and laugh, and regale each other with verse in the evening at the regular local poetry recitals. My mother's best buddy was Surita, who lived next door but one when we lived in Warwick Avenue. There was constant to and fro flow of food: *bhaturas* from Surita's, *bhindi* from ours. Children were constantly in each other's houses. So it was only natural for Saliha and Indu to form a lifelong, indestructible bond. As my father used to say, 'there is no partition here'.

Shortly after I joined LWT, our son Zaid was born. I was a devoted husband during Saliha's pregnancy. I maintained a calendar of prenatal visits, and accompanied her to all the appointments. Unfortunately, I wasn't there at the crucial moment of birth. I was on assignment filming a report on racism against Asian doctors. This was my second categorical mistake: an error of a jobbing reporter. Saliha saw that as a lack of devotion. 'There was a twinkle in her eye', says Indu, when she held Zaid for the first time. She was exceptionally proud. A photo of the proud mother holding a few-hours-old Zaid adorns our house. There was a great deal of joy and happiness in our home. We had a little celebration when Saliha became a naturalised British citizen in July 1984.

One day, we were doing our weekly shopping at Sainsbury's, the local supermarket. Saliha was leading from the front, examining every item for undesirable haram ingredients as well as price, pushing Zaid in his pram, and me lagging behind holding Maha's hand. A young Asian woman recognised me, came over, and embraced me without a hint of hesitation.

'You are the reporter from Eastern Eye', she exclaimed. Saliha's face turned red. When the woman left, Saliha turned around and snapped: 'me or television?'. 'You', I replied, with a smile.

5.

But it was not easy for me to give up television. I was working hard, but also enjoying myself. I was destined to be a star as one of the TV executives once told me. Being recognised on the street gives you something akin to a sugar rush. It also does something to your soul. Your Self, *nafs ammarah bi-su'*, urges you to move away from what you understand as virtues and towards their debasing counterparts. The movement is subtle, but definite. I became arrogant (even more than my usual quota) and boastful. Too full of myself. I was not ready to give up my nascent television career just yet.

I often left home early and came back late. She felt neglected. First she accused me of paying more attention to the children than her. I pleaded guilty. Then, she even accused me of paying more attention to Lucy, our cat, than her. This time I pleaded not guilty. One day, Saliha pronounced: 'I want another child'. I wasn't keen. 'Two are enough', I replied. She looked a bit despondent, but I thought nothing of it. A few weeks later, she asked: 'why are you being mean? Why can't we have another child?'. I explained, we are just about coping with two. Think of all the problems we will have with schools, universities, marriages. We took our children everywhere with us. I wanted to travel and write travel books, and lugging three children around would be a burden too far. In any case, I pointed out, the population of the world is increasing too fast. Better to have fewer children for the sake of the planet. She was not convinced, but said nothing.

The question emerged again a few weeks later. *Why can't we have another child?* This time I lost my temper. 'We can't, ok', I shouted at her. 'Stop asking'. She kept quiet, but that evening moved out of our bedroom into the small guest room. That was my third and most serious categorical mistake. An error of conceited modernity. I failed to realise that the lives of traditional women revolve around children. A home is not a home unless it is spotless and orderly (ours always was) and full of children running around destroying the created order, making mess everywhere.

Two just won't do. Saliha's parents had five. Her grandparents had eight or nine. Ditto other relatives.

She said nothing. She didn't speak to me – at all. Like an ideal housewife, she would do all the chores perfectly. As soon as I returned from work, she would retire to her room, leaving me to have dinner alone or play with the children. All my attempts at cajoling failed. She would not utter a single word. This went on for days, then weeks, then months. Eventually, I too stopped trying to talk to her. We were like two strangers in a home. Then, she packed her bags and left for Pakistan, leaving me with the children.

I was confused. Was she suffering from postpartum depression, feeling sad and anxious after she had given birth to Zaid? Was she leaving me? The demands of the job at LWT were also taking their toll on me. It was not easy to look after two kids while trying to file reports and features for a demanding television programme.

I had a regular crew that accompanied me on shoots: director, camera man (in those days they were all men), sound person, sparks (electricians) and production assistance (who kept the whole lot together and made sure we were at the right place at the right time. Sometimes the director would be replaced by a female assistant director. The director and I were very chummy and often mocked each other: he referred to me as 'the luminary' and I called him 'Mr Morgan', after the self-admitted dreamer of the 1966 film, *Morgan: A Suitable Case for Treatment*. But I was rather close to the assistant director. We often found ourselves together on long shoots, or working late at night. Her goal in life was to turn the romantic novels of the French playwright and novelist, Françoise Sagan, into a mini-series for television, which she would direct. She wanted me to write the screenplays. I saw it as a challenge and was eager to try my hand at a different kind of writing than I was used to. I was trying to balance work with looking after two children, while trying to write a script till late at night. She volunteered to help with looking after the children, which I readily accepted. And, for a period, she moved into our house. We worked together on Sagan's first 1944 novel, which Sagan wrote while only eighteen, called *Bonjour Tristesse* (Hello Sadness).

Saliha returned after six months in Pakistan. Still silent. The only person she talked to was Indu. One evening I returned after a long day of editing to find my collection of tapes and newly acquired CDs all over the living room floor. I thought the children had been up to their usual naughtiness. But then I heard a familiar sound. I rushed upstairs to the main bedroom and found Saliha sitting on *our* bed, crying. My portable cassette player was by her side. The tape was playing Munni Begum:

> *Bewafa se bhi pyar hota hai*
> You can even love the unfaithful
> *Yaar kuch bhi ho yaar hota hai*
> Friends are friends whatever they are
> *Saath mein uske hai raqeeb toh kya*
> So what if my fate is tied to him
> *Phool ke saath kaante hota hai*
> Even flowers have thorns with them.
> *Jab woh aate nahi shabe waada*
> When he doesn't return on promised nights
> *Maut ka intazaar hota hai*
> I wait for my death.

She broke her long silence when she saw me. 'I love you *jani*', she sobbed. 'I can't live without you'. She opened her arms and I rushed to embrace her. 'You are going to…'. She could not get the words out of her mouth. 'I want..'. I put my hands gently on her mouth. 'You don't have to say anything', I murmured. 'I am not going anywhere'. I changed the tape in the cassette player to another Munni Begum *ghazal*: *Ek Bar Muskura Do*:

> Paradise will swing,
> The atmosphere will smile,
> If you smile,
> God will smile.
> Smile once (again)

Our third child, Zain, was born nine months later.

Once again, I was not there at the crucial time. By now I had quit LWT and started to work for East-West University in Chicago. My first task there was to organise a major international conference on '*Dawa* and

Development'. When Zain was born, I was in Mecca running the conference. But I was able to talk to Saliha immediately after the birth, and that was a consolation – a last-minute goal. I think Indu organised the 'long-distance call' as they used to be called in the 1980s. My friend, and the children's god mother, Merryl Wyn Davies, who was about to join me in Mecca, drove her to the hospital. The two women had some warm words with the proud mother. When Merryl joined me in Mecca, we jumped up and down in joy and had a glass or two of 'Jeddah Champagne' (orange juice and soda water) in celebration.

The first few years after the arrival of Zain were difficult. He was born with his feet facing inwards and had to have a string of operations to have them corrected. There were numerous visits to the hospital and to see the consultant, who was called 'Mr Angel'. Saliha used to say, 'Zain arrived with a *farishta* (angel) in toe'. The boy had his feet in plaster for months. He would hobble around the house damaging and breaking things with plastered feet which had the gravity of a small boulder.

By now, our modest dwelling in Colindale had become sizeable. As the children arrived, we turned the garage into a room, added another with an extension, then transformed the attic into a study, and finally added a conservatory. The children attended the local primary school. I left East-West University to work, along with Merryl, in Malaysia with my friend Anwar Ibrahim, who then held a number of ministerial portfolios; and commuted between London and Kuala Lumpur – often with wife and children, who instantly fell in love with the country. It was a joyous time with a great deal of travel within Malaysia – we spent a memorable few days in a tree house in the National Park trying to see a tapir without success. There were 'intellectual discourses' in Kuala Lumpur, where local, regional, international and Islamic issues of the period were analysed. It was also a prolific period for me as a writer. I did most of my writing in London, cooped up in the attic where I was seldom disturbed. I only came down when Saliha would shout, from the kitchen: 'Zia, lunch!', 'Zia, tea!', and 'Zia, dinner!'.

Life changed a gear when it was time for the children to attend secondary school. And Saliha had had enough of being a housewife. Now she wanted to work.

6.

Most of our arguments were centred around the children – how we should bring them up, how they should they play, what school they should attend, what they should study at university. Saliha wanted her children to grow up with a strong sense of right and wrong, good and bad, virtue and vice. They could not be left to their own devices and had to be told what they should, ought, and must do. I wanted my children to be people with imagination, perception, observation and reasoning, which I thought they possessed, by virtue of being children. I also thought they would develop a sense of right and wrong as they grew. So there was always a tug of war. But somehow we reached a middle ground. Dolls with the entire package of adult pornography (with big breasts, slender waist and long legs) were out. But Maha could play with more locally made 'halal dolls', made of cotton or wood, that I bought back from my travels. In general, modern toys were out – such as Teletubbies, Hollywood-inspired nonsense, and Playstations – but toys that involved building, thinking, and creative play were allowed, such as modelling clay, wooden blocks, and jigsaw puzzles. Television was restricted but the kids could watch what the parents were watching. This was easy for Saliha, as she almost exclusively watched Pakistani television dramas and Bollywood films. But rather difficult for me, as I watched Hollywood and foreign films. Pop music was discouraged, but Bollywood singing and dancing was accepted. Most of all, however, reading was promoted at every opportunity. The children usually received books for their birthday presents.

When it came to schools, there was no way Saliha would allow Maha to attend a mixed, co-ed establishment. Fortunately, there was a reasonably good girls school not too far from our place. She toyed with the idea of sending Zaid to a private school. There was a famous and highly recommended one relatively close. We couldn't afford the astronomical fees. But we had Zaid sit the entrance examination anyway. He passed with flying colours. We used the result to get him admitted to the most sought after boys school in our borough. She wanted Zain to go to an Islamic school. But accepted my suggestion for a Catholic alternative. It took some effort and threats involving letters from the Vatican, which both Saliha and I visited that year and where I had contacts, to get him admitted. The daily school runs were a nightmare as the three schools were in three different locations. Saliha dropped the children in the morning. I collected them in the afternoon. Sometimes. Other times, she took it all on her shoulders.

She was happy when Merryl and I gently ushered Maha towards law. We got her interested by sitting with her to watch endless episodes of *LA Law*. Zaid liked building things so it was natural for him to study engineering. But we had a long running battle with Zain. I wanted him to study philosophy and got him interested at a young age by reading Plato – we began with *Symposium* and went on to *The Republic*. She was incensed. 'What good would that do?', she demanded. 'What kind of job will he get as a philosopher?' No answer would satisfy her. The battle raged for years and became worse when Zain decided to attend the University of Kent, which meant he had to leave home. It took long, protracted negotiations before she reluctantly agreed to allow her youngest child to leave home to pursue university education outside London. But she wasn't happy. And she made that clear.

With the children at various universities, she had more time on her hands. She wasn't satisfied by just being a housewife. She wanted to work, and there was only one job she wanted to do. To work with children. She had an infinite love for children. Not just her children, but children *per se*. Not just in her household, where she was Begum, but everywhere. She would use the Urdu word *bacha* – child – when talking to her own kids, even when they were mature adults. 'When I start work', she asserted, 'what I earn is mine. You have no right over it'. I agreed. 'And what I earn is also yours', I teased. 'I already know *that*', she shot back.

During September 1980, she started to work part time at the Village School, a short drive from our house. It caters for children from three to nineteen, with special or complex needs or disabilities. Some are on the autistic spectrum, but most have severe and profound needs relating to disorders such as cerebral palsy, Down's syndrome, cystic fibrosis, and disorders of movement and coordination. For her, it was not so much 'work' as a cherished vocation. That's just what she always wanted to do: to care for special children. When she started to work full-time, she undertook a string of courses and training programmes: health and social care, multi-sensory cues training, manual handling in a care environment, life support, risk assessment, muscular skeletal injury, supporting complex needs, infection prevention and control, the moving and handling of specialised equipment (such as hoists), food allergy awareness. With all these she had no problem. But when it came to such things as legislation and 'Diploma in Team Leading', she sought the help of her family. We all ran in different directions. 'Please, I need help with this', she would plead. Eventually, Maha or I would sit with her and see her through the course.

I agreed to help her on a particular course on organisation management. We went through various sections of the course. The first section was on vision. She learned that a 'vision is an image of the future that an organisation wants to achieve in the future'. I asked: what is your vision? 'I envisage', she replied, 'playing with and looking after my grandchildren in the future'. The second section was on mission. We were told: 'mission is the goal an organisation sets itself in answer to such questions as what, how and why we do what we do and who are we doing it for'. What is your mission in life? I playfully asked Saliha. 'My mission', she replied without a second for thought, 'is to get my children married as soon as possible so I can have grandchildren'. The course went on to strategy, objectives and targets. 'My target is to get the boys married within a year'. The boys had their own ideas.

She worked at the Village School for over forty years and never missed a single day. She would go to work even when she was not feeling too well. 'My children need me', she would say.

Her love was reciprocated: her pupils as well her colleagues adored her. Every now and then, her colleagues would come after school, or at weekends, for tea. Our living room would witness lively conversation and laughter, which would reverberate all the way to the attic, where I would be working.

Just before her fortieth birthday, Saliha complained of a stomach ache. I suggested she should go and see our GP. But she was reluctant; she just did not like the idea of seeing a doctor. The pain continued. One night it was obvious that she was in considerable pain and I could not contain myself. 'We are going to the hospital', I asserted. 'No, no', she squeaked. But I wasn't going to take no for an answer. I took her to the Northwick General hospital. We waited for about three hours before she was seen.

The A&E doctor sent her for an x-ray. We sat for another four hours and it became obvious that she wasn't going to have an x-ray any time soon. By now, it was early morning and we were exhausted. 'Enough of this shit', I bellowed. 'We will go private'. We drove to a private hospital not too far from where we live. But before we could reach the entrance we were stopped by some firemen. 'Turn back, turn back', they shouted. The hospital was on fire. 'You see', Saliha snapped. 'God does not want me to see a doctor'. 'He does', I replied, as I reversed and drove towards another private hospital some distance away. She was immediately seen by a specialist who diagnosed cholecystitis – inflammation of the gallbladder. He prescribed a cocktail of medicines, which worked.

On Saturday 31 January 1998, we celebrated with some fanfare the joint fortieth birthdays (a couple of days late) of Saliha and Indu. The celebrations were held at Indu's house, where families and friends of the boon companions gathered. There were tributes, speeches and much Bollywood dancing. Zafar and Sameena, who by then had moved to Chicago, came for the anniversary. Sameena had written a poem for the occasion, which she read in her amiable style.

Saliha

You've turned the big four O
All these years you maintained a glow

My first recollection of you
A hurried introduction at Heathrow
Simply dressed in black and white
With an obedient smile

You began your life with Zia, Jeddah bound
Soon that turned your world around

In contrast to your serene self
Zia was wrapped, only in himself

All these years...past
Quietly you've won...at last

Children, home, cat and all
Love, affection and patient stand tall
Your friendship I truly treasure
Twenty years of real pleasure

Hats off to you
Now, that's my view

7.

Sameena was right. I tended to be wrapped in myself. I suspect that most writers are. I needed time and space to write and had to travel for research. But Saliha came to appreciate this. When people asked me how I had managed to write so many books, I always replied: it's thanks to my supportive wife. In one respect, she is the invisible but ever present co-author of all my works, and she actually features in a few. When someone visited our house, she would point, with a beaming smile on her face, to the bookshelf that held most of my titles: 'my husband wrote these'. However, she seldom agreed with what I had to say.

She loved to travel, but only with me. The only place she would travel to on her own was Pakistan. She visited her family there quite regularly, whenever she got a break from work. Elsewhere, we travelled together – to Malaysia, Singapore, Turkey, Spain, Bosnia and Herzegovina, Sweden, France, Morocco, Egypt, Tunisia. We spent quite a lot of time in some of these places – and revisited them, again and again. But Saliha preferred to go to new places every time. 'We have already been there', she would complain, 'let's go somewhere new'. 'Like where', I would reply in annoyance, 'the North Pole?' I would save money for her to spend on trips. It would be handed to her when we reached our destination. 'Here', I would say, 'some bread for your delectation'. She would take the money, wander around shops and bazaars all day, pulling me here, pushing me there. And at the end of the gruelling essay, hand all the money back. She liked everything she saw. Never bought anything she saw. Unless she was with her daughter, who is a spendthrift.

The last twenty years of my life with Saliha developed into joyful sets of choreographed routines. We had worked out what we needed and what made us happy. She would leave for work in the morning. I would have my constitution coffee and work till one o'clock, and then come down from the attic for lunch. The days when she used to call out 'Zia, lunch' had long gone. I had to make my own lunch, and then get back to work. She would return near four o'clock by which time I had to have her tea and biscuits (usually, one McVities digestive, one Jaffa Cake) prepared. As soon as she opened the door, she would shout: 'Is my *chai* ready?'. We would have tea together. I would return to the attic. She would watch some Pakistani news channel till six and then prepare the dinner. Around seven, I had to come down for dinner as soon as she called. The meal could not be allowed to get cold. We would dine together while watching the Channel 4 News.

Thorny issues raised their head after dinner. Saliha had established two strict rules that had to be followed, or, as the proverb has it, hell hath no fury. First rule: Islam and Pakistan were above criticism. Criticism of these subjects was to be limited to my books, and not made in front of her. If I made a comment on some story on Pakistan that we had watched on the news, it would be taken as a vile calumny, even if well intentioned, on the sanctity of the Land of the Pure. As far as Islam was concerned, I had better keep my mouth shut – something that was practically impossible for me. One afternoon, I was watching a Pakistani news channel with her at tea time. The host was interviewing the famous singer, Junaid Jamshed, who gave up a highly successful career in pop music, grew a preposterous beard, and became a missionary. The host asked the singer: what do you love most about Pakistan? Jamshed replied: the devotion of the people to Islam. Pakistanis are fervent in prayer and rush to their mosques as soon as the *azan* is called, he said. During Friday prayers, he pointed out, the mosques are full to the brim. Pakistanis are very observant of Ramadan. Et cetera. The interview ended with the suggestion that God was looking favourably towards Pakistan and its people.

I just could not contain myself and burst out in laughter. Saliha saw this as a double whammy: not only had I laughed at Pakistan, I had also somehow denigrated Islam. She was incensed. 'Begum', I tried to explain. 'Think about it. If God was showering his blessings on Pakistan the country would not be in a complete and utter mess'. She frowned. So I went further. 'Consider that over 250 million Pakistanis have been fervently praying five times a day for over seventy years asking God to sort out their country. But no reply has been forthcoming. So there are only three possibilities. One: God doesn't exist. Two: He is not listening to Pakistanis. Three: if He is listening, His answer is no. Get lost you rotten sods'. She dismissed my analysis. She had her own critical take on Islam, which was idealism peppered with hope and wrapped in tradition. She moved out of our bed for three days – the specified *fiqhi* time for being angry!

Second rule: films and television shows containing sex and violence were totally forbidden. As a news junkie, I would proceed from Channel 4 news to Sky News at eight, BBC News at nine, ITN News at ten, and end the evening with News Night or Press Review. Saliha saw this as demented. After dinner, she would get her iPad out, put on her headphones, and watch Pakistani dramas and comedy shows. On selected days, we watched *Poirot* or *Murder in Paradise* together, programmes where the murder takes place off stage and no sex is involved. She also liked *Bake Off* and other cooking shows and *Doc Martin*. We usually sat at the opposite end of the sofa, engaged in our chosen activity. But there was a sublime connection: we kept an eye on each other, sometime leaning sideways to hold hands when no one was around. When I was watching something that was not on the approved list, or a sex scene or violence appeared on screen, she would mutter, without moving her gaze from her iPad, 'change the channel, change the channel', or 'fast forward, fast forward'. If I was watching something tragic, howls of laughter would be coming from her side as she watched a Pakistani comedy. Watching something like *Game of Thrones*, where sex and violence are the order of the day, was well nigh impossible. '*Astaghfirullah!*' (I seek forgiveness from Allah) she would exclaim, without lifting her eyes from the iPad, followed by a very loud: '*Auzubillah Minashaitan Nirajeem*' (I seek refuge from Allah from the accursed Shaitan). That was a signal for me to switch off, while she continued to regale herself with whatever she was watching.

Sometimes, however, I would not concede defeat. I had a trump card up my sleeve: *Coke Studio*, the truly brilliant, and long running, Pakistani music show. Its strength lies in its synthesis of traditional and classical music – *ghazals*, *qawwali*, folk and Sufi – with contemporary rock and pop. I would turn to YouTube and start listening to the latest season. She would slowly raise her eyes from the iPad and then put it down. She knew that I had pulled a fast one. We would both become immersed, mesmerised. Just to annoy her a little, I would play a particular *ghazal* that I really liked again and again, savouring the words, looking for metaphorical connections. The only time I got her to abandon her iPad completely was when we watched all 448 episodes of the Turkish show *Ertugrul: Resurrection* on Netflix. Indeed, the whole family watched it together. No one was allowed to watch ahead on their own. Here the problems I usually faced with Saliha were reversed. The show, which revolves around the exploits of the father of the first Ottoman caliph Osman Ghazi, is full of endless sword fights, numerous elaborate marriage ceremonies, and sermons on Islam. Now it was me saying, 'fast forward, fast forward'. But Saliha wanted to watch every second. Even the violence didn't bother her.

We had a division of labour. She had this strange ability to instantly pick out that one damn thing you'd missed. If I spent all day painting a room, for example, she would walk in and immediately point to the square inch that had escaped. It was perhaps her most annoying ability. Consequently, I was not allowed to wash the dishes or clean the house as, inevitably, I did a bad job. So I did the gardening, which I loved. On the whole, she approved. Every spring, when I brought the garden back to life, she would make a video and send it to the extended family: 'this is our garden'. But there had to be an issue. So it became: Saliha versus weeds. I couldn't be bothered with sorting out the weeds on the paved areas of our front and back gardens. She could not stand them. There would be determined and protracted battles between the two adversaries. She would pour weed killer on them but they would return reinvigorated in a few days. She would meticulously rake them out but the blighters would come back as soon as she had finished. I got her a device to burn them. That didn't help either. Finally, we got an electric weed remover that seemed to do the job. But it was chargeable. So the charge often ran out during the battle. It was a campaign she was destined to lose.

She never threw anything away. If anything could be used in some distant future, it had to be kept. The trouble was that she had a very loose definition of what could be used, and it included boxes. All kinds of boxes. Boxes which were used for her wedding jewellery. Perfume boxes (perfume finished decades ago!). Boxes for beauty products. Shoe boxes. Gift boxes. Cookie boxes. If something came in a box, the thing itself may or may not be used, but the box itself was kept for use in the future – which, of course, never arrived. (The future has a habit of doing this). So boxes kept piling up – in cupboards, cabinets, up in the attic, down in the garage. Her side of the house was full of boxes. My side was brimming with books. Books and boxes constantly fought each other for dominance and extra space.

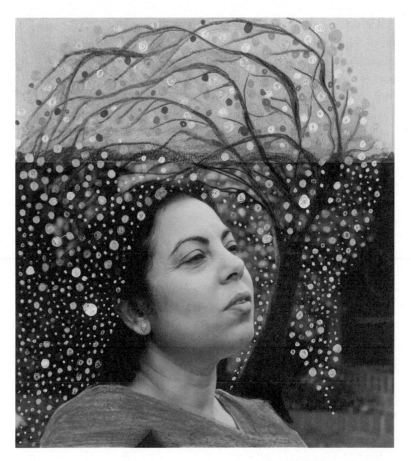

She was always discreet. Never said a bad word about me, or expressed affection, in front of the children. But love was showered when we were alone in bed, along with all the complaints. We spoke in Urdu. She would laugh at my comments in gatherings. But at night: how could you say such and such, why did you mock him, why did you criticise that. I would offer no defence, for the things I often said could not be defended as far as she was concerned. Anxieties about her children would be whispered. She had acquired the habit of repeating herself – especially when she thought her complaints were not being listened to or were ignored – so I would let her talk. She would give an endless list of my shortcomings.

Occasionally, she would complain about the injustices of the world, the suffering she saw every day on the news that she could no longer watch, the wars and destruction she could not endure. But she said it as though I was to blame for all these ills. I would exclaim in exhaustion: 'Why stop at violations of human rights? Why don't you also blame me for nuclear holocaust?' But it would all end with mutual expressions of undying love.

I thought she was the most pure and kind hearted person God had created on earth. She was grateful for, as she wrote in her 'Moment's Journal' on 29 January 2018, 'having loving children and husband'.

8.

In early October 2022, Saliha complained of pain in her stomach. She went to her GP who fobbed her off with antibiotics. They didn't work. She went back: this time the GP organised an ultrasound and blood tests. She was then referred to a gynaecologist, who organised a CT scan on 17 October, followed by an a MRCP on 25 and a PET scan on 31 October. During this time her pain continued to increase. She became jaundiced and started vomiting, had little or no appetite, and lost five kilograms in weight. She was in acute agony. Maha took time off work to look after her, as her symptoms became worse and worse. On 4 November, Maha, Zaid and Zain went with her to see a consultant at the Royal Free Hospital, Hampstead, in London. They were told that a biopsy confirmed gallbladder cancer – 'an adenocarcinoma'. The treatment would be chemotherapy with the aim of disease control rather than eradication. But if the disease was confirmed as locally advanced and she had an excellent response to chemotherapy, other treatments could be used to expel the cancer.

I was unaware of all this.

An election was on the horizon in Kuala Lumpur. And I was working on Anwar's campaign. I would ring Saliha every other day. But she never told me anything was wrong. 'I am fine. Don't worry about me', she would say. 'Just make sure Anwar wins the election'. A week after her diagnosis, I was in Tambun, a major town of the Kinta District in Parak, the seat Anwar was contesting. There was some doubt that he would win the seat. So, I went there with my colleagues to judge the situation, a couple of days before Anwar was due to arrive in the town to launch his campaign. I went to the airport to meet him and to communicate what I thought he should push at the hustings. But before I could say anything, he shook my hand, and pulled me near him. 'Has Maha rung you?', he asked. 'No', I replied. 'She has something important to tell you'.

I became concerned. I rang Maha immediately. 'I can't talk now', she told me. 'But *we* will ring you in the evening'. The *we* increased my anxiety.

That evening there was a meeting in Anwar's suite at his hotel. The entire election team of some thirty people were there. I was sitting next to Anwar when Maha rang. He asked me to take the call in his bedroom.

'Zaid, Zain and Mum are here', Maha said. 'And Zaid needs to talk to you', she handed the phone to her brother. 'We have something important to tell you', Zaid said. There was a long pause. 'Mum has gallbladder cancer'. He could hardly get the words out of his mouth.

I was stunned. 'What, what?', I mumbled. Another long silence. Then I became angry. 'What has happened to my wife? Why did you not tell me earlier?'. I started sobbing.

Maha came to the phone. 'Mum did not want us to tell you. She did not want you to worry. She wants you to concentrate on your work'.

'I will leave immediately', I exclaimed. 'I will be with you by tomorrow evening'. 'Let me speak to her'.

Maha gave her mobile to Saliha. 'I did not want to worry you', she said. 'And I don't want you to worry. I will be alright'. She paused. 'And there is no need to for you to come back immediately. Stay there till the election, till Anwar becomes the Prime Minister. You have waited a long time for that'.

So typical, I thought. Even in her darkest hour she is concerned about me rather than herself.

Both Saliha and Maha insisted that I stay and continue my work in KL. Saliha's chemotherapy was supposed to begin on 15 November, and I could return the day after the election. I agreed reluctantly. But I was angry that Anwar knew, my sister and other members of family had been told. But I knew not.

A week later, Maha rang in panic. It was middle of the night in London. 'Mum is vomiting continuously', she sobbed. 'I can't cope. Come now'. I took the first flight out of Kuala Lumpur.

I arrived early in the morning and ran straight to the bedroom. Saliha and Maha were sleeping together. They got up when they saw me. I ran to embrace my wife. I could not believe her transformation: she had been reduced to a skeleton; her face was pale. She had been unable to eat for days. Yet she was composed. I held her in my arms for several minutes, sobbing. 'We need to take her to hospital – *Now*!', I asserted. Saliha was reluctant. 'I hate hospitals', she said. But we took her anyway.

On 10 November, she was kept in the hospital for a night. A procedure was performed to sort out her severe constipation. She was given medicine to stop her vomiting. And we brought her back home the following day. She felt and looked much better, and very happy to see my sister, Huma, who had arrived from California that day. We anxiously waited for her chemotherapy to start.

I took her to the Royal Free Hospital on 15 November, when her chemotherapy sessions were to begin. But it was not to be. She was too malnourished. The bilirubin levels in her blood were too high. The first part of her small intestine (duodenum) was totally blocked. She was immediately admitted to hospital. A week later, she was taken to theatre to have a stent inserted in her bile duct. The procedure went horribly wrong. It was done using local anaesthetic, so she was conscious throughout and heard the surgeons talking. 'It's not working'. 'Too much fluid'. 'I can't get to it'. 'She's losing a lot of blood'. Saliha came out of the theatre terrified and upset. 'I don't want this. I don't want this', she kept saying. I consoled her, but it took a while for her to unruffle.

Later that day, when she had returned to her ward, she was in a great deal of pain. 'I can't imagine your pain', I grieved. 'No you can't', she replied. 'Only those with pain know what it is like to suffer'. She thought for a while, then she said: 'Jani, I don't want to be a burden on my children'. Then she prayed: '*Ya Allah*, don't turn me into a burden for my husband and children'. 'No, no,' I said. 'Begum: you are the centrifugal force of our lives. Our lives revolve around you. You can never be a burden on us. Please don't have such thoughts'. She smiled, turned over, and tried to go to sleep.

A second attempt was made a week later. This time a senior surgeon was called. Two stents were simultaneously inserted in the bile duct. The procedure went well.

We visited her daily. The kids. My sister. Her friends and colleagues also came to see her. She seemed happiest when her friend Indu and her colleagues from the school came to see her. I got jealous. 'You seemed happier to see them than me', I complained. 'You are my husband', Saliha replied. 'You are naturally bound to me. You have to be with me. You can do nothing else. You and I have no free will. We are bound together in eternal love'. She paused to adjust her intravenous drips. 'They are my friends and colleagues. They have their free will intact. They don't have to visit me. Yet they come. So I am happier to see that they too love me'.

After two weeks, she returned from the hospital feeling much better. She started to eat. Albeit mostly liquids, and slowly. Her vomiting had stopped, although she was still having problems with constipation. We saw her consultant on 9 December. We were told that she was very happy with Saliha's progress; her bile duct issue was 'now almost completely resolved'. Her first chemotherapy went well, and three weeks later, the second was even better. The cancer nurse rang to say that she had made 'remarkable progress'. It was all very encouraging We felt relieved and admired the courage that my Begum had shown during this tough period.

My sister felt confident enough to return to California. Her departure coincided with the arrival of my niece, Hana. Indu was a daily visitor. And her colleagues too came to see her regularly. She was so happy. And on her way to a semblance of recovery.

On 17 January she had her third session of chemotherapy. By all accounts it went well. But she couldn't sleep the following two nights. She was severely constipated and the vomiting returned.

On the morning of 20 January, she looked pale and unwell. We thought she needed another procedure to relieve her constipation. She was not keen to go yet again to the hospital. But we thought, and assured her, that she would only be there for a night. After all, the treatment was going reasonably well. 'You will be back by tomorrow, once the procedure is done', I said. Maha had a work-related matter to attend to, and I suggested she should go. She had taken enough days off work. I wanted to take Saliha to the hospital but Zaid said he would take his mum and look after her. 'You stay home and rest', he said. 'I will keep you posted'. 'I will come and see you in the evening as soon as the tests are done and you have been admitted', I said to Saliha. Maha and I hugged her as she left with Zaid at 11am.

At one' clock, Zaid rang to say that she would have a blood transfusion. A couple of hours later, he informed me that she was going for a scan. At around five o'clock he rang again. His voice was shaking. 'Dad', he murmured, 'Mum. She is very poorly'.

I dropped everything and called an Uber. I wanted the driver to get me to the hospital as fast as he could. But he took his time and insisted on telling me his life story.

When I got to the hospital, I ran straight to the emergency ward. A nurse took me to Saliha's bed.

Zaid was standing next to her weeping. I saw my beloved lying on a stretcher motionless. For a minute or two, I was totally paralysed. I couldn't speak. Then I shouted: 'What happened? My wife is dead? How could that be?' I held her hand. I stroked her face. I kissed her cheeks. 'Saliha! Saliha! Saliha! My Saliha'. I had no control of myself. I could not look at her in that state. I ran out of the ward and into the hospital compound. I was howling. I rang Maha. 'Your mum, your mum has died'. There was a loud scream at the other end. Then the phone went silent. I rang Zain: 'Our world has collapsed. Your ma has passed away'. I rang my brother. I rang Indu. All the while I was inconsolable. I was in shock. Disorientated. Despondent. Highly distressed. I walked up and down, round and round, in front of the hospital. And started attracting undue attention from the passers-by. Eventually I ran back to the ward.

I paced nervously in front of Saliha. I kept stroking her hand. Kissing her on her cheeks. While trying to regain control of myself. Soon Zain arrived, and stood motionless in front of his mother, next to his brother. Bewildered. Confused. Then a hospital Chaplin – an Imam – arrived and began to recite the Qur'an. That had some calming influence on us all. Then he prayed for Saliha to be forgiven. My insides exploded. 'Forgiven? What is there to be forgiven?' I bellowed. 'How can God forgive when there is nothing to forgive?' It is I, her husband, her *jani*, I thought, who needs forgiveness. 'Saliha, my Saliha, please forgive me'. 'Please forgive me'. '*Mere jan mujay maaf karu*. My Begum, forgive me for all my categorical mistakes, for everything'.

The junior doctor on duty took me and Zaid to a secluded part of the ward. 'My sincere condolences', he mumbled. 'We were waiting for the results of her scan', he continued, 'when her gallbladder ruptured. We did everything we could. The cancer had spread all over her body'. He handed us a 'document' – a printed sheet which stated the time of death: 18.11. Just a few minutes before I arrived. I asked Zaid if she had said anything to him. 'Yes dad', he replied. 'She said make sure you ask the doctor if my cancer is in recession'. She wanted to live. And she had so much to live for.

I looked around. There was no Maha. She was on her way to hospital, devastated with grief. I had to see her first. I ran out of the hospital and waited outside the A&E entrance. She arrived in a taxi within a few minutes. She was wailing. I put my arms around her and held her tightly. I walked slowly towards the ward, all the time with a firm grip on Maha, while trying to console her. But she continued to scream 'mum, mum'. By the time we entered the ward, her screams had become quite loud. A female nurse came, blocked our way, and threatened to call security if Maha did not calm down. 'Get out of my way', Maha shouted. 'How dare you stop me from going to my mother'. A male nurse rushed towards us. He was of Middle Eastern background, and seemed to understand our grief. He pushed the female nurse aside, and escorted us to Saliha.

We were soon joined by my brother, his wife, Farah, and daughter, and Indu and her sons Ashis and Anish. Everyone in disbelief and in tears.

Our grief had now grown exponentially and flooded our entire being. I was drenched in tears. Maha sobbed uncontrollably. Zaid wept incessantly. Zain stood motionless, tears in his eyes, as though, for him, time had stopped. I felt as though my very being had disintegrated. My innards were only loosely attached to my body. They were falling off, bit by bit, and I was disintegrating into so many atoms and molecules. The glue that held me together had dissolved. Half of my Self had gone. And the remaining half was falling apart.

Saliha's illness had been kept hidden from her mother – my *khala*. Now she had to be told. It was not possible for me. When she was eventually told by her son, she rang me. '*Khala*', I sobbed, 'please forgive me. I could not look after your daughter. *Khala*, pray that Saliha forgives me. I let her down. I was not even there when she took her last breath. Please forgive me'. Crying ceaselessly, she replied: 'No Zia, *baitay*. It was the will of God. He will forgive us all'.

There was a huge crowd at her funeral. My niece, Hana, was the first to arrive with her family the day after Saliha died. Then my sister and nephew,

Atif, who had returned one last time to see my Dulhan. Her school gave the day off to the staff to attend the funeral. My friends, her friends – we lost count. She was buried in Mill Hill cemetery, not far from where we live.

Over the next three or four weeks, messages and mails of sympathy poured in. There was a continuous flow of visitors who came to convey their condolences. Indu came almost every day, loaded with food. Saliha's colleagues visited us a number of times, encumbered a string of dishes. My sister's friend, Sadia, came and went, and every time she returned with even more fare. There were many visitors we hardly knew. And a couple we did not know at all. They claimed that they had once met Saliha! The house was full of people – day and night.

Then, they stopped coming. My sister, niece and nephew went away. The house became empty.

The absence of Saliha was a mournful presence. She had turned the house into our home. Every corner of our home was touched by her style, charm and elegance. She was everywhere. But nowhere. I couldn't sleep at night; I spent most days in tears. Every second, every moment, I longed for my Begum. I could not bear to be in the house without her. Eventually, I summoned the strength to go back to Malaysia, where Anwar Ibrahim was now Prime Minister, after three decades of our grinding struggles – all of which had been witnessed and shared by Saliha. Maha and Zaid decided to go with me. Zain wanted to be left alone. 'This is the most traumatic event of my life', he said. 'I need to be alone. I need to find my own way to overcome my grief'. While we flew to Kuala Lumpur, Zain went hiking.

9.

Our house has a recognisable black door. For me, it is pregnant with expectation. I opened it with great joy. Wherever I went in the world, whenever I returned, I opened the door to a loving embrace. If it was too early in the morning, and she was still sleeping, she would murmur '*Aa Gai*' – you are back. If it was a little later, and she was getting ready to go to work, she would come and embrace me and say: 'your lunch is in the fridge'. If it was at night, I would just slip in bed beside her. She would turn around, embrace me, and whisper: 'I love you *jani*'.

But this time, after a few weeks in Kuala Lumpur, and a couple of months after her death, I returned and could not open the door. Our neighbour, Farhan, son of my Malaysian friend, Ahmad Nazri Abdullah, was leaving for work, along with his wife Sara. They said Salaam. Then, Sara remarked: 'Uncle, the weeds have taken over your front garden'. I hadn't noticed. All I saw was the door.

I stood in front of the door for several minutes, shaking. Tears rolled down my cheeks. The key dropped from my hand. As I bent to pick the key, the words of Omar Khayyam echoed in my head:

There was a Door to which I found no key:
There was a veil through which I could not see
Some little talk awhile of Me and Thee
There seemed - and then no more of Me and Thee.

It took a little while for me to compose myself. Eventually, I opened the door, and went inside the house. I threw my luggage in the doorway, and sat in the living room. The house was truly empty for the first time. She was not there; there was no '*Aa Gai*', no loving embrace, no murmurs of *jani*. I could hear nothing. I could see nothing. I yearned for her voice. I longed to see her radiant face. I felt a haunting sense of incompleteness – exposed, as though I had been skinned, my body was just bones and flesh without the protective layer of the skin. The protective layer was always at our home, the fulcrum of my life. That is where I found myself and my body united with my skin, my soul with my being. But our home for over forty years did not feel like a home. It was just a house. How can the body survive without the skin? How would I survive separated from my soul mate? There was an absence, an eternal absence that I could not bear. I wept uncontrollably. After some time, I managed to get up, climb the stairs to our bedroom, and throw myself on the bed.

I fell asleep, or rather drifted into a state of suspension, somewhere between asleep and being conscious of my surroundings. I heard a movement. I thought it was the rattling of internal doors, and ignored it. Moments later, I heard another rustling sound. Then I felt as though someone had sat at the end of the bed. I looked up in fear. But my fear evaporated instantly as I gazed at the serene face of my Begum. She was looking and smiling at me. My Dulhan, swathed in garments like the day she married me. But not in red. She was covered with a soft white blanket that my sister had brought for her when she was going through her cancer treatment. I got up to embrace her. As usual, at first she was reluctant; then she threw the blanket around me. The eternal absence transformed into a perpetual presence. I walked down to the living room, and then all over the house, with Saliha wrapped around me, as though she was a life-enhancing blanket. The two as one. A door was ajar. She turned my grief into grace. Even in death she was concerned about me. In life, she displayed a bundle of virtues to be emulated. She was my life. She *is* my life. *Meri Jaan.*

10.

How fortunate I was to have her in my life. How unfortunate I am to lose her. Left with a longing that knows no bounds. What remains is just a name that was built over 64 years. Her birth certificate read simply Saliha Begum. The Pakistani passport of 1977 has Saliha Basit in blue, to which was added Sardar in black. Since then, she took the name as her own, no longer an afterthought. She expanded what meaning can be put in a name.

Enriching our moral compass so that it may always point towards justice and compassion. Ensuring the Sardars would not be without virtue. She was Saliha Begum Basit Sardar.

In the distance, I can hear Munni Begum singing.

> I don't know how the evil eye
> Of the world fell upon me
> My nest is broken
> I sit in a gathering, head bowed
> Kill me, just kill me.

VIRTUE AND VICE

Abdelwahab El-Affendi

There is an interesting contrast between the Biblical and Quranic accounts of the fall of Adam and Eve. In the first, Adam and Eve were warned against eating from the Tree of Knowledge of Good and Evil; and when they did, the concern in Heaven was about how dangerous the couple have become because of their newly acquired knowledge. They had to be expelled from Heaven and the Garden of Eden, not just as punishment, but to cut them down to size. In Genesis 3:22, God is reported to have said: 'Behold, the man has become as one of Us, to know good and evil', and he must now be expelled from the Garden of Eden, 'lest he put forth his hand and also take of the tree of life and eat and live everlasting.' It is not clear what 'Us' refers to here, to who the proclamation was addressed, since there is but one God in the end. This is a suspicious portrayal of the Biblical Jehovah as rather insecure, and worried about competition from His own creatures, in particular of their acquisition of knowledge that could make them more powerful.

This problematic outlook is also reflected in another Biblical story, that of the 'Tower of Babel' (Genesis 11:1–9,) where humans have allegedly posed another threat to Heavenly power and authority through an attempt by Babylonians to build a tower that reaches up to the heavens, after the Deluge. According to the biblical story, God intervened to foil the plan by so confusing the language of the workers, thus disrupting their ability to communicate and coordinate their work. According to extra-biblical sources (in this case, the first century Roman-Jewish historian Flavius Josephus), one of the aims of the human plot was to be as powerful as God Himself and deter the Almighty from ever sending another Deluge to drown the world. The tower in the mighty city would be too high for the waters to submerge it. This is also described as a revenge against God for destroying the Babylonians' forefathers.

We will only in passing point out some gaping hole in this story. Since the story describes the Babylonians as descendants of Noah, it is incongruous to accuse God of drowning their ancestors, since Noah has been saved, not drowned. This would be like the Jews holding a grudge against God for drowning the Pharaoh. Even more congruous, given that the story of the Deluge was alive in the rhetoric of the offending Babylonians, where the Almighty has demonstrated his absolute ability to completely destroy a community to the last individual, would Heaven be at all worried about such a prank by the apparently ignorant Babylonians?

Both stories seem to have echoes of polytheist myths and cultures, where Jehovah is portrayed like a Greek God, vulnerable to machinations from competing gods and their human allies, (including frequent successful) human attempts to 'steal' knowledge from the gods (the way Prometheus did with fire).

In contrast, the Quranic version of the story shows God as the source of knowledge for Adam. That was how God reinforced Adam's advantage when the Angels complained about his designation as God's vice-regent on Earth. The Angels questioned his worthiness of this honour, protesting that he was going 'to wreak havoc on it and spill blood,' (in contrast to the obedient angels who 'glorify Thy name and worship Thee'). God then 'taught Adam all names,' and tested the angels' knowledge in that department. They failed. Adam was then instructed to display his mastery of language by enumerating the names of objects; his superiority was thus based on his divine-imparted knowledge. This is the complete opposite of the claim that God was in fact jealous of Adam's capacity to acquire knowledge.

The contrast is that it was God who endowed Adam with the knowledge he had acquired, the Almighty being the source of all knowledge. This favour was deliberate and meant to enhance Adam's worthiness of being God's chosen creature to take charge on Earth. God, being Almighty and All-Knowing, has no insecurities vis-à-vis His creatures, and was not worried about their acquisition of knowledge. While eating from the forbidden Tree is said to have made Adam and Eve aware of their nakedness (and ashamed of it), it is not this 'knowledge' that was the focus of God's displeasure with Adam and his wife, but the act of disobedience that precipitated it. The seducer is not a 'serpent', but Satan, the creature who was jealous of God's favouring of Adam; he had already refused to prostrate himself to Adam when ordered by God. When banished from Heaven for this insubordination, Satan swore to corrupt Adam and his descendants, and encourage them to disobey God. Adam was duly warned against the machinations of this devil, who could drive him out of Eden. He did not heed that warning and fell in the trap when Satan indicated that the Tree could grant him and his wife 'royal immortality'. It was thus Adam's ignorance and gullibility that caused his fall, not his superior knowledge. In the Quranic version, Eve is not blamed for the sin, since Satan addressed the couple together, and they both accepted his dubious narrative. Adam is constantly singled out as *the* culprit.

Ignorance as Faithlessness

On this basis, the 'original sin' was ignorance and gullibility, rather than knowledge or the search for it. Adam was provided with knowledge about the threat posed by the Devil to his welfare, but he ignored this valuable knowledge, and acted contrary to it. In spite of knowing that God was his benefactor, having favoured him over the angels, and even asked them to bow to him, and warned him against the evil intents of his enemy, he believed that the Devil has got his interests at heart more than God. He believed that God had in fact withheld from him beneficial information about the value of the tree he was prevented from touching, and that this knowledge was possessed by his enemy who, 'out of the goodness of his heart', readily volunteered it to him. The problem here does look like a surplus of knowledge, but the opposite, serious misjudgement that ignored the true knowledge he already had.

This an interesting manifestation of ignorance, in that it is acting contrary to what one already knows, making this knowledge useless. It also conforms to the Dutch philosopher Rick Peels's so-called New View of ignorance as 'lack of true belief rather than lack of knowledge.' According to this view, Adam was indeed ignorant, in that he wrongly believed that eating from the forbidden tree would have made him immortal and granted him limitless powers, that God has deceived him by concealing from him this important truth in order to deprive him from these benefits, and that the Devil has benevolently revealed those 'truths' to him. It is also a question of trust/mistrust. Here, one is trusting information from a dubious source, in contrast to information from a source with absolute credibility.

This in turn, highlights the relation between knowledge and faith. The latter is a form of knowledge in the sense of 'true belief' based on trust. It is supposed to reflect true knowledge about the universe, its origin, its purpose, how it works, and how to conduct oneself in it. Religion, as the universe's 'operations manual' that comes with the product, is supposed to project such a body of knowledge. The problem is not obtaining this manual and the power that comes with it. Rather, it is losing it, or not having it in the first place, or having a faulty version, that is the catastrophe. This knowledge is by its nature problematic to verify, and is based primarily on trusting the immediate source.

However, the biblical point about some knowledge being harmful, even though problematic in the instance above, is not entirely invalid. The Quran does recognise some types of knowledge as harmful. The primary example offered is dabbling in magic, which, we are told, was originally taught by two angels in Babylon. But they always gave a warning when responding to requests for tuition: 'We are a seduction; so do not become an unbeliever [by learning what we are going to teach you]'. Here, 'knowledge' becomes a gateway to unbelief, even synonymous with it. However, this appears the odd case out. The reason given is that magic can only be used to do harm, never good. In this it is a unique form of knowledge, given that most types of knowledge are commendable, or at least harmless. Most types of information can be used for good and evil. Not magic, apparently.

Other forms of harmful knowledge include prying into other people's private affairs, which is seriously discouraged in the Quran, as is gossip and the spreading unsubstantiated accusations against other people. In particular, attacking a woman's chastity is regarded as a cardinal sin. Interestingly, even if a person does have direct compromising information about a woman, he is not permitted to share it, unless he can bring three other witness who have direct supporting information. Any allegation not backed by four witnesses is described in the Quran as a lie. Its purveyor is branded a liar, and his/her testimony can never be trusted again, regardless of the actual veracity of the claim. Sharing negative or derogatory information about others in their absence (aka gossip), even if true, is also a grave sin. These are instances where selective ignorance is indeed a virtue. It is a sin to investigate and seek such information, a burden to know accidentally, and even graver sin to share.

The connection between faith and knowledge is additionally complicated by the challenge of verification. For even if the knowledge on which faith is based is supposed to refer to undisputable truths, such knowledge cannot, by its very nature, be verified directly. In fact, if and when such claims are verified, it would usually be too late, and it *will not be faith*. A person who is not a prophet, would encounter angels usually when one is about to die, or to be smitten by heavenly chastisement. Then one will indeed have *direct knowledge* of the angelic phenomenon. But that will not be *faith*; it is true, direct and undisputable *knowledge* indeed; but superfluous, and utterly useless.

Faith is a type of inference, based on cumulative evidence. Its validity depends primarily on trusting the veracity of the primary narrator, usually a privileged person who has direct and exclusive access to the Truth (a prophet). Such an agent ascertains a direct communication line to Heaven. Through this channel, a series of self-reinforcing and mutually supportive messages are received, confirming the veracity of the narrator. The character of this narrator is also supposed to be a testament to this trustworthiness and reliability.

In the Abrahamic tradition, a corroboration is found in the continuity of the tradition itself: its key tenets and ruling values. Here, successive prophets confirm and re-confirm the stories and injunctions over generations. This is often linked to practical communal experiences of suffering, salvation, punishments and rewards. Individually, prophets may provide 'miracles' as indirect corroboration. The success of the mission, through the fulfilment of promises, spectacular victories, or dramatic changes, is also supposed to be corroboration. However, even the apparent initial failure of the mission, as in the case of Christianity, could be reformulated as the ultimate victory.

Refusal to subscribe to these narratives is branded as ignorance. It is often self-imposed ignorance, since those hostile to the message usually refuse to listen to it. It is reported in the Quran that opponents of Prophet Muhammad in Makkah would plug their ears so as not to hear his words, on the belief that it may have a 'magical' impact that would overpower their will. This was also reported about Noah's people. The enemies often murder prophets and/or drive them out in order to suppress their message.

This is probably one reason that the pre-Islamic period in Arabia is not referred to as an era of ignorance (*jahl*), but as a culture of ignorance (*jahiliyya*). This culture is not just about the refusal to learn, but could also incorporate other negative traits, such as racism. Prophet Muhammad reportedly reprimanded one of his companions for using an abusive racist swear word against another companion, calling him 'son of a black woman.' The Prophet told the culprit: 'Did you insult him by referring to his mother? You are someone with traces of *jahiliyya* in you!' Thus, ignorance may not manifest itself merely in the deliberate rejection of 'true' knowledge, or the failure to attain it, but also in having the wrong attitude: arrogance, racism, disdain for others, etc. Here, ignorance is an ethical, as well as a cognitive, issue.

Enforced Ignorance

It is also ironic that religious knowledge is often restricted by its own guardians. This is evident in Judaism, which is not a proselytising religion, keeping religious knowledge only for internal circulation. However, while Islam and Christianity are essentially 'missionary' religions, with the spread of the message obligatory on the community, they still maintained mechanisms for limiting the circulation of religious knowledge, or at the minimum, restricting the authoritative interpretation to a small circle of 'learned men'. The regimentation of religious authority was more formalised in Christianity, where a closed hierarchy of priests controlled access to religious knowledge, including the authority to perform or preside over religious rituals. Only priests can officiate at ceremonies of christening, weddings, and funerals; and only they could lead prayers. These restrictions were enhanced by official decrees from the Catholic church restricting lay access to the scriptures and outlawing their translation into local languages. An early translator of the Bible into English, William Tyndale, was in fact burned at the stake in 1536 for this offence. The Catholic Church only permitted the conduct of religious services in languages other than Latin in the mid-1960s.

Islam was more permissive in this regard, since it has no official priesthood, and any modestly informed believer could conduct or lead services and rituals. These could also be conducted anywhere, and not necessarily at a mosque. However, a clerical hierarchy has evolved over time, and religious teachers and imams need to be endorsed by some formal authority to be recognised by the community. Arabic is still the official language for prayers and Quranic recitations. And although the Quran has been widely translated, usually by enterprising individuals, leading clerical hierarchies insist on endorsing translations before being allowed to circulate.

While it has become fashionable for clerics in both religions to extend their quest to knowledge to non-religious subjects, especially languages, final authority usually still resides with clerics whose main expertise is in religious learning. A person who immerses himself too much in secular disciplines might disqualify himself as a religious authority. Thus interestingly, the authoritativeness of a cleric is enhanced proportionately to what he ignores (outside traditional religious disciplines), rather than what he knows. The more ignorant you are about things mundane, the higher your status becomes. Paradoxically, however, these clerics also present themselves as authorities on how people should conduct themselves in daily lives, being requested to offer fatwas on anything from medical procedures to financial transactions.

This systematic 'promotion of ignorance' by restricting access to religious knowledge is condemned in the Quran as an unforgiveable sin. 'Verily, as for those who suppress aught of the revelation that God has bestowed from on high and barter it away for a trifling gain - they but fill their bellies with fire. And God will not speak unto them on the Day of Resurrection, nor will He cleanse them [of their sins]; and grievous suffering awaits them.' (2:175) The reference to this interconnection between the promotion of ignorance and worldly gain points to a close link between ignorance and power. Maintaining exclusive access to authoritative religious knowledge by restricting access and circulation is meant to enhance power over others. However, it defeats the whole purpose of religion as the source of indispensable 'salvation knowledge,' a characteristic that imposes on the 'custodians' of this knowledge not just a duty of 'full disclosure', but an active obligation to make this information as widely available as possible. They are certainly not permitted to conceal it or obstruct access to it, and overall not to seek to benefit from such obstruction.

In the Quran, the custodians of the scriptures are described as 'people of the book', which indicates that they were 'communities' built around the scripture. It is an important aspect of their defining identity. As a community, they have been 'granted' the revelation, or 'made to inherit the book'. They have been 'selected', 'chosen', carefully picked for this role. Just as humanity has been selected through Adam to reign on Earth, various communities have been selected as guides about how to perform this mission. This is a privilege as well as a burden and a responsibility. The two are interrelated: being the object of divine choice is indeed a great honour; but it is linked to a heavy responsibility. The dereliction of the associated duty will obviate that privileged status and turns it into a curse. Literally so, as one verse of the Quran puts it:

> Behjold, as for those who suppress aught of the evidence of the truth and of the guidance which We have bestowed from on high, after We have made it clear unto mankind through the divine writ - these it is whom God will curse, and whom all who can judge will curse (2: 159).

These custodians fall, in relation to their privileged position, into three categories, according to their fulfilment of the burden: those who fail or wilfully abuse their position; those shoulder the duty, but maybe only just; and those who excel in being both teachers and exemplary practitioners. The latter position marks a higher level of selection.

> And so, We have bestowed the divine writ as a heritage unto such of Our servants as We chose: and among them are some who sin against themselves; and some who keep half-way [between right and wrong]; and some who, by God's leave, are foremost in deeds of goodness: [and] this, indeed, is. a merit most high! (35: 32).

Of course the custodians could argue that their manipulation of access to the scriptures is not only well-intentioned, but in fact a sacred duty. The holy texts should not be made available to all and sundry. This could lead to desecration and/or exposure to abuse. The 'ignorant' might misinterpret the texts, or use them for questionable purposes. Blocking access is in fact a form of teaching; people must strive to access the holy texts: learn the language, be fit to read and understand exegeses. They must genuflect for decades in front of the learned and learn and practice humility, before they can become part of the authoritative inner sanctum of custodians. The 'ignorant', on the other hand, must be locked out; they should be kept ignorant.

The Construction of Ignorance

It is to be recalled the direct followers or disciples of Moses, Jesus, and Muhammad, were mostly illiterate 'ignorant' individuals, often in multiple senses of the term. They had not gone to universities or spent most of their youth in seminaries. They were simple carpenters, fishermen, labourers, slaves, women, teenagers. They listened directly to the words of those prophets and, as a result, became teachers themselves.

Later generations, however, constructed an elaborate body of knowledge designed to exclude, rather than simplify and inform. The development of modern science has gone even further in making knowledge esoteric and exclusive through jargon. As 'disciplines' and sub-disciplines multiply, each produces its own specialised language and techniques, mastering them tends to require years and prohibitive expenses. That is usually coupled with heavy regulations of professions. Authorities (governmental and professional) restrict the access of 'outsiders' to learning or practicing all sorts of professions, from electric repairs and plumbing to medicine, pharmacology, and even law, without elaborate training and procedures. This is usually justified in terms of safeguarding the interest of 'ordinary people' and preventing harm. Of course given the current situation, that is indeed justified. For it is impossible for anyone who has not spent many years in law and medical schools, or long apprenticeships in engineering professions, to perform even the most preliminary tasks in these areas. The majority of us are almost completely ignorant of almost everything other than our own professions. A doctor is usually an ignoramus in law or engineering, and vice versa.

However, the question arises: is this the fault of the 'ignoramuses' or of a system that has turned the most learned individuals into ignoramuses? There is certainly a minimal body of medical, legal, technical knowledge that can be made available to most people, and it is essential for their health, the protection of their rights, or just getting about with their daily lives. Many people have acquired such knowledge. Many of us find lawyers and doctors less helpful in certain cases than an informed 'lay' person, who can give more sound, and less costly, suggestions for solutions.

Modern societies and their institutions have replicated religion by constructing new spaces of taboos, prohibitions, areas and modes of silencing, and types of imposed ignorance. In addition to the professionalised taboos, the state has its own 'official secrets' laws, where actions, deliberations and internal operations of state institutions cannot be disclosed to the wider public, under the pain of severe punishments for transgressors. Corporations and other institutions, including universities, the bastions of learning, also have their secrecy norms. In such cases, unauthorised 'knowing' about such things, let alone disclosing them to others, can be a grave sin. Ignorance is highly recommended, and in fact imposed; any attempt to discover or 'research' such forbidden areas is punishable as espionage. Related to this are various types of intellectual property regulations, where professional information regarding the manufacture of items, use of processes or techniques, the composition of medicines, and even the right to re-publish material already in the public domain without permission of the 'copyright' owner, could be very risky.

Here, 'ignorance' is not the absence of knowledge but the enforcement of exclusion from a certain knowledge community, being prevented from knowing (or sharing your knowledge, if you had access to it). You are designated by some authority or another as someone who is not permitted to know. You may not be literally burnt at the stake for defying or infringing the prohibition, but you could still be hunted in that foreign capital where you have taken refuge, extradited to face punishment, or just incinerated by a drone hit in your desert hideout.

A trend championed first by the Frankfurt School in the 1930 about interdisciplinarity has now gain wide acceptance. According to this principle, scholars should not restrict themselves to narrow specialisations, but must familiarise themselves with the findings of other disciplines, reach out across specialisation, and set up cooperative research groups from multiple disciplines to research social issues. There is a rationale for this, since specialisations can get rather myopic, missing the bigger picture.

Social phenomena are too complex to be treated with a few sets of abstract concepts and a small number of tools. Human beings are social and political animals, but they are also literary constructors of narratives and imaginary worlds, economic actors, and spiritual beings. They associate as neighbours, professionals, members of political parties, sports fans clubs, concert goers, civil activists; they congregate as families and clans, religious communities and sects, nations, groups, etc. And investigators thus need to have wider horizons in order to grasp what is going on around them, just as disciplines are shifting towards micro-specialisations. Otherwise, the most learned can become an emblem of ignorance.

Ironically, the current system promotes narrower and narrower specialisations, since academics and other professionals advance more in proportion to how narrowly focused they are. This means ignorance about most things outside your specialisation, in fact even most things within your specialisation. Do not try to complain about the sudden headache that gripped you to a family member who specialises in neo-natal acute medicine. You will be wasting your time.

Still, multidisciplinarity has its advantages. I have personally resorted to interdisciplinary strategies (both as cross-disciplinary reach from politics to economics, literature, sociology, history, and as collaborative effort with colleagues from other disciplines) in studies of mass violence and genocide. This has yielded important insights that were unavailable for researchers who concentrated on just one dimension of the phenomenon.

The custodians of the system could argue that restrictions on knowledge acquisition and dissemination serve the public interest. Government institutions, or even universities and businesses can barely function if their daily deliberations are open to unrestricted outside access. It could also be argued that confidentiality is important for many processes, judicial, bureaucratic, and even academic, where it should be possible for individuals to express their opinions freely or look at private or secret information for the more effective functioning of institutions. The same can be said about the protection of intellectual properties or trade secrets. These are vital for the economy and scientific progress.

Custodians of religious knowledge or other specialisations can also argue that preventing dilettantes from accessing privilege/authoritative knowledge is an important precaution against abuse. Clerics and their supporters often compare the two, complaining that all and sundry are permitted to pontificate on religious matters, regardless of their ignorance. They are allowed to attack the opinions of qualified religious sages, and even denigrate their knowledge qualifications. However, the same people would insist on consulting only qualified and certified doctors, or an accredited engineer or computer expert, when the need arises. And they would not dare challenge the opinions of doctors or nuclear physicists in their specialisation.

There is a difference, however. There are no restrictions on direct access to the available information in medicine, pharmacology, or engineering. Anyone can independently study those specialisations. However, they are not allowed to practice in that field without certification and tests that ensure the person is not a danger to others. For this reason, they are supposed to acquire the knowledge and training, and pass multiple tests, within authorised institutions. So the restrictions are not on acquiring the knowledge, but on using it. Additionally, there is no obligation on any authority to make such knowledge available on demand. In fact, there are prior tests for eligibility even when one seeks to join a recognised institution. Not anyone can be admitted to medical school.

Religious knowledge is different in many respects. It is supposed to be available on demand. In fact, it is usually made available even to those who are unaware of its existence, or those who explicitly reject it and show intense hostility to it. Restricting its availability is a violation of its own logic and provisions. The argument against abuse is of course important. However, if God Himself insists that this knowledge must not be withheld, it is not up to those 'made to inherit the book' to have other opinions about who to choose as privileged recipients. As the Quran repeatedly affirms to the Prophet your duty is only to deliver the message. You are not accountable for the actions of recipients after this delivery.

Conclusion

The biblical and Quranic versions of the story of Adam and Eve offer diverging judgments about the nature of the sin that caused the couple to be banished from Heaven. In the biblical version, their sin was acquiring forbidden knowledge, and the potential to access empowering but dangerous knowledge; in the Quranic version, it is gullibility, naiveté and ignorance. In one version, knowledge was a threat; in the other it was an asset and a sign of divine favour. It was what caused the envious Satan to trick Adam into losing his advantage, naively and erroneously believing his sworn enemy to have superior knowledge that had been withheld from him; and that the same enemy against whose wiles he had been warned, will be so generous with this privileged knowledge as to share it with him.

It was thus ignorance and gullibility that was the original mother of all sins responsible for Adam's downfall, and not the acquisition of 'forbidden knowledge'. In religious terms, harmful knowledge does not refer to true knowledge about the universe and human affairs. Rather, it is the acquisition and use of skills that could only harm innocent humans, such as magic. While it could of course be argued many other harmful arts do exist, in particular the art of war. Even indispensable arts and professions, like medicine, could be used for harming others. However, the presupposition is that magic is a single-purpose art, while the others do have dual or multiple purposes.

Other types of forbidden knowledge, such prying into other people's private affairs, are also problematic because of their potential harm to others. Such a knowledge is acquired against the will of the person concerned, and its sharing and use is necessarily harmful. It is an infringement on the very integrity of the human being, a serious violation of her very personhood. In this day and age where the power of technology and increasingly concentrated power of states and conglomerates combine in a sustained assault on privacy and integrity of every human being, this infringement on the very personhood and inner integrity of the human being is the greatest threat to humanity, and certainly the mother of all modern sins.

However, this poses a paradox. Some pursuits of knowledge is indeed ethically questionable. We would not be happy if others wanted to invade our privacy and make (usually uninformed) judgements about our intimate affairs. So we should not subject others to such processes. But this should not be a justification for clamouring for the strictest restrictions on seeking and disseminating information. Ignorance is not a virtue to be promoted, even if it may look like it sometimes.

This is especially so since ignorance is often 'constructed' and imposed by various authorities, religious and secular. The powers-that-be often exercise power through restricting access to knowledge, and discrimination between citizens by designating many as ineligible to access vital information. Even religious authorities practice such selective imposition of ignorance. State and business bureaucracies also rely on enforced ignorance to bolster their grip on power.

The professionalisation of knowledge has also spread ignorance even among the most learned and has become adept at creating a coalition of 'ignoramuses' in order to sustain a mesh of compartmentalised knowledge. This is alright as long as each understands that she is just an insignificant cog in a big machine that produces knowledge by rationing ignorance. The problem arises when someone who only studied genes starts to think of himself as a judge over God himself.

However, the maxim we should adopt is that knowledge is generally beneficial, and not the other way round. Areas in which ignorance appears to be a virtue relate to a general ethical rule of reciprocity and the duty not to cause harm. The issue depends more on the person's own ethical commitment and restraint. It is not a matter of 'ignorance', but of decency and restraint. Human beings should generally abstain from prying and slandering others out of their own will; and there should be legal means of redress and restraint in an era where such infringements have become professionalised and exploited for huge economic gain.

In the end, the pursuit of knowledge remains the virtue of virtues, but has to be combined with other virtues, such as integrity, honesty, and concern for others. Many professions claim to safeguard such values, even though this may involve the promotion and 'imposition' of ignorance. Their argument is that, on the balance, the 'safeguards' benefit the community and learning in general. Similar arguments are advanced by other authorities and bureaucracies that restrict access to knowledge as several levels. Again, while there are valid justifications for some of these restrictions, the balance is still on keeping them to a minimum.

THE BEDROCK VIRTUES

Colin Tudge

The task for all humanity, I modestly suggest, should be to make the world a better place – and that requires us first to decide what a 'better place' would look like. Without that, we can have no Goal, and no proper sense of direction. Specifically, I suggest, our Goal should be to create - convivial societies; personal fulfilment; and a flourishing biosphere.

All three are important – no single one has priority. The three vital ingredients of a truly agreeable and secure world are like the legs of a three-legged stool, if any of them is compromised the whole structure collapses. But of course, in most modern societies, and most societies from the past, one or more of the three is neglected, which is one good reason why the world is in such a mess. Note, please, 'fulfilment' rather than the more usual 'happiness', which all too easily is taken to mean hedonism. So it is that farming for example - or nursing or teaching or building houses or anything else that is really worthwhile - is infinitely fulfilling for those who love it but it's certainly not all fun and games. Note, too, the term 'biosphere' which means the living world rather than 'environment'. 'Environment' simply means 'surroundings' and in these neoliberal days it is equated with real estate. Nature is reduced to stage scenery.

Movement towards the Goal is what ought to be meant by 'progress'. Progress should not, as is now the norm, be equated simply with technological innovation or increase in material wealth. But modern governments do not define their Goal in any satisfactory manner. They focus instead on 'targets' which should simply be seen as means to an end – but they rarely if ever spell out clearly what the end is that they have in mind, if any. Thus, in Britain right now both the major parties are intent, and in the Tories' case obsessed, with economic growth – or 'Growth, growth, growth' as the fly-by-night Prime Minister Liz Truss put the matter. But perpetual growth is of course impossible in a finite world - and doesn't necessarily or usually raise the wellbeing of humanity as a whole and still less of our fellow creatures even when it is achieved.

I suggest that if we are ever to achieve our Goal (of 'convivial societies; personal fulfilment; and a flourishing biosphere') then we need first to address three basic questions:

What is it *right* to do?
What is it *necessary* to do (in order to do what's right)? And
What is it *possible* to do?

If what is necessary exceeds what is possible then we are in deep trouble – which seems to be the case right now as the world collapses around us. But in truth we have merely overestimated what is necessary. For example: the present, prevailing economy, geared single-mindedly to the global market, requires us to produce as much meat as it is possible to sell so as to maximise return and profit. But it isn't possible to produce all the meat that it's possible to sell without wrecking the biosphere. But then it isn't necessary to produce all that meat in the first place. Good cooks make a little go a long way, and a little (from animals that have been raised kindly, on diets that are as near as possible natural to them) is all we need. More generally, the ultra-competitive, ultra-materialistic neoliberal mindset encourages us all to strive for material wealth - Ferraris and private swimming pools all round - which indeed is impossible but is also quite unnecessary. So we need to ask, as Gandhi asked, but very few modern governments do, what really *is* necessary? Of course, many millions of people worldwide are truly deprived but in the western world at least most of us already have far more than we really need. Yet in the present economy all industries are encouraged to expand – to produce and sell more stuff. But it's not more stuff we need. It's more fairness.

Which brings me at last to the point. In order to address the three fundamental questions and to move towards what should be our Goal, we need to root all our thoughts, plans, and actions in what I suggest should be called the 'Bedrock Principles' of Morality and Ecology. Indeed, the principles of morality and ecology are the only concepts that deserve to be called 'principles' at all. What politicians and economists call 'principles' are mere ideologies, which is not the same thing at all.

Moral philosophy is the study of morality – it aspires to tell us what it is *right* to do; and ecology should be able to tell us what is necessary to keep the world in good heart, and what is possible within the physical and biological limits of this Earth. Modern education tends to discuss morality in various contexts but in this neoliberal world it is mainly concerned with 'getting on' – with competing successfully for wealth and position; while the science of ecology has typically been down-played – not considered front-line in the manner of molecular biology or particle physics.

Ecology must be a broad church. As in medicine, the first requirement is to give a damn – truly to *care* about our fellow creatures and the state of the biosphere in general; and so (like medicine) ecology must be framed by ideas and feelings that belong in the realms of morality, aesthetics, and spirituality.

Yet the core of ecology is serious science, rooted in disprovable hypotheses. Indeed, ecology must partake of *all* the sciences – a grand coalition of biology, earth science, chemistry, physics, and what you will. Physics sets the gold standard of science because it deals primarily with the grand principles that are seen to underlie all reality, and because it seeks ideally to express those principles in mathematical formulae (such as $E=MC^2$), which are commonly seen to be irrefutable. All in all, then, science in its purest form deals in abstractions.

Ecology must accept those abstractions of course – the laws of physics, if we've got them right, must apply to everything. But ecologists must go one step further. They must seek to show how the underlying physical principles play out in the real world, when the pot is stirred by the realities of chaos and complexity and non-linearity, and indeed by the vagaries of evolution; and then show how the physical realities interact with the endless details of natural history – the interactions of trillions of individuals (when we include the microbes), and thousands of species, in any one place.

Indeed, ecology is not the poor relation of science. By seeking to apply the abstractions of science to the endless details of real life it emerges as the most complete of sciences, the grand coalition seeking to understand reality. Yet in the end, too, ecology must be a practical pursuit. It must indeed be rooted in science, but it must also be an art and a craft, and framed overall by precepts of a moral and spiritual kind.

Then again, despite the protestations of some of its practitioners, and despite its wondrousness, science in general has serious limitations. It does not and cannot deal with absolute certainties as was once believed, but its ideas are at least *robust*. Its ideas may not represent absolute truth but neither are they simply speculation. For to qualify as bona fide science, ideas must be of a kind that are testable and theoretically disprovable. To be sure, we may sometimes feel certain that the ideas of science do represent the absolute truth, but in all but the simplest of matters (as in tautologies and matters of definition) we can never be certain that our certainty is justified (as of course is true of all ideas of every kind). But at least we can be sure that the ideas of science that qualify as theories have survived the best attempts to date to show that they are *not* true – and this is robustness of a kind.

But can moral philosophy ever be comparably robust? Is it even reasonable to speak or indeed to dream of 'bedrock' principles of morality? Can there be principles of morality that are deeply rooted and can apply to all humanity at all times? Clearly, after all, different societies have different mores and moral codes – some for example embrace the idea of 'honour killing', which others find utterly repugnant. So can moral 'principles' ever be more than 'relative'? Isn't morality in the end just a matter of opinion, shaped by the irredeemably fickle hands of history and custom?

Well, I suggest that despite appearances, and despite what it is widely fashionable to believe, we can nonetheless discern moral principles that at least are well-nigh universal – and to that extent can be considered 'bedrock'. And those principles are of the kind known as *virtues*.

The three main threads of moral philosophy

I owe to the Oxford-based philosopher and theologian Timothy Bartell the insight that moral philosophy in general throughout the past few thousand years of written history has been of three kinds: Utilitarian, Deontological, and Virtue ethics.

Utilitarians judge the goodness or the badness of any particular action according to outcome; so utilitarian philosophy is also called 'consequentialist'. The idea of utilitarian ethics emerged in its more or less modern form in the Enlightenment of the eighteenth century. It's all very rational, as the Enlightenment aspired to be. The whole philosophy of it was perhaps best summed up by the English philosopher Jeremy Bentham

(1748–1832) who said that a good action is one that leads to 'the greatest happiness of the greatest number'. This approach obviously has its uses – it is indeed 'utilitarian'. Thus it should help us to decide for example what medicinal drugs or vaccines we should put our efforts behind – those that help just a few or those that could cure or protect a great many (and clearly, at the moment, the world favours the wealthy few over the impoverished many).

But as the ultra-rational Scot, David Hume (1711–1776), had long since pointed out, matters of morality *cannot* in the end be decided by rational means alone. Mere arithmetic does not get to the bottom of things. In the end what we consider to be good or bad is a matter of *feelings*. So it is (this is my example, rather than Hume's) that if six Hooray Henries beat up one old tramp who nobody apparently cares about, then we are left with six well-connected and happy roisterers versus one lonely old chap made miserable, which arithmetically may seem to satisfy Bentham's criterion of goodness. Yet most of us – all who are not sociopaths - feel in our bones that such beating up is *wrong*. Moral philosophy, surely, should ask where this bone-feeling comes from and how much store to put by it. But I'll come to that.

The idea behind deontology is that we should act according to some set of rules or 'principles'. To obey the rules is good, and to flout or defy them is bad. Thus, a morally good solider is one who obeys orders; a morally good executive is one who carries out company policy, according to his or her contract of employment; and a good priest or imam or monk or nun is one who conforms to the norms of his or her religion.

In truth, my own suggestion – that it is good to try to create convivial societies that encourage personal fulfilment and look after the natural world – is a form of deontology. It defines a good thought or action according to whether or not it is in line with this particular objective. So I cannot logically argue that deontology *per se* is bad. Again, though, it clearly has its limits. Are soldiers right to obey orders if they feel in their bones that the order is wrong? Should a soldier set fire to a village simply because some general tells him or her to do so? Is it enough to say, as many a Nazi said at the Nuremberg trials, 'I was only obeying orders'? Should a corporate executive help to sweep aside traditional societies and landscapes and ways of life just in the interests of company profits, even if he or she is contracted expressly to maximise returns to the shareholders? Should politicians conform to party policy even when their conscience says 'No'? Clearly many do feel that obedience is right, come what may. Politicians make a special 'virtue' of party 'loyalty', and of overriding their own misgivings. Or then again: does the God from whom the clerics of Christianity take their lead always behave well? Thus, in Genesis, Exodus, Numbers, Deuteronomy, Joshua, Judges, and Samuel God constantly threatens to 'smite' transgressors without mercy, or exhorts the Israelites to do so. Thus in Samuel-1 15:3 he tells the Israelites to 'go and smite Amalek, and utterly destroy all that they have, and spare them not; but slay both man and woman, infant and suckling, ox and sheep, camel and ass'.

Many nowadays might well feel it is over the top, even though the Amalek were constant thorns in the Israelites' side. Similarly, Leviticus 20:10 tells us in the King James version that 'the man who commits adultery with *another* man's wife, *he* who commits adultery with his neighbour's wife, the adulterer and the adulteress, shall surely be put to death'. And we learn from the Gospel of St John that putting to death means stoning – which led Jesus in chapter 8 verse 7 to tell the self-appointed, vigilante executioners, 'he that is without sin among you, let him cast the first stone'. Clearly, Jesus felt that that God's original command (as least as transmitted by the prophets of the Old Testament) could and should be overridden. If even God can be questioned, then it seems that *no* authoritarian voice can be taken to be absolute.

Virtues, when you boil them down, are the special qualities that people seem to have (or lack) which lead us to feel that they are indeed good people (or not). Incidentally, or not so incidentally, it seems to me that the expression 'virtue ethics' is unfortunate. 'Virtue-based morality' would be closer to the mark. Ethics, from the Greek *ethos*, is specifically about what is good behaviour – in effect without regard for motive. Morality in contrast seeks to define what is good – including behaviour but also including thoughts, feelings, and motives. But 'virtue ethics' is conventional, so I'll go with it.

Of the three approaches to morality, virtue ethics may seem the least satisfactory even though it was espoused by Aristotle no less. It seems to be the most subjective, the hardest to pin down, and so to be the least 'robust'. But we might reasonably ask an empirical question in the manner of a naturalist (which Aristotle was): what qualities of the many possible candidates have most of humanity through most of history (and presumably also of pre-history) recognised as 'virtues'? What actually *do* we feel is right and wrong? We can ask later where such feelings come from, and whether they have any substance apart from being what we feel. But it is surely pertinent, first, to ask what it is that most human beings do *in fact* feel is right and wrong – what qualities *in fact* are widely recognised as 'virtues'. From there we might reverse engineer and seek to discover what those virtues have in common, and get some further insight into what virtue actually *is*.

In truth throughout their long history human beings have proposed that many different qualities should be recognised as 'virtues' including 'loyalty' and honesty, and the four Cardinal Virtues proposed by Plato and espoused by Christianity: prudence, justice, fortitude, and temperance. But, I suggest, among the plethora of candidates, just three are outstanding. They are: compassion, humility *and* the sense of Oneness. All three are at the core of all the great religions and of many traditional, 'indigenous' religions too.

All in particular emphasise compassion: true concern for the wellbeing of other people and (I would say) of other creatures. Those who are truly compassionate do not merely feel sympathy for the suffering of others. They feel *empathy*: they share at least to some extent the others' suffering. Compassion is the wellspring of Christianity, or at least of the teaching of Christ (which is not quite the same thing) – though historically Christians have preferred the term 'love'. (A theologian tells me that the Christian concept of 'love' is distinct from 'compassion'. But at the least, the two concepts clearly overlap very considerably). Compassion too is at the root of Islam: every chapter of the Qur'an bar one begins with an appeal to 'the Compassionate One'. Many a good Muslim has pointed out that the violence so often associated with Islam is very much against the spirit of the core teaching. In Buddhism: the Dalai Lama told students at the University of California, in 1997, that for him 'the Revolution of Compassion is in the heart, the bedrock, the original source of inspiration for all the others'. And as he said in a lecture in Oxford some years ago (which I attended), when faced with a moral dilemma of whatever kind 'always ask yourself what is the most *compassionate* thing to do'.

All the great religions too stress humility; and for the old Greeks, the opposite quality of *hubris* was and is the great sin and folly of all, and those who were guilty of it were struck down. For hubris didn't simply mean arrogance or pride. A person guilty of hubris was one who flouted the rule of the gods – who sought indeed to usurp their power. Sophocles made the point beautifully in *Antigone*. King Creon of Thebes refused to bury the body of Polynices, slain in war, as the gods ordered must be done – and from then on, he is plagued by misfortunes which break his spirit. Our treatment of the natural world and the attempts of well-endowed nations to create empires may all be said to be hubristic and humanity as a whole, and the rest of nature, are now paying the price. But the hubris continues.

Humility must be espoused at all levels. Thus, beyond doubt, some people are more talented than others, at least in some things. I freely admit that I could never have run as fast as Usain Bolt or played the piano like Alfred Brendel even if I'd trained and practiced as hard as is physically possible. Many have trained and practiced with the utmost dedication but still there is only one Bolt and only one Brendel. The American myth that anyone can succeed at anything just by working hard is just that: a myth.

But the difference in skills and abilities between different people should not be taken to mean that some are innately better than others, and more worthwhile, and that those who are more talented or otherwise privileged have a right to look down on those who are less endowed. More broadly, no society should assume it is innately superior to others just because it is richer or has smarter technologies – and more guns. Still less should any society use its material superiority as an excuse to mistreat or enslave other peoples. Imperialism and the self-righteousness that goes with it reflect an underlying lack of humility. More broadly still: it's clear that human beings have the ecological edge over most other creatures but that does not give us the right to dispose of them at will. Neither should we assume that our own ideas are right or are the best. As Oliver Cromwell said (and the Quakers say it too) 'always consider that you may be mistaken'. But then, thank goodness, some of the most talented people are also among the most humble.

Oneness means what it sounds like: a sense of unity – with other human beings; with all other living creatures; and indeed, with the Universe as a whole. The Eastern religions – Buddhism; Hinduism; Sikhism; Shintoism – are especially strong on the idea that human beings are one with other creatures of all kinds. So too are many indigenous peoples. Highly pertinent is the African concept of Ubuntu: basically, the idea that human beings *cannot* exist in isolation. Our very existence depends on the existence of other human beings. Satish Kumar, the Indian-British activist, and the Scottish philosopher Sir John MacMurray have written very cogently along such lines.

I like to think too that Darwinian science, when properly construed, reinforces the sense of oneness. Darwin is often remembered (or misremembered) primarily because of the emphasis he placed on competition as the spur to natural selection and hence to evolution. Less well remembered is that Darwin also stressed the importance of cooperation – and I like to argue that in reality, cooperativeness is the most universally effective of all survival tactics and ought therefore to be favoured above all by natural selection. But also, Darwin argued (albeit not quite accurately) that *all* Earthly creatures must have descended from a common ancestor. Thus, all Earthly creatures are *literally* related. Chimpanzees are our first cousins and fish are our third cousins and mushrooms are our fifth cousins and plants are our nth cousins and so on, all the way to the bacteria and archaeans. Many traditional religions acknowledge the same core idea. Among Hindus it's common to regard elephants as our brothers and sisters even as they trash the crops, and hunters in traditional societies commonly apologise and give thanks to the animals they feel obliged to kill for food. Alas, though, ancient peoples who felt such affinity with our fellow creatures were not necessarily good conservationists. Their modern descendants may seem to live in harmony with the natural world (when they are allowed to do so) but the archaeological and fossil record suggests that their ancestors drove many an ancient species to extinction, nonetheless. Conservation surely does require some sense of oneness, or at least a sense that other species *matter*. But it also requires sound ecological know-how, which includes good science.

Christians on the whole are weakest on the idea of oneness. In general, they seem bogged down by the passage in *Genesis* 1:26 which tells us in the King James translation: 'God said, let us make man in our image, after our likeness: and let them have dominion over the fish of the sea, and over the fowl of the air, and over the cattle, and over all the earth, and over every creeping thing that creepeth upon the earth'.

There's no sense of oneness in this. The idea that we were made in God's image rather implies that the rest weren't, and 'dominion' reinforces the sense of separation and indeed of hierarchy – the mediaeval Christian idea of the 'great chain of being', with God at the top and then the angels and then humans and then animals and then plants. Many have sought to suggest that dominion really means stewardship but even the idea of stewardship has an 'us and them' quality. It is often suggested that St Francis had a sense of oneness with nature but as Roger Sorrell points out in *St Francis of Assisi and Nature* his attitude to other creatures was primarily chivalric. He certainly felt that we ought to care about our fellow creatures and take care of them (*noblesse oblige*), and he preached to the birds. But he regarded other creatures as our wards, rather than as fellows.

Two points. First, it seems to me that if all human beings - or at least enough to qualify as the norm - fully espoused these three cardinal moral principles then the human societies really could be convivial, and the individuals within those societies would at least have their best chance of achieving fulfilment; and if enough of us fully grasped the idea of oneness then we really could achieve harmony with the natural world. As Keats said about truth and beauty, these moral principles are ' all ye know on Earth/ And all ye need to know'.

Secondly — and encouragingly — these three moral principles seem to be so widespread and, I suggest, so deeply embedded in the human psyche that they may reasonably be seen to be part of our biology — part of what makes us human beings. Indeed, since many other sentient creatures behave in ways that suggest that they too share such sentiments — including chimpanzees, dogs, elephants, horses, parrots, and crows — we might reasonably infer that these three moral principles are part of what is entailed in being an intelligent social animal. In truth this idea has never been prominent in biology — the mainstream seems rooted in Tennyson's concept of 'nature red in tooth and claw'. But the idea that other animals are moral beings (even if they don't formally practice moral philosophy) has nonetheless been espoused by a whole string of excellent scientists from the Russian Peter Kropotkin (1842-1921, a younger contemporary of Darwin) to the modern Dutch primatologist Frans de Waal.

In contrast, modern evolutionary biologists seek to explain morality simply as a variation of the theme of the 'selfish gene' — the idea that genes can sometimes increase their own chances of being replicated by prompting their possessors to be nice to each other. Well, such a mechanism surely does apply. The idea that there is evolutionary advantage in behaving morally does make perfect sense, and surely one reason for this is that genes that promote moral behaviour may thereby improve their own chances of replicating.

Still, though, we may ask – *should* indeed ask if we really want to get to the bottom of things – is the evolutionary/ genetic explanation of morality, sufficient? Or is there more to it? Let's speculate. All serious inquiry must begin with speculation.

Where do our moral sentiments come from?

Here we come to the dichotomy that seems to have run through philosophy and bedevilled theology since the year dot, whenever that was. Those we might call out-and-out *materialists* insist that the world of things that we can see and hear and bang our shins on, is all there is. Others, though, have a sense of what I suggest can properly be called *transcendence*: the general idea that behind the scenes there is, or may be, more going on. Many feel indeed that the universe and all the creatures that it has given rise to must be guided by an intelligence – consciousness; 'mind'. Some indeed suggest that behind the universe there is or may be an agenda, a plan – a *purpose*.

The questions then abound. Is this hypothetical guiding intelligence built into the fabric of the universe itself? Is it all around us? Do we in fact create intelligence in our own heads, or do we simply partake of what is already out there, just as we partake of light, via our eyes and visual cortex? Are our minds in part at least like radio receivers?

Or does this hypothetical guiding intelligence emanate from some separate being who sits above the rest and presides? And did this hypothetical being create the material universe, and all the creatures within, as described in *Genesis*? Or is this hypothetical being simply the *reason* why the rest exists at all which is the way that Hindus envisage *Brahma*, in effect the super-god among the hundreds of specialist gods? Some Christian theologians envisage the God of Abraham in the same kind of way: not as a mere builder and doer – a 'demiurge' – but as the source of all.

All such questions, including those of theology – and indeed of science – belong in the realm of *metaphysics* which asks what many have called 'the ultimate questions' – including asking what goodness actually *is,* as opposed simply to asking what it is good to do in any particular circumstance. Such questions are of endless interest to all who do not deliberately shut their minds to such deliberations but they do not lend themselves to straightforward answers of a scientific kind that can be reduced to mathematical formulae. Indeed, all our explorations of metaphysics lead us in the end to mystery. Many hate the idea of mystery. It makes them feel insecure. It threatens their sense that we, human beings, have full control of our own destiny – for how can we be in full control if we don't really understand what is going on?

Indeed, many scientists evidently feel that it is their role in life to dispel all mystery – to provide 'robust' explanations for all that is. But as Albert Einstein, indisputably one of the greatest scientists of all time, observed in *Living Philosophies* in 1931:

> The most beautiful thing we can experience is the mysterious. It is the source of all true art and science. He to whom the emotion is a stranger, who can no longer pause to wonder and stand wrapped in awe, is as good as dead —his eyes are closed. The insight into the mystery of life, coupled though it be with fear, has also given rise to religion. To know what is impenetrable to us really exists, manifesting itself as the highest wisdom and the most radiant beauty, which our dull faculties can comprehend only in their most primitive forms— this knowledge, this feeling is at the center of true religiousness.

Those scientists who see it as their role to explain all aspects of existence clearly begin with the premise that complete explanations are actually *possible*. This is in line with philosophy of *logical positivism,* which maintains that the only ideas that should be taken seriously are the ones that can be 'verified' – and further argues the only ideas that can be verified, shown to be true, are those of conventional western science.

Logical positivism arose in Vienna after World War I and had a great impact – but it soon began to look very shaky, not least because the Austrian-British philosopher (Sir) Karl Popper showed that in truth *no* idea that is not simply a definition or a tautology (as in 2+2=4) can ever be shown beyond all possible doubt to be true, or more than a fragment of the truth; and largely due to Popper logical positivism had more or less run its course by the 1970s. But it lives on in spirit in the form of 'scientism': the idea that science can tell us everything worthwhile that there is to know and that everything else, including the ideas of metaphysics are mere woolgathering. The ideas that underpin all *bona fide* religions are metaphysical in nature – which means that those who embrace scientism perforce must be materialist-atheists.

I suggest that although we surely should pursue the ideas of science with all possible vigour, we should not assume that they really do represent the truth, the whole truth, and nothing but the truth. Neither should we assume that because science so often provides us with satisfying accounts of what is in the universe and satisfying explanations of how the universe and life actually work, that no other kind of explanation is necessary or worthwhile. For it is perfectly possible to be an excellent scientist and yet be deeply devout. So it was that Newton no less spent more time on his somewhat recondite brand of Christian theology than on physics. Einstein rejected the religion of his birth (Judaism) along with all formal religion but as his writing clearly demonstrates he had a deep sense of transcendence, which of course is a key component of all *bona fide* religions.

In short, the old and still prevalent idea that science and religion are mutually exclusive and are bound to be at odds, is simply not true. Many scientists of the highest calibre have had a strong sense of transcendence and of mystery – and a feeling for transcendence is I suggest what is properly meant by 'spirituality'. Spirituality does not simply imply heightened emotion. And although some, like Einstein, nonetheless reject formal religion, many others are devout followers of Christianity, Islam, Sikhism, or what you will. More to the point, materialist explanations simply do not preclude the possibility that some transcendent intelligence created the material universe and all its forces in the first place, and/or is the reason that the universe exists.

All this is a build-up to saying that there are many other ideas out there besides those of evolutionary biology that seek to throw light on the nature of morality – including ideas that emanate from theology and of course, more broadly, from metaphysics. Obviously, the ideas that spring from or feed into our sense of morality cannot be as 'robust' as the established theories of science may claim to be but that does not mean they should be dismissed out of hand. How seriously we take such ideas is not a matter merely of what is called 'rationality' which relies on direct observation and mathematical analysis. Indeed, in the end, whether or not we take any particular idea seriously depends on our *intuition* – and that applies to the ideas of science as much as to the ideas of theology or of metaphysics in general. Thus, for my part I like very much the idea that I associate with the Tao, and is reflected in some versions of the idea of the Dharma – the idea that the universe is fundamentally harmonious. This leads on seamlessly to the idea that a good action or thought is one that enhances the universal harmony, and a bad action or thought is one that detracts. Such ideas do not lend themselves to direct scientific investigation and so achieve the status of scientific theory. But then, even within the realm of science, when all the available lines of investigation have been explored and the weight of evidence is enormous and the logic and the maths are impeccable, scientists must still rely on their intuitions, on the feeling in their bones, to tell them whether the theory, however widely accepted, is actually true. So, for example not every modern physicist accepts the idea that the universe began with a Big Bang even though the Big Bang is at the heart of what is called 'the Standard Model'. As one renowned cosmologist remarked recently in a BBC TV documentary, 'It just doesn't feel right'; and note the word 'feel'.

And although ethical committees feel obliged to give rational *reasons* why they reach particular conclusions, in the end they too must rely on their own intuitions - what they feel in their bones is right. In the end, all big decisions in all fields are made by the bones. As St Augustine advised (as quoted by Pope John Paul in his encyclical *Faith and Reason* in 1988): 'Do not wander far and wide but return into yourself. Deep within man there dwells the truth'.

And deep within all of us, or at least the vast majority, and perhaps too in the hearts and minds and bones of our most intelligent fellow creatures, is the feeling, the intuition, that the fundamental virtues of compassion, and humility, and the sense of oneness, are *right*. We need to develop our rational minds beyond doubt. But we also need, perhaps more urgently now than ever before, to cultivate our intuitions.

Coda

The world is dominated by a fractured and fractious but nonetheless dangerously coherent oligarchy of big governments; the corporates, which may be far more powerful than most governments; various forms of financiers: and their selected expert and intellectual advisers, largely recruited from an otherwise cash-strapped academe, who for the most part tell them what they want to hear. All are focused on money and power; and since the oligarchs are indeed rich and powerful those who seek to change the world commonly feel that it's necessary – 'realistic' – to seek to engage directly with them. So those who want the world to be a better place – perhaps, indeed, as suggested here, to be more kind and just and perhaps to take better care of the natural world – tend to seek political and economic solutions to our many and increasing ills. Those who are most radical are wont to invoke some pre-existing economic formula or system of governance of an extreme kind, either far-Left or (as now seems to be increasingly the case) far-Right.

But as almost all the great religious leaders have taught, from Buddha to Jesus to St Augustine to Muhammad to the present Dalai Lama, the change we really need must in the end come from within: a change of *mindset*; and central to that is morality.

Religion in practice plays a huge part in this for in practice it's the world's religious leaders – rabbis, priests, imams, many other kinds of elders - and theologians of all persuasions who spend most time discussing morality and its spiritual underpinning. Religion properly conceived should therefore be widely and indeed universally acknowledged, as once it was, as a vital component of governance. It falls short of this however largely because clerics spend far too much of their energies fighting recondite points of theology among themselves – Christianity *vs* Islam; Catholic *vs* Protestant; Lutherans *vs* Calvinists; and so on. Clerics and indeed all who give a damn should instead be seeking common ground, and the common ground is that of the bedrock morality suggested here: the three great virtues of compassion, humility, and the sense of oneness, all underpinned by a sense of transcendence.

If the world as a whole was focused on these bedrock virtues we surely could find ways out of the present disasters, horrendous though they obviously are. But if we simply seek solutions of a political or economic kind, geared in the end to power and the *status quo*, and typically invoking some existing, off-the-shelf 'ism' like Marxism or neoliberalism, then we surely have had our chips.

THREE DEPARTURES ON ANGER

Gordon Blaine Steffey

Anger is the one common ground.
Peter Baker, *New York Times*,
Jan/Apr 2021

Well, the people were very angry.
Donald J. Trump, *March 18, 2021*
interview with Jonathan Karl on the Capitol Riots

Departure 1: 'A virtue, being self-sufficient, never needs the assistance of a vice: whenever it needs an impetuous effort, it does not become angry, but rises to the occasion, and excites or soothes itself as far as it deems requisite' - Lucius Annaeus Seneca, *On Anger*.

Stoicism is 'back,' though it is more a rebuild than a resuscitation of Stoicisms of yore. But why Stoicism, and why now? In the cant of Howard Beale from the 1976 film *Network*: 'We know things are bad, worse than bad, they're crazy! … Things have got to change! But first, you've got to get mad. You've got to say: I am as mad as hell, and I'm not going to take this anymore.' It's axiomatic that 'if you're not outraged, you're not paying attention,' which is to suggest that your anger is a measure of your moral compass. That axiom became a clarion call for antiracists following the 2017 murder of Heather Heyer (whose social media adopted the dictum) at a 2017 white supremacist rally in Charlottesville, Virginia. Though the inventory of items stoking our anger is somewhat altered, we are mad as hell, all of us, but as anger has become more continuous script than episodic release, it has proved to be less cathartic and cohesive than destructive and divisive. The adverse psychological and physiological impact of prolonged anger and associated behaviours is well-established. A brimming slate of popular books, retreats, and media bloom hail Stoicism as a nostrum against the negativities of anger. Anger management techniques are on the rise, and some of the same forces that prompted the distillation of mindfulness-based programmes and the mindfulness movement from traditional forms of Buddhism are now at work on premodern Stoicisms. These modern secularised phenomena are making common cause with cognitive behavioural therapies and other psychological modalities and emerging as potentially useful techniques for managing difficult emotions like anger, anxiety, and fear. Some 'modern' Stoics extol the overlap with therapy and seek to integrate Stoic concepts and practices with modern psychotherapies. Others mine Stoicism for 'life hacks' purged of any fine-grained cultural or ideological freight.

What did Stoics think about anger? In short, that it is a form of self-harm, that it is communicable, that it is antisocial, and (critically) that it is manageable. Stoics taught that virtue/happiness is an 'inner' path. In the view of the formerly enslaved Stoic sage Epictetus:

> The primary work of life is this: to discriminate and sort among circumstances, and say, 'Things outside [me] are not up to me; choosing is.' Where shall I seek the good and the bad? Within, among those things up to me.

This so-called 'dichotomy of control' sourced the Stoic ideal of eliminating emotional responses to outcomes not decided finally by my will. Far from intending to ennoble frigidity, Stoics strove to avoid the false judgments those emotional responses implied. The path to this outcome wasn't repression, but discipline and the development of mental and physical practices to support virtues like working for justice, reconciliation, truth, and gratitude. Their ideal did not keep them from messy political involvements, though they had a spare tradition of political discourse for the same reason they were ill-adapted to radicalism, namely, ordinary incitements to political reform were typically held to belong to that network of cause and effect not 'up to me.' The inner path was sufficient for Stoic objectives, and that path was available whatever the nature of government. As David Sedley observes, 'ultimately Stoicism had to allow that no form of government would make the happy less happy or the wretched more wretched.' And should tyranny so thoroughly restrict opportunity for the expression of virtue, the 'exit' of Seneca, the 'open door' of Epictetus, and the examples of Socrates and Cato the Younger remain: 'Do you ask what route leads to freedom? Any vein in your body.'

The political conditions that might render such an exit well-advised did not give license to anger, which Seneca reckoned a 'wholly violent' and the 'most hideous and frenzied of all emotions.' In the well-worn words of Epictetus: 'Do not look for things to come about as you wish them to come about but wish them to come about as they do and you will flow well.'

The attraction of Stoicism lies in its resources of self-overcoming (its therapies of self) and not in its politics, which, despite the pleading of its advocates, is complicated both by its quietist lure and lack of any collectivist practice. Consider emperor Marcus: 'don't go expecting Plato's *Republic*; be satisfied with even the smallest progress, and treat the outcome of it all as unimportant.' At first glance, Marcus' advice seems sensible: resist fantasy, celebrate small steps. Fair enough, but why *unimportant*? Because happiness isn't 'out there' and the 'smallest progress' (even dragging in Stoic notions of justice and commonweal) is entirely consistent with the embrace of inequalities that arise from differing positions in a hierarchically ordered society (a reflection of Stoic metaphysics). All this has a bit of an archaic (and weirdly contemporary) feel, which isn't at all dissipated by new Stoic popularisers who scale down actionable political space to individual responsibility and self-improvement.

The advocacy of indifference to outcomes is out of step with a soaring new politics powered by anger and resentment at the rabid and conclusive failure of modern democracies to make good on longstanding promises of more than *merely* formal equality. Indian writer Pankaj Mishra identifies this failure as the root of a 'global turn to authoritarianism and toxic forms of chauvinism.' Mishra joins American philosopher Martha Nussbaum and others in seeking to come to terms with the increasingly outsized role of anger in political spaces and the abiding failure of labour liberal politicos to reckon with it and the success of anger merchants in exploiting it. In an interview given to *The Atlantic*, social psychologist James Averill recalled his initial impression of 2016 candidate Trump: 'He understands anger and it's going to make voters feel *wonderful*.' Seven years later Americans are perhaps farther than ever from Martha Nussbaum's vision of a 'public culture of compassion,' where education, policy, and culture producers severally create emotional support for principles of inclusive, just futures.

Nussbaum accepts the Stoic critique of anger as 'pretty on target.' She argues that 'anger is always normatively problematic' because its cognitive content affirms payback, which leans on 'magical thinking' about payback rebalancing some structural disproportion in the cosmos. Comeuppance and the fiction of rebalancing is a myth many live by. Though it may slake the hidden thirsts of Jungian shadow, payback as rebalancing does *not* work except to 'put me relatively up' against an offender who has done me a status-injury. This is not at all to recommend 'narcissistic error' and the spiralling preoccupation with relative status. Nussbaum allows for something she terms 'Transition-anger,' an anger seemingly more attuned to active love and compassion than 'garden-variety anger.' Transition-anger is metabolised in the immediate transition to pragmatic solutions for remedy: 'how outrageous! Something must be done about this.' It is exceptionally uncontaminated by the payback wish. Nussbaum offers the example of parents who punish errant children with the intent to shape different futures rather than to deliver comeuppance. Here is anger already pivoting toward futures-focused strategies and projects for repairing institutions, policies, and behaviours that prompted the initial outrage.

Nussbaum elevates the radical practice of Martin Luther King, Jr., who struggled with intense feelings of anger and recognised through disciplined self-inspection the perils of 'garden-variety' anger. Revisiting the Montgomery bus boycott negotiations of 17 December 1955, King recalled a powerful inner dialogue: 'I was weighted down by a terrible sense of guilt, remembering that on two or three occasions I had allowed myself to become angry and indignant ... Yet I knew that this was no way to solve a problem. 'You must not harbour anger,' I admonished myself. 'You must be willing to suffer the anger of the opponent, and yet not return anger. You must not become bitter. No matter how emotional your opponents are, you must be calm." On the 100th anniversary of the birth of Du Bois in 1968, King praised Du Bois for not seeking in polemic mere 'emotional release,' and for recognising that 'the supreme task is to organise and unite people so that their anger becomes a transforming force.'

King unswervingly tied his experiences of anger to the moral sinkhole of 'corroding hatred,' from being made to surrender his seat to whites in high school, to the bombing of the Montgomery parsonage where he lived with his family. He acknowledged the anger he felt naturally in the suffocating grip of oppression, recognised the danger hidden in pleasant thoughts of oppressors and despots suffering some measure of the agony

they wrought, and nevertheless managed anger as an accelerant to the
embers smouldering at the surface of most conflicts. Anger was morally
corrosive *and* impractical. In the spirit of Gandhi's view that 'anger
controlled can be transmuted into a power that can move the world,' King
transmuted his justifiable anger for moral and pragmatic reasons so as to
shape more equitable political futures with those who contributed to and
benefited from his oppression and resisted his liberation.

Departure 2: 'Dear Black Folks, Your Pain Matters, Your Rage Matters,
Your Life Matters' — *Handmade protest sign at Maastricht, Netherlands on 7
June 2020*

Anger is 'back.' Dare I say, it's all the rage? The inverted commas mean
just that any explanation of its absence and return requires a hedge or two.
The mid-1980s registered burgeoning interest across academic disciplines
in retrieving emotion from the sidelines to the centre of cultural analysis.
Anthropologists and psychologists began to reconsider the public, social,
and cognitive dimensions of emotional experience. Normative questions
about the role of difficult emotions in political life remained unsettled.

To characterise emotion as historically sidelined may mislead because it
suggests that retrieval is mainly a matter of getting emotion into the game.
Far from riding the sidelines, emotion has long been in play as the
antithesis of reason. The foundational reason/emotion binary empowers a
linked series of binaries constituting an episteme rightly described as
sexist, racist, xenophobic, and otherwise supremacist. It has been a key
construct in the privileging of male above female, white above black and
brown, cultural above natural, native above foreign, mind above body,
modern above medieval or traditional, and the like. Reason/emotion
polices a network of patriarchal power relations it was instrumental in
defining. Anthropologist Catherine Lutz calls it a 'master symbol,' integral
to the 'our ways of looking at ourselves and others.'

To be sure, one thinks immediately of vile tropes like the angry Arab/
Muslim so thoroughly exposed since the onset of Orientalism critiques.
Incredibly (for all that is new in the Orientalism scholarship), Orientalist
representations haven't strayed too far from the pattern set by Victorian
imperialist Evelyn Baring's *Modern Egypt*. There the imperial Consul-
General of Egypt described the 'subject race' as driven purely by emotional
needs in contrast to the European, a 'natural logician.' In the wake of actor

Riz Ahmed's 2017 speech to the House of Commons on screen diversity, the 'Riz Test' emerged 'to measure how Muslims are portrayed on Film and TV,' with a failing grade assigned to programming wherein an identifiably Muslim character appears as 'irrationally angry.' Hit television programmes like Netflix's *Fauda* demonstrate the enduring energy of the angry Arab/Muslim. This trope, so thoroughly dug into knowledge production in the global north, drove Bernard Lewis' infamous exposition of 'Muslim rage' as ressentiment and irrational retaliation against secularism and the legacies of colonialism. Lewis fatefully termed this conflict a 'clash of civilisations,' an expression later extrapolated to geopolitics and international relations by American political scientist Samuel Huntington. Lewis' performance of 'Western paramountcy' relied on an Orient construct wherein the Muslim man constituted that emotionally driven inferior of European self-reflection. Like the Orient construct in which it participates, the binary of reason and emotion is not a tagging of phenomena found lying on the ground—it is not 'out there'—but is rather a mythic reality by means of which a northern self constitutes itself for itself and haunts intercultural interactions with its distorted preoccupations.

Attempts to quarantine emotion from political space—a corollary of which is the subordination of groups identified with emotion—on grounds of its subversion of clear thinking is a longstanding discursive practice. Acknowledging that emotion can sometimes encumber knowledge acquisition (for example, lovers oblivious to their surroundings), philosopher Alison Jaggar argues that the ideal of 'dispassionate inquiry' is myth serving a classist, masculinist, and racist ideology that identifies men with pure reason and women and people of colour with emotion and emotional instability. Reared in societies where that ideology operates, we come to experience as natural those responses in which the values of the dominant group are expressed. In short, the emotions we experience 'reflect prevailing forms of social life,' and thus 'limit our capacity for outrage' and blind us to alternative lifeways. But hegemony is never total, and 'subordinated individuals' often have emotional responses out of step with those prescribed by convention.

For Jaggar, such 'outlaw' or conventionally inappropriate emotions are key to the formation of oppositional subcultures and the delineation of futures beyond the status quo. They do this by provoking new analysis that *may* reveal that the 'facts have been constructed in a way that obscures the reality of subordinated people.' Indeed outlaw emotions may sound the first alarm that the ostensible facts are otherwise, but they should not be affirmed uncritically. Their appropriateness must be assessed against their capacity for shaping a society wherein all humans and some non-humans 'thrive.' Jaggar accords 'epistemological privilege' to the subordinated as a guardrail against the imprecisions of 'thriving.' Especially in the case of outlaw emotions, the emotional responses of the subordinated offer a 'less partial' view of reality and are 'more likely to incorporate reliable appraisals of situations.' Such epistemological privilege would entail giving the benefit of the doubt to a cohort of younger, often BIPOC (Black, Indigenous, People of Colour) and women scholars now pushing back against the prohibition of political anger.

In her 2016 review of Nussbaum's *Anger and Forgiveness,* philosopher Amia Srinavasan argues that calls to eliminate anger from politics underline the 'limits of the liberal worldview.' What are those limits? Srinavasan criticises Nussbaum for cherry-picking 'liberal fairy tales about the power of civility' and ignoring how the 'angry politics' of Malcolm X conditioned Lyndon B Johnson's acceptance of King's vision of racial harmony, and for failing to register anger's 'psychic importance' to the oppressed, whose historical and ongoing exclusion from the public square figures not as a miscarriage of the principles underpinning US society but as the 'perfect realisation' of commitments shared by many Americans.

Srinavasan defends the expression of *apt* anger against the criticism that it is counterproductive. Anger is apt when motivated by and proportional to someone's reason for being angry, namely, a violation of 'how things *ought* to be.' Counterproductivity critiques urge us to avoid anger, apt or otherwise, because it subverts the process by which desirable outcomes may be achieved, say, gun control or policing reforms. French philosopher Jean-Paul Sartre offered a counterproductivity critique when he argued that anger is an 'escape' from complexity, a shabby substitute for higher order solutions to conflict.

For some, counterproductivity critiques run past questions of the inherent value of anger. Granting that anger can be imprudent, is there anything to recommend *counterproductive* apt anger? Srinavasan contends that apt anger adds to the knowledge of injustice an affective appreciation of it, which is to say that getting angry about racial bias and wrongful conviction has a value distinct from merely knowing it to be unjust. It attests publicly to that injustice and invites solidarity in shared attestation, though (again) such anger may complicate policy objectives. The ugly ditch between the world as it is (generative of apt anger) and the world as it ought to be (the achievement of which may require setting anger aside) is a conflict of competing goods.

For Srinavasan, to insist on the priority of the pragmatic is to commit an unrecognised form of injustice she terms 'affective injustice.' That priority is a by-product of the hegemony that both induces and proscribes anger. Affective injustice occurs when someone is confronted by the incompatibility of an apt emotional response to an unjust situation and the desire to change that situation for the better. Srinavasan characterises this incompatibility as a 'kind of psychic tax that is often levied on the victims of injustice.'

Inquiry into the second-order injustice of affective harms and disadvantages caused by structural racism and other forms of oppression is still in a nascent state. Srinavasan proposes to remedy affective injustice by dismantling the hegemonic reason/anger binary and thereby short circuiting recourse to an 'efficient rationalisation for excluding those who most threaten the reigning social order.'

Canadian philosopher Laura Luz Silva has recently challenged the commonplace that anger is counterproductive in the political struggle against injustice. She cites empirical studies supportive of a 'correlation' between the expression of anger in collective political action and 'conciliatory action tendencies on behalf of dominant groups.' Against Nussbaum's monochromatic view of anger, Silva offers an account of anger as desire for recognition rather than essentially retributive. Anger fuelled by a desire for recognition seeks 'epistemic change' in the offender; it aims for the offender to share the offended's moral appraisal of the offense. The most significant variable here is the offender's openness to change: 'when the targets of anger are seen as capable of change, anger tends to involve desires for recognition. Desires for recognition typically trigger actions that are primarily communicative, and which make clear the reasons for anger. This allows the targets of anger to share in the appraisal of a relevant situation as unjust.' For Silva, constructive anger is far more common than allowed by Nussbaum's 'Transition-Anger' (which Nussbaum herself suggests might *not* be anger at all: 'Is Transition-Anger a species of anger? I really don't care how we answer this question'). The 2020 murder of George Floyd ignited waves of anger culminating in global protests against police brutality and the lack of accountability. In the wake of the anger, federal, state, and local governments passed a wide variety of legal measures to redress racial bias in policing. Was this Transition-Anger? If so, it strains a bit against the example of the parent whose anger expresses the intent to reform rather than to retribute.

The young American philosopher Myisha Cherry is among the new advocates of anger or rage (she uses the terms interchangeably) in the struggle for racial justice. Against views of anger as uniformly destructive, Cherry proposes a catalogue of five political angers in the context of racial injustice. What differentiates one anger from another is its target, its aim, its perspective, and the action it is likely to motivate. For example, 'wipe rage' targets 'racial others' whom the enraged believe to source their experience of being hard done by. Think here of the simplification of economic inequities by scapegoating immigrant and migrant workers for 'taking our jobs.' In August 2017, tiki torch-wielding white supremacists in Charlottesville, Virginia, chanted 'You will not replace us!' and 'Jews will not replace us!' The aim and likely action of wipe rage are the same, namely, to 'eliminate' the scapegoats. Its zero-sum perspective commits wipe ragers to eliminating their competitors lest they be eliminated. Wipe rage and three other political angers (rogue, ressentiment, and narcissistic) are 'morally and politically problematic' and threaten to obscure a morally and politically salutary form of anger Cherry terms 'Lordean rage' after the Black feminist scholar and poet Audre Lorde.

Lorde saw focused anger as a powerful source of energy serving progress and change: 'I have tried to learn my anger's usefulness to me, as well as its limitations.' Cherry's 'Lordean rage' targets the perpetrators and accomplices of racism and racial injustice. It aims precisely to change the ideological supports and the behavioural and institutional expressions of white supremacy. Its seeks to 'metabolise anger'—in Lorde's terms, to 'translate' it into liberating activity—and its perspective is inclusive of all those who discern in the shackles of others their own unfreedom. Cherry distinguishes this ordinary and transformative rage from that rare

Transition-Anger where anger passes quickly into the love of Nussbaum's King. Indeed, she rejects the notion that 'Lordean rage' needs replacing by presumptively nobler emotions, which is not at all to suggest that rage requires no tending. As the millennia-spanning library of anger management literature presumes that anger is (almost) never apt or proportional, Cherry proposes an alternative discipline for capitalising on the transformative potentials of 'Lordean rage' in the antiracist struggle. She argues that rage *should* be expressed lest we undermine the values that have been infringed and suffer the 'psychic tax' identified by Srinavasan. Moreover, she contends that expressing rage facilitates the formation of solidarities for the pursuit of change and justice. Cherry invites us to resist those who seek to 'squelch' 'Lordean rage', whether 'anger police' who serve the status quo or 'anger dismissers' who gaslight the angry by renaming anger bitterness.

Departure 3: 'The density of History determines none of my acts.' – Frantz Fanon, *Black Skin, White Masks*

These two departures represent rival discourses of anger in contemporary philosophy and the public square. They agree that it is imperative to pay attention to our angers and to examine the role they play in personal and political life. They agree that not all anger is of a piece and that serious self-scrutiny makes anger available to nuance and correction. The first discourse has deep roots in Stoic philosophy though it outgrew its native soil to become a formative source for thinking about anger in northern epistemes. It is anxious about the destructive psychosocial effects of anger generally and lately about affirmations of social anger in politics. It worries that anger, contaminated by retributive desire, narcissism, and liable to excess, undermines the rule of law and is toxic to the deliberative cool required by the exigencies of legislative politics and policymaking in democratic governance. Stoics developed practices to exclude this 'temporary madness' from the daily grind and to attain *apatheia* (indifference, or perhaps equanimity), but contemporary advocates argue that non-anger is continuous with revolutionary justice as well as 'deep loves, friendships, and other commitments.'

Anger-critical discourse often benefits from our vernacular about anger, from what Robert Solomon terms the 'hydraulic model' of emotion where an analogy is made to fluid moving through a system under pressure. To 'blow your top' or 'flip your lid' or 'erupt in anger' frame anger as a volatile hazardous material requiring close control. Anger must not be 'bottled' but rather 'channelled' into more appropriate states. This shifts focus from the triggers of anger like racism and structural injustice to individual anger management in prudential pursuit of salutary outcomes. For Nussbaum, anger isn't a manageable bodily humour, but an intelligible moral response to wrongdoing *even if it is also normatively problematic*. Her work on political anger seeks to persuade us 'to see clearly the irrationality and stupidity of anger' with the caveat that 'it's hard not to be stupid.'

The second discourse on anger is a comparatively recent phenomenon and tethered tightly to the struggle for social justice. It suspects that shibboleths about necessary deliberative cool obscure important questions about who decides and polices the nature of political space, who decides and polices justifiable anger. Anger-discerning advocates hold that anger must be assessed in terms of the intersecting social locations and complex power dynamics that shape identities and access in society. Those 'with their backs against the wall' enjoy an epistemological privilege because they suffer from systemic injustices often unseen by the privileged groups who benefit from them. It is in this sense that, as social critic A. Shahid Stover contends, black rage is 'lucidity,' a revolt against the 'spiritually pacifying epistemology' of a violent empire. Anger is not a virulent fluid to be channelled away from public space but a truthful response of healthy human beings and groups to structural injustices and the legacies of racism. Far from valorising pathological expressions of anger (like wipe rage), advocates of this discourse defend the aptness and prophetic necessity of rage in the antiracist struggle.

Anger-critical advocates argue that anger bends toward morally dubious outcomes and is counterproductive to mechanisms by which justice is achieved in democratic society. Anger-discerning advocates argue that *some* anger is socially desirable and epistemically useful if we are to identify and respond properly to injustice especially if the mechanisms by which justice is achieved in democratic society suffer from systemic racism. *With so much at stake clear answers seem critical.*

In contemporary US society, partisan differences eclipse demographic differences on political values even where opinion in both parties moves in the same direction. Retreating from the centre, congressional Republicans and Democrats are ideologically more distant from one another than they have been in fifty years. Meanwhile, Americans at either end of the ideological spectrum are more politically engaged across several measures than moderates. In their work on polarised polities and democratic erosion, political scientists McCoy and Somer define 'pernicious polarisation' as a by-product of political entrepreneurs using polarising strategies around grievances for their own self-aggrandisement (for example, mobilising voters by demonising a political opponent who fails to renounce critical race theory) and the failure of opposition elites to develop nonpolarising responses. The short-range benefits of polarisation to campaigns and political parties are offset by the threat of democratic erosion due to the undermining of democratic institutions and norms. McCoy and Benjamin Press compared fifty-two democratic polities with pernicious polarisation, finding 'no peer analogues for the United States' current political divisions.'

In his *American Rage*, political scientist Stephen Webster marshals a rich array of data to show that political anger erodes trust in governing institutions and weakens commitment to democratic norms and values. In follow-up research, Webster and his collegues establish that 'when people are politically angry, they are less likely to create new social ties and are more likely to cut off current social ties with out-partisans.' In most cases neither gender nor race moderate these effects. They find that anger 'produces' social polarisation, contributing to a sinister cycle of social polarisation, social sorting, and more anger. Distressingly, these findings confirm that anger is an accelerant of social polarisation '*above and beyond* the extreme social polarisation that already exists.'

Additionally, the empirical literature paints a grim picture of the effects of anger on thinking. Anger disposes me to a sense of certainty consistent with other high cortisol and adrenaline emotions, disposes me to attribute blame and responsibility to others, and disposes me both to perceive less risk and make risk-seeking choices. Moreover, and perhaps most problematic for anger-discerning advocates, anger disposes me to rely more on stereotypes and simple heuristics in my judgments. Psychologists Lerner and Tiedens conclude that angry decision makers 'approach a situation with the tendency to feel confident, in control, and thinking the worse of others,' and 'unlikely' to indulge in careful analysis or 'to ponder alternative options before acting.' Shallow processing joined to myopia and high confidence (call these the toxins of anger) is a dangerous recipe for political engagement in any environment, especially in the perniciously polarised United States, which still seems to be holding its collective breath after the past and perhaps future ravages of Donald Trump.

The 'case for rage' has merit. It expresses a knowledge born in struggle. Audre Lorde warns that 'when we turn from anger we turn from insight.' Her powerful concluding litany to 'The Uses of Anger' bears repetition:

> It is not the anger of Black women which is dripping down over this globe like a diseased liquid. It is not my anger that launches rockets … It is not the anger of Black women which corrodes into blind, dehumanising power.

Her anger did not get us here, to be sure. It may seem that the counsel to turn from anger is counsel to turn from those who have just cause for anger or from the moral violations that precipitated this anger. The counsel to turn from anger (even when it acknowledges the ideological function of such counsel) can seem to reinforce existing hierarchies and hegemony. Existing institutions of the liberal democratic order must soon demonstrate a will to remedy the structural injustices and growing inequalities that drive anger and uncertainty, as many did in the US in the aftermath of the murder of George Floyd. Any counsel to turn from anger affirms with Reverend Dr. King that "Wait' has almost always meant 'Never.' We must come to see … that 'justice too long delayed is justice denied."

Pankaj Mishra diagnoses a present vexed by 'a fierce politics of identity built on historical injuries,' and Myisha Cherry aims to refocus debate about political anger on the causes of social ills, meaning 'analysis of the social context from which anger arises.' The Lordean rage she prescribes (which, she admits, risks the malice of anger in the absence of discipline) is 'about coming to grips with our past and our future.' The oppressed surely have the most compelling reasons for their anger, and no discussion of anger can eventuate without bringing to mind, for example, the dire costs of visible anger for the oppressed under the US slaveholding system, in the Jim Crow South, and today. This is to say nothing of the dire costs of visible anger for the undocumented workers constituting the spine of the US economy. In this broader historical context, anger can signify agency regained, a rejection of subjugation and servility, silence, and social control. It can insist on recognition and accountability. And, to be sure, it is unfair that those oppressed by racism and sundry forms of structural discrimination must put so much effort into managing tensions between apt emotional responses to injustice and political remedies.

Still, to conduct the debate on anger *strictly* in the register of oppressor versus oppressed is *untimely* (so too the competing invocations and interpretations of moral saints like King, Mandela, and others— biographical proof-texting is largely inconclusive and invariably reductive and the contexts in which they made sense of and used their angers are not ours). Debate about apt angers—even the useful drive toward discriminating between angers ranging from destructive and inapt to constructive and apt—soar too far above ground level as to lose sight of this tenuous moment - the fragile, postnormal present.

Aptness has so far been thought in terms of the properly motivated and proportionate response of individuals and groups to moral violation. There is something at once salutary and strangely clinical about that vantage. A richer account of aptness might include analysis of the fit of apt anger with 'local' political moments, and not strictly anger-generative social contexts. Some will see in this cavil a counterproductivity critique, but, and here I agree with anger-discerning advocates, anger is *not always* counterproductive to salutary social change, and occasional counterproductivity in the broader interest of underscoring values can be endured. Timing is everything.

In an oft-quoted text from his *Nicomachean Ethics*, Aristotle writes: 'anybody can become angry; that is easy ... But to be angry with the right person and to the right degree and *at the right time* and for the right purpose, and in the right way—that is not within everybody's power and is not easy' (1109a25). I have emphasised 'at the right time' because in claiming anger as a licit motive force in social justice activism, in making the case for rage, anger-discerning advocates fail to take seriously enough that even well-regulated apt anger may be maladapted not just to policy but to a moment in a nation's political life. Apt anger may act destructively in a polarised polity suffering from democratic erosion. The anger industry, inclusive of anger merchants in media and government who bundle populist rhetoric and other polarising strategies, are keen to activate the shadow of anger in support of narrow partisan objectives. Social media accelerates the velocity at which anger moves even as it shrinks its epistemic horizons. Research confirms that the steady infusion of anger and more anger into our politics acts as an accelerant to the polarisation spiral. To be sure, anger is easy, though that claim needs to be nuanced by attention to the ways in which anger expression has been fraught with the play of power, and therefore how any proposal to be more suspicious of adding our angers to political space may be received like a repetition of brutalising past protocols. It is nevertheless critical that we take into account more than our 'right,' more than history, more than this policy or another, and adapt our activism and behaviours to the deceleration of polarisation and the (re)construction of a political environment where frank disagreement conduces to good policy and the commonweal.

In the waning days of the Trump presidency, the president and his party manufactured and peddled (and continue to peddle) a dense tissue of false claims designed to generate anger, subvert the electoral process, and reverse the outcome of a legitimate election. More alarming, the president refused to disavow political violence, flirting with and grooming extremist groups in service of the Big Lie. As rioters surged through the doors of the US Capitol on 6 January 2021, they chanted *Hang Mike Pence! Hang Mike Pence!* Interviewed by Jonathan Karl in March 2021, Trump was invited to express disgust and disavowal, but instead replied, 'well, the people were angry.' This verbal shrug is a textbook case of how racial rules operate in white supremacist society. What is the rule? White male anger is natural and privileged and must therefore be expressed. In the aftermath of 6 January, several comparative treatments of BLM protestors and Capitol rioters underscored differential racialised treatments both in terms of the initial posture of security forces and how those conflicts evolved and resolved.

Anger is finally ineliminable, individually and collectively, but to say so is not to surrender. Anger is valuable as a signal that something may have gone wrong. If it is persistent, readily available, and under-regulated, anger itself *has* gone wrong and is likely to compound suffering. Anger is also its own satisfaction, which is why Trump 'makes voters feel wonderful.' He understands that policy is largely irrelevant to political advantage, and that anger satisfies the angry. What we learn from the Stoics is that there is no straight path from the world to my anger, and from anger-discerning advocates that being angry does not represent a moral failure and that there is no straight path from my anger to reparative work on that world.

The counsel to turn from anger is counsel to develop a protocol that seeks to humanise others in the thick of disagreement, to seek the humanising potentials always available in any situation and to activate those potentials even at the risk of 'affective injustice.' The counsel to turn from anger is an alarm bell to rally now to democracies, to take up the difficult work of depolarisation to arrest democratic erosion; a corollary of this urgent work is a more collaborative environment in which to enact policies for increasingly just futures. Americans, as well as others, must demand of themselves, policymakers, civic leaders, and activists a new priority, namely, the dismantling of incentives fortifying the poisonous binary logic of pernicious polarisation. Political actors must disavow political violence, renounce exclusionary nationalist rhetoric, oppose antidemocratic measures like voter suppression and gerrymandering, and redress representation deficits using ranked choice voting and proportional representation. It is time for conscientious citizens everywhere to turn from anger and take the field, to prioritise humanising political activity, and to form solidarities in defence of democracy *and* justice.

CONFUCIUS, HE SHOWS

Jinmei Yuan

Logic has a bad reputation. Complaints vary from it being too abstract to it being reductive, and famously for it being too 'mathy'. But what is too often overlooked is the window logic provides us into the foundations of our language. Thus, we can peer into the mental processes that structure our thought and give way to the epistemological megaprojects our societies take on. Logic rules start to make sense when people practice them in their real life. Ethical arguments are only convincing when they sound logical. Yet ethical principles vary depending on where you are. Therefore, logic also can be used as a very revealing comparative tool. Chinese logic rules, for example, shaped and entailed a different logical structure of thinking from the logical framework of Western civilisation. It starts with a different presumption about living in a changing world. Being aware of these significant logical differences between Chinese and Western traditions, one can re-examine statements and arguments in Confucianism more accurately and appreciate Confucianism as it is – beyond being simply stereotypes of non-western worldviews.

Thus, it will not suffice to simply compare the Confucian thinking process to the Aristotelian tradition, the prominent system of logic in the West. Instead, it is important to shift one's perspective from a one-to-one comparison of the two styles to looking at both traditions using the concept of a set. Borrowing from Set Theory opens a new opportunity for mutual understanding. In so doing, I hope to offer an accurate picture of what classical Chinese philosophers have to say about virtue and some of the moral arguments made by them.

According to Western logic, ostensive definition is a kind of denotative definition, in which the objects denoted by the term being defined are referred to by means of pointing, or with some other gesture. Buried in many logical concepts, rules, and principles, ostensive definition does not play a major role in the Western traditional logic. Instead, when introducing it, logicians always point out the limitation and ambiguity of ostensive definition. For example, it can only point at particulars, not forms or abstract concepts. It is not accurate and is ambiguous. For instance, when one points at a desk, and says, 'It is a desk', whether the books on the desk are included or not cannot be determined. The claim remains vague.

But, when reading Confucius (551–479 BC), one can immediately discover that ostensive definition, referred to as 'Pointing Out' or *zhi* by Chinese logicians – including the School of Names and Later Mohists (479–221 BC) – was practiced by Confucius in his *Analects* as a crucial logical approach to convince his disciples. Later on, Mencius (372 – 289 BC; alt. 385 – 303/302 BC), another key Confucian scholar, used this rule frequently in his moral reasoning. Confucius used Pointing Out to define his basic virtuous terms, such as *ren* (being benevolent in associations) and *xiao* (filial piety). Mencius used Pointing Out to define his four moral sprouts: compassion, righteousness, propriety, and wisdom. Nearly every moral principle discussed by Confucius and his disciples is associated with the Pointing Out rule, in one way or another.

If the reasoning is done simply by giving examples, and without the application of deductive rules, can one still make a valid argument? According to Aristotelian logic, the answer would be 'No'. Validity associates with deductive arguments only.

Responding to this question carelessly resulted in two common attitudes used in judging Chinese ways of thinking. One of these pushes with great effort, and ultimately with futility, to match Chinese logical thinking with that of the West. The other is simply to completely deny that there is such a thing as Chinese Logic. These two attitudes are, in fact, looking at Chinese logic from the very same perspective – that of Aristotelian logic. As the American philosopher David Wong notes, Western studies, on the one hand,

> sometimes promotes a tendency to read into Chinese thinkers an acceptance of a top-down model when there is no such acceptance, on the other hand, when the absence of a top-down model in a Chinese thinker is correctly noted, an equally mistaken conclusion is the absence of any ethical reasoning at all in the thinker.

A top-down model is a kind of moral reading to be governed from the top down by the most general and abstract principles. This is seen in

Immanuel Kant's *a priori*, categorical imperative and also in utilitarianism, the Great Happiness Principle. Those most general and abstract principles serve as the primary premises for people to build up moral arguments in making moral judgments and decisions. But no such general and abstract principles can be found in Confucius's and Mencius's teachings. Rather, their discussions refer to particular men or specific cases. But still, it would be foolhardy to deny that Confucianism is one of the most serious moral philosophies and core ideologies of a culture. With billions of followers in China, as well as in other Asian countries, Confucianism has been practiced for three thousand years. If their moral arguments are not appealing, if their thoughts moving from one step to the other are inconsistent, and if their reasoning is not logically strong, then how could Confucianism become so attractive and convincing?

I suggest that instead of either fitting Confucian teaching into an Aristotelian logical framework, or denying that Confucian teaching follows any logical patterns, it would be fair to hold a position that we accept the fact that Confucius's and Mencius's ways of thinking and reasoning follow the rules of an alternative logic – Chinese logic. In studying classical Chinese philosophers' thoughts, it would be better to avoid an Aristotelian perspective. A set of very different logical rules backs up classical Chinese philosophers' thoughts. These rules are not only practiced by the masters, but also fully understood by their listeners and followers.

So how does Chinese logic functions; and what are the major rules one should learn, in order to fully understand classical Chinese philosophers' ways of distinguishing correct from incorrect reasoning.

Chinese logic begins with the very language. The Chinese language is a pictographic language. Chinese characters are divided into six categories, *liushu*. The first category is pictographs or imitative drafts, for example, ㄱ is the right hand. These characters are the basic radicals and function as building blocks to make other words. In total, there are 364 radicals in the first category, most of which can also serve as individual characters. These basic radicals function as building blocks to make other words The second category is indicative symbols, called 'ideographs.' For example, a more abstract concept, 'brightness' 明 is made of radices, the sun 日 and the moon 月. These two categories include basic radicals and characters, which is about 10 percent of the total characters. The remaining four categories make up the 90 percent. The characters in the other four categories almost all are associated with the first two basic pictographic categories in one way or another. Among the four, phonetic compounds use similar sounding words to generate new meanings, making the majority of Chinese characters. Those phonetic compounds imply pictographic radicals to group words. For example, almost all names for insects have an insect radical, *chong*, 虫; almost all the objects associated with water contain a water radical, *shui*, 氵 . Even the concept *virtue*, *de* 德 , which is a phonetic compound, contains the radical of two persons 彳 on the left. The meaning of moral conduct is indicated pictographically as virtues starting when there is more than one person.

The Chinese pictographic language naturally impacts and shapes Chinese ways of thinking in its own way. For example, in his research on the issue of moral self-cultivation, comparative philosopher P. J. Ivanhoe points out the uniqueness of understanding virtue, *de* in Chinese language. Ivanhoe says that in the early contexts, '*de*, 'virtue' was a kind of power.' It relates to another character *de* 德 , 'to get' or 'gain,' which shares the radical of two persons 彳 with virtue, *de*, and is also pronounced as *de*. The connection of the two concepts is etymological, graphical, and semantical. Having examined a few other moral concepts, Ivanhoe says, 'one can begin to see how the trajectory of this line of thinking leads naturally to a concern with moral self-cultivation'.

To demonstrate how Chinese logic works, one needs to examine a common rule of Pointing Out. Ostensive definition or Pointing Out is almost the only rule that Aristotelian and Chinese logicians practiced in a similar way, although the former group pays way less attention to it than the latter group. Ostensive definition in Aristotelian induction is a primary step for pursing the abstract form of a concept, while ancient Chinese thinkers showed no interest in pursuing abstract forms. Pointing out a particular is the best way to recognise meaning in a changing world. It offers the most accurate definitions to start a reasoning or to explain the changing situations in a process. Catching one hundred fishes in a running river is the best way to demonstrate what a fish is.

The basic structure of Chinese logic could be further clarified using case studies from some famous moral reasoning in Confucius's and Mencius's texts. When Aristotelian logicians do reasoning, they take abstract forms, patterns, and principles as real knowledge and treat them as a safe ground to build up their arguments. In Aristotelian deduction, the validity can be proved in a logical world with a pre-fixed order. The task of reason is to represent this order. Living in the world, we experience change, but the logical order remains as is required by the rules. However, unlike Western traditional logicians, classical Chinese philosophers never separate the logic world from the real one. They treat particulars as the elements in a real word and clarify what a particular is for starting a good argument. Unfolding the truth in time has been a serious logical practice for many ancient Chinese thinkers. Inseparability of the logic world from the real-world requires one to examine the consistency between one's practical actions and ethical codes taught by Confucian sages throughout history continuously up to the present.

Chinese philosophers saw the world as constantly changing. Living in a changing world, they might not have had an intention to seek the most general and abstract principle, which does not change. As the Canadian comparative philosopher Roger T Ames says:

> Chinese thinking does not presuppose the unity of Being behind beings, a One behind the Many. All you have in the Chinese world view is 'the ten thousand things' as an ad hoc summing up of beings and events. Correlations among these 'ten thousand things' are nonfoundational since they are only a matter of empirical experience and conventional interpretation.

'The ten thousand things' are clearly particulars, but not principles. If they are nonfoundational, then pointing them out in associations turns out to be a possible way to view them accurately in a changing world. Accordingly, thoughts are more structured when ancient Chinese thinkers discuss the relations among 'the ten thousand things'. Thus, while Western philosophers sought to define what is good and how it can be known, Chinese philosopher focussed on the problem of how to become good.

In Aristotelian logic, a term can be understood as referring fundamentally to either essences, or membership. In creating an objective language, which can be understood by anyone objectively, classical propositional logic focuses only on membership readings. A proposition is require to be either true or false, as stated by the law of excluded middle. A sequence of such propositions forms an argument. As long as the patterns (rules) are correctly followed, one can make a valid argument.

A proposition is made of a subject term and a predicate. The distributive relations between terms are determined based on a presupposed order of membership in classes. A proposition distributes a term if it refers to all members of the class designated by the term. For example, 'All horses are animals' is a proposition which must be either true or false. To confirm that it is true, its subject term must distribute to the predicate. In other words, all the members of the species *horse* must distribute to the genus, 'animal', which is higher up on the hierarchy. The truth value of a proposition is pre-determined by the relations of terms in the hierarchical system of genus and species. A hierarchical system of relationship by 'genus and species' is required to decide the truth value of a proposition. Within this system, laws of identity and noncontradiction work smoothly. This can be seen in hierarchical, dichotomous trees which often hold two characteristics: hierarchy and distribution. A pre-existing order guarantees a stable position to locate a member. Aristotle did not encourage people to think that things might outrun their essence based on a presumption that there is a fixed order in this world.

Studying how ancient Chinese thinkers categorise 'ten thousand things', one quickly sees there is no need for hierarchical organising trees as categorical propositions cannot be found in Chinese logic.

To explore how Chinese logic works in the changing contexts, and why Pointing Out is the best rule to practice in such contexts, I shall start with an examination on how Confucius defines *xiao*. A common translation of *xiao* is filial piety but it is better seen as 'filial conducts'. In actuality, *xiao* refers to a set of particular conducts required in a Confucian society.

When Socrates and Euthyphro discuss filial piety, regarding whether Euthyphro should turn his father in for his murder case, Socrates pushes Euthyphro to explain the essence of the term. That he should not merely tell an attribute of it. They reached an agreement that 'the holy is that which the gods love.' Socrates still pushed Euthyphro to search for 'the absolute truth' or the Form.

In the *Analects*, Confucius does the opposite. When discussing *xiao*, he points out one and then other examples of filial conducts to illuminate the concept:

Meng Yizi asked about filial conduct (*xiao*). The Master replied: 'Do not act contrary.'

Meng Wubo asked about filial conduct (*xiao*). The Master replied: 'Give your mother and father nothing to worry about besides your physical well-being.'

Ziyou asked about filial conduct (*xiao*). The Master replied: 'Those today who are filial are considered so because they are able to provide for their parents. But even dogs and horses are given that much care. If you do not respect your parents, what is the difference?'

Zixia asked about filial conduct (*xiao*). The Master replied: 'It all lies on showing the proper countenance. As for the young, contributing their energies when there is work to be done, and deferring to their elder when there is wine and food to be had. How can merely doing this be considered being filial?'

Now, questions arise: why does Confucius neither give a clear definition, nor encourage his disciples to explore the absolute true definition? When Confucius teaches his disciples, without giving clear definitions to the basic terms, how could Confucius make people understand him correctly? Is it possible that Chinese logic does not require a universal agreeable definition to start reasoning logically?

Of course, reading the above quotes from the perspective of Aristotelian logic, one can criticise that Confucius creates ambiguities. He fails to give his students a general definition of *xiao*, instead giving different examples to different people accordingly. If no clear definition is given to the term in a proposition, the starting point in a process of inference will be problematic. If premises change meanings according to different individuals, one cannot infer from a starting point to an ending point without fallacy. According to Aristotelian logic, categorical propositions are the building blocks for constructing arguments; the terms in a proposition must be defined clearly so that each proposition can be either true or false.

To understand Confucius's unique methodology of distinguishing good from bad reasoning, an explanation from an etymological perspective is necessary. Most Chinese characters contain pictographic elements, which could often present the meaning themselves. In other words, a character has already carried out some sort of demonstrative meanings itself without the need for a further definition. Forming thoughts in Chinese language naturally carries some pre-set unique features, even before one realises or practices Chinese logic intentionally.

Looking at the following samples of pictographic characters in ancient time, we see how they themselves are examples of Pointing Out:

Mountain: 山

Water: 川

Woman: 犬

Elder/Senior: 老

Child: 子

Xiao, filial conducts was written as: 孝

The pictographic character *xiao* itself represents a clear demonstrative definition, which conveys the meaning of a filial conduct: a senior sits at the top; a child stands at the bottom. Younger ones listen, obey, and provide service for the elders. According to an ancient etymological dictionary *Shuo Wen Jie Zi* by Xu Shen (circa the second century BC):

> The character *xiao* demonstrates doing kindly service to the parents. It represents the connotation of the relationship between an elder and his son. The son supports the elder

孝, 善事父母者, 從老省, 從子。子承老也。

Xiao, filial conduct as a virtuous code, expresses its meaning in the above pictographic character. Having learned this character, one gets the ostensive definition of *xiao*. When Confucius discusses *xiao* with his students, by bringing this character in, he has introduced the definition. No misunderstanding occurs when one reads out *xiao*. It is like pointing at an apple in the set apple and saying, 'this is an apple'. Or like pointing out one hundred fishes, and saying, 'they are members in the set of fish'. According to Set Theory, a set is defined by all members or elements of the set. The elements or members in a set can be either particulars or even subsets. Pointing out a member in a set is a way to learn about the set.

When ancient Chinese people first learned how to read and write, they had to practice Ostensive Definition or Pointing Out over and over in order to identify elements in a given association. Ostensive Definitions are used everywhere for pointing out 'ten thousand things' in the world. The process of learning the language is, indeed, a process of understating the meanings of words by Ostensive Definitions. Pointing Out is a way to recognise a set of elements which working together to define the set.

With an understanding that the world is made of 'ten thousand things' (particular elements), and that they are changing all the time, Chinese logicians overlook universal affirmative and negative statements. There is no categorical membership presupposed. 'All' for Chinese thinkers means all the members in a given domain of a set; while 'some' means some members in a given domain of such a set. This understanding made the Aristotelian Traditional Square of Opposition fail to match Chinese oppositions, which are limited within particular affirmative and negative statements only.

Classical Western logic deals mainly with arguments based on the relations of classes of objects to one another. Four kinds of categorical propositions, A (All S is P), E (No S is P), I (Some S is P), O (Some S is not P), are used to build categorical syllogisms. The underlined logical order is determined by classes of genus and species so that the categorical syllogism can be built by categorical propositions. In Chinese logic, using pictographic language, one points out not only the meaning of a word, but also the relationship can be pointed out demonstratively. Chinese language even contains special pictographic characters to mark out an affirmative or a negative statement.

Claiming that a copular, 'to be,' was unknown to Chinese philosophers in the Period of Hundred Schools (the golden age of Chinese philosophy), the Chinese Aristotle scholar, Jiyuan Yu says,

> together with the fact no copular is needed to connect subject and predicate, the logic structure 'predicating something of something else' that is central to Aristotle's theory of categories, plays little role in Chinese. Propositions of the form 'S is P' are expressed in various ways in classical Chinese. They might simply be expressed in the form 'SP'.

If both subject and predicate are particulars among 'ten thousand things', and if no categorical membership is involved between the two, then determining the relationship between which two particulars among 'ten thousand things' becomes an important job for the ancient Chinese thinkers. When the form of 'SP' works as an affirmative statement in the Chinese language, an affirmative character *ye* 也, serving as an affirmative marker, is put at the end of a statement. A relation or an association is confirmed. When the form of 'SP' works as a negative statement, a negative character *fei* 非 is put between S and P, serving as a negative marker. A relation or an association is denied. These two markers, *ye* and *fei,* are pictographic characters, which carry meanings. It is important to know that using Chinese language to express thoughts, even affirmative and negative relationship, can be demonstrative too.

For example，in Classical Chinese, an affirmative statement, 'A horse is an animal', is written as '豸 嘼 也 (*Ma shou ye*, 馬兽也)'. The last word, 也 (*ye*, 也) is an associative marker, which confirms relations.

Some associations can be more appropriated for a specific context than others. When *ye* is used to confirm a relation of two kinds against the contexts, learning of the relationship among 'ten thousand things' can be positively done by demonstration. *Ye* marks out an affirmative statement, which, at least, represents more appropriate associations between two particular sets in this case. In other words, if 'horse' refers to one set and 'animal' refers to the other set, then *ye* marks out that there is an object, horse, that can be cross-listed in both sets.

A negative statement, 'A horse is not an animal', is written as ' 豸 非 嘼 (*Ma fei shou*, 馬非兽)'. 非 is also demonstrative character. The connection between S and P is blocked by 非, which means separation or no connection. It is similar to say that '*a* ∉ H' (*a* is not a member of set H). The image of *fei* 非 demonstrates two fences and a ditch to separate the subjective and predicate terms.

If the images of Chinese characters carry meanings pictographically, then one should expect to see a different logical structure in classical Chinese philosophers' arguments. However, is it possible that ancient Chinese thinkers built their arguments with the knowledge of sets? Or more specifically, could it be possible when Confucius defined *xiao* that he did it in a way that is similar to modern logicians' discussions on set identity?

I have no ambition to claim that classical Chinese philosophers knew Set Theory. But I do want to emphasise that the written form of Chinese classical language offers a natural base for the language users to practice or play with sets and their domains. The latter is determined by context in ordinary language. This might share some commonalities with the original concept of Set Theory introduced by the nineteenth century Russian mathematician Georg Cantor (1857-1918). 'A set S is any collection of definite, distinguishable objects of our intuition or of our intellect to be conceived as a whole'.

In the very beginning of his book *The Order of Things,* noted French philosopher Michel Foucault (1926-1984) writes an interesting quote, which arose out of a passage from the Argentine writer Jorge Luis Borges, 'out of the laughter that shattered all the familiar landmarks' of Western philosophy. This passage cites a 'certain Chinese encyclopaedia', in which it is written that:

> Animals are divided into: (a) belonging to the Emperor, (b) embalmed, (c) tame, (d) sucking pigs, (e) sirens, (f) fabulous, (g) stray dogs, (h) included in the present classification, (i) innumerable, (j) drawn with very fine camelhair brush, (k) et cetera, (l) having just broken the water pitcher, (m) that from a long way off look like flies.

Western philosophers would be confounded by this. But if ancient Chinese thinkers did think within sets, then the definition made clear sense to them. Of course, animals are among 'ten thousand things', which ancient Chinese thinkers had strong interests to discuss over and over. If 'animal' is a set, and could be pointed out from the 'ten thousand things', then the above definition, in fact, gives a domain and lists the elements in the domain of the animal set clearly. If a domain, like in modern Set Theory, could be any size and consist of any object which associates with the set, then the domain here is the 'Belonging to the Emperor'. All the other listed creatures are pointed out as particular elements within this domain. Particular elements in the domain can be extended if necessary.

As long as a domain of the set is given, the association of a member in this domain can be pointed out. And since it is a domain, any number of objects can be included. The number of members can be extended if more creatures are discovered. But it does not matter whatever they are and what order their positions are arranged; as long as they are animals, they are the belongings of the Emperor.

Let me provide another example using the following etymological data.

First, the Chinese pictographic character for a set is *Ji* 集 . This character demonstrates that when a few birds sit on a tree, they are collectively in a set *ji*. One domain is given, which is the tree.

Secondly, Chinese pictographic characters are arranged in this way that the 364 primary radicals can serve as different primary units for different sets of characters. The related compound characters are listed under different individual primary radicals, like they are listed within different domains of sets. The image of birds collectively sitting on one tree represents this way of listing or sorting elements. Learning characters as elements in sets has been an effective way to master the language. For example, in the classic text, *Shuo Wen Shuo Wen Jie Zi,* 'horse, *ma* 馬' is a domain-radical. which holds many members, such as, 'Black horse', which is written as '*li* 驪 (α)', and 'one year old horse', which is written as '*ju* 駒 (β)'. They both associate with horse in that they all have a 'horse' radical, *ma* 馬 , on the left. They are members within the 'horse radical' set with a given domain. 'Examination' seems to have nothing to do with horses, but indeed, it has. 'Examination' is written as '*yan.* 驗 (ε)'. The left side has a 'horse' radical. The right side has a 'human' radical, *ren* 人 at the top, 'mouth' radical, *kou* 口 and 'walking/following' radicals, *cong* 从 follows. It is 'examination.' For instance, when a person examines the mouth or legs of a horse to determine its health. According to *Shuo Wen,* '*yan* 驗' can be the name of examined horses 馬名從馬驗. Similar to 'examination', 'stopping at a place' seems to have nothing to do with the general term 'horse', but it does. The ancient character is written as '*zhu* 駐 (ω)', which represents 'a horse stands 馬立也'.

Thirdly, if every character that the classical Chinese philosophers use to structure their thoughts is associated with a set, and the members within a given domain of the set are extensive, then no rule would be better than the rule of Pointing Out for one to recognise one after another element in a set, which could refer to a context during a discourse. Therefore, when Confucius did his logical reasoning, he points out one after another example in *xiao* (a set of 'filial conducts') to help his disciples identify the virtuous Set *Xiao.* Looking at the image of the character *xiao* 孝 and the list of filial conducts, which Confucius points out, one can understand *xiao* as a set with a domain containing a list of filial conducts. The set of *xiao* is understood as following: α : Do not act contrary; β : Give your mother and father nothing to worry about besides your physical well-being; ε : respect your parents in addition to providing food to them; ω : young works, parents drink…

Chinese ancient thinkers let context be involved in determining the domain of the discourse for ordinary language. A set in Chinese logic has two significant features: one is associative, and the other is extensive. Particular elements in a domain of a set can be different objects, like the modern understanding of a set, but they are all associated with the given domain of the set in one way or another. And the quantity of members in a set can be extensive according to the contexts. Classical Chinese philosophers' reasoning is to point out what these particular elements are, and how they relate or belong to the different sets as members or elements in a set.

Similar to his discussion on *xiao*, Confucius defines another main virtue, *ren* by offering particular examples. All these examples are associated with the set of humanitarian conducts. The left radical of the Chinese character, *ren* 仁, is a person and the right one is number two. The character itself conveys clear meaning of being humane when more than one person is involved. Confucius says:

a. 'Love the multitude broadly and be intimated with humanity, ren 仁.'

b. 'Authoritative persons [ren] establish others in seeking to establish themselves and promote others in seeking to get there themselves.'

c. 'Through self-discipline and observing ritual propriety (*li*) one achieves ren.'

d. 'In striving to be authoritative in your conduct (ren), do not yield even to your teacher.'

e. 'A person who is able to carry into practice five attitudes in the world can be considered authoritative. 'What are these five attitudes?' Confucius replied, 'deference, tolerance, making good on one's word (xin), diligence, and generosity.'

...

The various ways that Confucius describes ren from passage to passage could be considered as a list of authoritative conducts which is associated with the same domain of the Set Ren. What Confucius does is to point out the particular authoritative conducts in the domain of the set, humanity. The set of ren indicates: there is at least one authoritative conduct, which is a conduct of ren, humanity. Such conduct is an element in Set R. The list of authoritative conducts can be continued and added on. The extension of this set gives infinite chances to define ren accurately by pointing out its elements. Doing Chinese logic of sets for accuracy can be achieved in time or process, although no Form of ren is required.

An example from Mencius discusses how the rule of Pointing Out works. Mencius has a famous argument in his Mencius, Book One 1A7, when he discusses compassion with King Xuan of Qi.

Mencius says, 'One cares for the people and becomes a king.' King Xuan asked whether he could become a king. Mencius pointed out that King Xuan had compassion in his heart, which could make him a good king. And then he argued that the moral sprout of compassion in King Xuan's heart still needed to be developed in order to make him a good king. The reason that Mencius gave was that he heard that when the king's people were going to consecrate a bell with an ox's blood, 'the King said, "Spare it. I cannot bear its frightened appearance, like an innocent going to the execution ground." Someone responded, "So, we should abandon the consecrating of the bell?" The King said, "how can that be abandoned? Change it for a sheep."' Then, Mencius argued that with compassion, killing an ox or a sheep should have no difference. King Xuan had a sprout of compassion, but had not developed it yet. The King should be able to act with compassion by putting a benevolent government into effect, letting people have a good life and teaching them filial piety.

Mencius tried to point out that King Xuan had no logical consistency of replacing an ox with a sheep and then killing it. But what is his own logical consistency when arguing that the King had compassion for an ox, but concluded that the King should run a benevolent government?

To determine whether or not the King was compassionate, Mencius argued, he had to demonstrate a subset relation of compassion. He chose love. The love that involves two living creatures. It is about the relationship. The King loves ox; the King loves sheep; the King loves people, all these elements or loving relations serve as subsets in the Set Compassion to define the virtue compassion. It turns out that King Xuan failed to love the sheep. By pointing out in one of the presented cases that the King's conduct failed to fulfil the requirement of being a subset in the domain of Set Compassion, Mencius proved, by way of example, that the King Xuan only had a sprout of compassion, therefore he was not fully compassionate yet. To run a benevolent government, the King needed to develop his sprout of compassion.

The consistency of Mencius's argument is demonstrated by pointing out that one's love can be different, but the loving relation is within the domain of the set Compassion and remains the same; or in other words, as individual elements, they hold the same value when defining the set Compassion. King Xuan failed to keep this consistency and thought that using a smaller animal to replace a bigger one could preserve his feeling of being a loving king. But it would not make him a good king if he was unable to love all forms of life impartially, especially his people. Therefore, there was a space for him to develop his moral character in order to run his government with compassion. Mencius's argument follows logically and is morally convincing.

Let me now point out how logical fallacies can be shown by practising Confucius's and Mencius's ethical wisdom illogically when doing moral reasoning in real life. China's One-Child Policy provides us with a good example. It was introduced in 1979 and was strictly enforced for decades. The policy led to a growing gap between the number of males and females, as male sons became a precious commodity. Many abortions took place and daughters were abandoned or even killed so that a son could be had where only one child was allowed. This resulted in fewer females available for marriage. It also led to a growing problem concerning the proportion of elderly people, as there were fewer children to support them. The role of the only child in a Chinese family after the introduction of the One-Child Policy fundamentally changed the family structures within the society which still abided Confucian tradition. The only child is often referred to as 'little emperor' or 'little empress' because they are the sole focus of their parents' attention and resources. As a result, only children are sometimes perceived as being spoiled, selfish, and lacking a sense of social responsibility.

To demonstrate the logical fallacy of enforcing the One-Child Policy in a Confucian tradition two logical steps are involved. Step One: Pointing out that the conducts associated with the One-Child Policy (*o*) can never be elements in Confucius's Set *Xiao*, although *o* could be in a subset with its own domain which includes, referring to the only child as 'little emperor' or 'little empress'; letting the child to become the sole focus. A subset including these conducts can never be an element in Confucius's Set Xiao because these conducts seriously incoherent with the core meaning of the set. In other words, the One-Child Policy has fundamentally flipped over Confucius's virtue, xiao. As a set, the set identity of *xiao*, as the image of the character shows, requires filial conducts which focus on the elders in a family. Young ones carry moral obligations to serve elders. The elements or conducts associated with the One-Child Policy, such as referring to the only child as 'little emperor' or 'little empress' in the family, and letting the child become the sole focus of their parents' attention and resources, cannot be members of Set Xiao. A logical inconsistency between the family structure and relationship enforced by the One-Child Policy and how this type of family structure and relationship defined by *Xiao* can be pointed out. Therefore, *o* does not exist in Set *Xiao*. Enforcing such conducts in a Confucian society involves a logical fallacy. Step Two: pointing out that this logical fallacy is caused by mixing up two different domains – conducts associated with One-Child Policy and those associated with *Xiao*.

With the guideline of Mencius's approach in moral reasoning, pointing out incoherent elements in an existing set, one can see the cause of the above logical fallacy. A one-child family/society requires a different set of moral codes to justify it. The conducts associated with the One-Child Policy are actions that belong to a different domain. Putting them in a Confucian moral system is either a logical fallacy or a forced exercise to diminish Confucian tradition.

Chinese logic is a practice of how to distinguish correct from incorrect reasoning. It has a clear feature of logic of sets. The rule of Pointing Out is a fundamental rule in Chinese logic of sets, which works together with some primary understanding of sets and domains. It helps classical Chinese philosophers to offer accurate definitions, clarify complicated relations, and point out missing objects.

As a crucial rule in Chinese logic, Pointing Out shapes the foundation of the structure of logical thinking in Confucianism. Starting from the Rule Pointing Out, Chinese logic of sets involves other rules, such as the rule of designing 'sets' and the rule of finding 'analogy'.

Logic rules start to make sense when people practice them in real life. Ethical arguments are convincing when they sound logical. Chinese logic rules shape a different logical structure of thinking. Being aware of these significant logical differences between Chinese and Western traditions, one can re-examine statements and arguments in Confucianism and appreciate the true wisdom of Chinese philosophy. The moral arguments in the works of Confucius and Mencius go beyond their own time and can still guide us to make moral judgments today.

VIRTUOUS WORDS

Jeremy Henzell-Thomas

The source of the English word *virtue* is Latin *virtus* derived from *vir* 'man', the source also of English *virago* ('manlike woman') and 'virile', and so etymologically it denoted 'manliness'. It passed into English via Old French *vertu* with the sense of 'valour, power, strength, moral excellence, goodness, uprightness, skill, efficacy.' From the sixteenth century it had also come to mean 'chastity, sexual purity' in women. The late fourteenth century Wycliffe Bible has *virtue* where the early seventeenth century King James Version uses *power*.

It is revealing here to probe the meaning of the Ancient Greek word *arete* personified in Arete, the goddess of virtue, excellence, goodness and valour. Usually translated, as 'virtue', it was nevertheless not a specifically moral term but was also used to refer to the full realisation of inherent potential, purpose or function, applicable also to animals and inanimate objects. A good bull had the virtue (*arete*) of being an effective breeder. A good knife could cut well 'by virtue of' its sharpness. The term denoted any sort of excellence, distinctive power, strength, capacity, skill or merit, similar to Latin *virtus*. The Italian word *virtuoso* preserves the sense of exceptional skill.

The connotation of 'excellence' in the word *arete* also comes through in the related word *aristokratia*, 'rule by the best people', from *aristos,* 'best of its kind, noblest, bravest, most virtuous.' Such an ideal should not be equated with its debased realisation in the form of government in which power is held by a hereditary ruling class of 'aristocrats' or other privileged 'elite' rather than by people of real merit, superlative ability or nobility of character, or, indeed, by people elected or formally chosen in line with the original meaning of the word 'elite' from Latin *electus*, 'chosen'.

Useful convergence can be found here with Confucian ethics, in which the most frequently discussed ideal is that of the junzi (or *chun-tzu*). The scholar of Chinese philosophy, David Wong, explains that the Chinese word originally meant 'son of a prince', a member of the aristocracy, but in the Analects of Confucius it refers to ethical nobility. The first English translations rendered the term as 'gentleman' but the more appropriate terms 'superior man' or 'exemplary person' have been suggested in more recent times. Wong also notes that 'before Confucius's time, the concept of ren referred to the aristocracy of bloodlines...but in the Analects the concept is of a moral excellence that anyone has the potential to achieve.' He adds that the sense of ren as 'all-encompassing moral virtue' is explicitly conveyed by some translators through use of the translation 'Good' or 'Goodness', although it is also commonly translated as 'benevolence' or 'humaneness'. It might be noted here that the Prophet Muhammad's reaction to boasts of ancestral glory was to warn those steeped in the arrogance of pre-Islamic pagan ignorance (jahiliyyah) that Islam had abolished such tribalism ('asabiyyah), and that all human beings are descended from Adam. The Qur'an (49:13) advises that there is no superiority of one over another except in taqwa, that consciousness of God which inspires us to be vigilant and to do what is right. This verse is an implicit condemnation of all ethnic, racial, national, class or tribal prejudice, a condemnation which is made explicit by the Prophet in his reported assertion that 'he is not of us who proclaims the cause of tribal partisanship, and he is not of us who fights in the cause of tribal partisanship, and he is not of us who dies in the cause of tribal partisanship'. Muhammad Asad reports in his note to Qur'an 28:15 that when asked to explain what he meant by tribal partisanship, the Prophet answered, it means helping your own people in an unjust cause.

In his epic poems, the *Iliad* and the *Odyssey*, Homer often associates *arete* with courage, but more often with effectiveness. The person of *arete* uses all their faculties to achieve their objectives, often in the face of difficult circumstances, hardship or danger. Odysseus is the epitome of the hero who is not only brave and daring but also wily, shrewdly sagacious (a particularly Greek quality) and resourceful, with the practical intelligence and wit (in the sense of quick thinking) of the astute tactician. Navigating a perilous course on his voyage home to Ithaca after the Trojan War, he has to steer through the Straits of Messina between two mortal dangers, that of Scylla, the hideous monster with six heads (each with three rows of teeth) which will inevitably devour some of his men, and Charybdis, the whirlpool, which will destroy them all. He makes the conscious decision to steer closer to Scylla and lose some of his men so as to avoid the greater danger of drifting too close to the whirlpool. Another Homeric exemplar is the warrior Achilles, described by Debra Hawhee , an expert on rhetoric, as 'a guarantor of *arete*' not only through his 'goodness and prowess' but also through the 'utmost glory' he attained in his destiny to die in battle at Troy.

Another hero of Greek mythology who exemplified not only courage but also the shrewdness and skill associated with *arete* was Jason. One of the greatest dangers he and the Argonauts faced on their quest for the Golden Fleece was the Clashing Rocks, or Symplegades, which guarded the entrance to the Black Sea like a gigantic pair of sliding doors, smashing together and crushing ships between them. In telling the story, the Ceylonese metaphysician, Ananda Coomaraswamy, relates how, as the Argonauts rowed along the Bosporus within hearing of 'the terrifying clash of the Rocks and the thunder of surf,' Jason released a dove and watched it fly ahead of them, and although the Rocks converged on the bird, nipping off its tail feathers, it got through. 'Then, as the Rocks separated, the Argonauts rowed with all their might. A well-timed push from the divine hand of Pallas Athene helped the ship through the Rocks just as they slammed together again, shearing off the mascot from Argo's stern. Argo had become the first ship to run the gauntlet of the Rocks and survive. Thereafter the Clashing Rocks remained rooted apart.'

Although, the Latin word *virtus* is associated with virility or manliness, Homer uses the word *arete* to describe not only male Greek and Trojan heroes but also female figures, such as Penelope, the wife of Odysseus, who embodies *arete* in her dutiful co-operation, for which she is praised by Agamemnon, as well as by exemplifying how misfortune and sorrow can be stoically endured to an excellent degree. Such is the virtue of *sabr* (patient endurance) in the Islamic tradition.

In the original Greek of the New Testament, *arete* is included in the list of virtues for cultivation in Christian moral development and is associated primarily with the moral excellence of Jesus. It figures in the celebrated 'Admonition of Paul' in *Philippians* 4:8: 'Finally, brethren, whatever is true, whatever is honourable, whatever is just, whatever is pure, whatever is lovely, whatever is gracious, if there is any excellence (*arete*), if there is anything worthy of praise, think on these things.' Other virtues in the New Testament include faith, knowledge (*gnosis*), godliness (*eusebeia),* brotherly affection *(philadelphia*), the highest form of love (*agape*) as the love of God for man and man for God, self-control (*enkrateia*) and steadfastness (*hypomone*). Virtue in the Christian tradition is also represented by the *seven cardinal virtues* (early fourteenth century) comprising the natural virtues of justice, prudence, temperance, and fortitude and the theological virtues of hope, faith, and charity.

In the field of education, Charles Terry, in a book entitled *Moral Education*, provides an example of the right balance between the pursuit of knowledge and the attainment of goodness and 'noble character'. This balance was the avowed aim of the founders of Philips Exeter Academy in New Hampshire in the US, a school I once visited to observe their teaching methodology. In the original *Deed of Gift* of 1781, John Phillips wrote: 'though goodness without knowledge is weak and feeble, yet knowledge without goodness is dangerous, and that both united form the noblest character, and lay the surest foundation of usefulness to mankind.' Yet, as Terry points out in relation to contemporary education, 'most secondary schools do much better in knowledge than in goodness – particularly those engaged in the uncompromising pursuit of academic excellence.' Although he is referring here to the situation in America, an incomplete and often one-sided view of excellence is widespread (though in different ways) in educational systems at all levels and in all societies. In the UK, for example, in line with the statutory requirements of the National Curriculum, 'moral and spiritual development' is often specified on school mission statements as an essential component of a broad and balanced curriculum, an indispensable dimension of its commitment to 'delivering' excellence. In reality, it may often receive little more than lip service. As for Muslim societies, it hardly needs repeating that deficits in knowledge production, independent enquiry, and critical thinking are repeatedly lamented, with the establishment of 'centres of excellence' often regarded as an important element in any strategy for educational reform.

One of the most challenging assignments I ever faced was the delivery of a keynote address at the Eid event held as part of the diversity programme at Goldman Sachs in London in 2010, bearing in mind that my audience would include a number of young Muslim trainee investment bankers. This was not long after the financial crisis in 2008 to which Goldman Sachs had contributed by packaging toxic subprime mortgage debt into securities and selling them to investors, an unethical practice that seriously damaged its reputation. I was well aware that I would need to balance the demands of diplomacy and honesty by delivering a message not from a 'preachy' high horse but from a position that would highlight corporate virtues and ethical principles while not alienating my listeners by pointing the finger too accusingly or ruffling too many feathers.

I chose 'Islam and Human Excellence' as my theme not only because excellence is so absolutely integral to Islamic values but also because it is a shared, universal value which figured strongly in the statement of Business Principles on the Goldman Sachs website. Opening my talk with the conciliatory words 'You will know your own principles much better than I do and know far better how you honour them in your work', I referred to one of those principles as follows: 'We take great pride in the *professional* quality of our work: we have an uncompromising determination to achieve *excellence* in everything we undertake'. Another of their stated business principles is 'integrity and honesty are at the heart of our business. We expect our people to maintain high ethical standards in everything they do, both in their work for the firm and in their personal lives.' I chose not to mention this, but rather to pick up on the terms *professional* and *excellence* so as to highlight the important distinction between them. 'We can talk about a professional hit man,' I said, 'but would it not be rather strange to say that Mario is an *excellent* hit man, unless we were members of the Mafia? The difference is that the heart of excellence is not simply about personal mastery of a skill or effectiveness in accomplishing a task but includes excellence of human character, and that has a moral and ultimately a spiritual dimension.' I added that 'some would go so far as to say that it's a healthy and distinctive aspect of the British character that we tend not to make an idol of so-called *professionalism* and do not confuse it with *excellence*.'

In retrospect, I can see that I was appealing for awareness of the moral dimension of excellence enshrined in *arete*. The aesthetic sense of refinement the Greeks also associated with *arete* converges at one level with that of *ihsan*, 'doing what is good and beautiful', 'behaving in an excellent manner'. In Islamic ethics and spirituality, *ihsan* embraces the aesthetic, moral and spiritual dimensions of a beautiful and virtuous character (*akhlaq* and *adab*). Beauty is thus inseparable from the attributes of Divine Perfection, and from the goodness, moral virtue, spiritual refinement and excellence of character which are the human reflections of those holy attributes. This integrated and elevated conception of beauty is fundamental to a proper understanding of what is meant by excellence in the domain of aesthetics.

In the same way as 'virtue' can be associated with Greek *arete* and with various connotations of *ihsan, adab, and akhlaq* in Islamic ethics and spirituality, it also converges with Arabic *futuwwah*, derived from the Arabic root FTY, the source of *fata* 'youth', and by extension 'manliness', 'nobleheartedness', the equivalent of the Western notion of 'chivalry'. The translator Aisha Bewley defines *futuwwah* as 'placing others above oneself as manifested in generosity, altruism, self-denial, and indulgence for the shortcomings of others.' The Prophet affirmed that all creatures are God's children, and those dearest to God are the ones who treat His children in the best way. In his celebrated letter to Malik al-Ashtar, Imam 'Ali writes: 'make your heart a throne of mercy towards your people. Show them perfect love and care. For they are in one of two groups: either your brother in religion or your fellow-human being.' This broad view, in total harmony with the Qur'an, embraces all races, all cultures, all tongues. It asserts the unity of the human race and the equality of all human beings, demanding compassion for all and not only to members of one's own group.

In his *Concise Encyclopaedia of Islam*, Cyril Glassé explains that 'before Islam, social responsibility was determined among the desert Arabs by blood ties alone, with little provision for the outsider apart from the prescribed rules of hospitality for guests.' However, as we know, when Mohammad was a young man, and not yet a Prophet, he took part in the Pact of the Virtuous (*hilf al-fudul*) in which tribal leaders pledged that it was their collective duty to intervene in conflicts and side with the oppressed against the oppressors irrespective of their clan affiliation. Years later, as a Prophet, Muhammad recalled the terms of that pact and said: 'I was present in Abdullah ibn Judan's house when a pact was concluded, so excellent that I would not exchange my part in it even for a herd of red camels; and if now, in Islam, I was asked to take part in it, I would be glad to accept.' The Prophet's admiration for the Pact teaches us that the principles of justice and morality are not the exclusive domain of any one group or ideology, and that group allegiance needs to be transcended in favour of primary loyalty to universal principles. The Prophet acknowledged the validity and nobility of the pact although it was established by non-Muslims and he saw nothing in it that contradicted the sacred principle in Islam to strive for justice and the common good.

The Qur'an teaches us that our intellectual faculties are not designed to exist in a moral vacuum. The various words in the Qur'an which denote these faculties (*'aql, albab, basirah, rushd*) also carry a profound sense of moral valuation. There is a criterion (*furqan*), a touchstone within our own hearts which enables us to distinguish between the true and the false, and between right and wrong.

To that layer of moral valuation, we should add too the imperative of right action, described so simply and beautifully by the Catholic monk, Thomas Merton: 'the activity proper to man is not purely mental, because man is not just a disembodied mind. Our destiny is to live out what we think, because unless we live what we know, we do not even know it. It is only by making our knowledge part of ourselves, through action, that we enter into the reality that is signified by our concepts.'

The same imperative to become what we know, to live out our knowledge, is encapsulated in the saying of the Prophet that 'my Lord disciplined me and taught me the most virtuous conduct.' The English word 'discipline' comes from Latin *discere*, 'learn' and also has the sense of a body of knowledge to be mastered (a discipline or subject). The word 'disciple' (learner) comes from the same source. The Prophet advises us that 'learning' is not merely an intellectual activity but a 'higher education', a training or discipline of the soul in the attainment of virtue.

Sadly, the economic pressures on modern students often have the effect of giving priority to the imperative to become unquestioning and conforming 'producers' and 'consumers' and to enter a narrow range of prestigious and well-paid occupations. We should never forget that when the Prophet spoke of the sanctity of the search for knowledge, and when he spoke too of the importance of acquiring *useful* knowledge ('I seek refuge from God from a knowledge which has no use'), he was not endorsing the kind of narrow, soulless, *utilitarian* curriculum-for-the-workplace to which our impoverished system of schooling has been largely reduced. That regime is designed to serve, above all, the rampant materialism embedded in the selfish and unsustainable illusion of perpetual 'economic growth'. That was not the vision of the Prophet. In speaking of 'useful' learning, he was upholding the education of the soul and the usefulness to others of well-rounded and wise people who have developed their character and nurtured their higher faculties. This may certainly entail the mastery of a domain of knowledge and practice, but that mastery serves higher and more altruistic ends, nurturing the beauty of character and conduct which distinguishes the Islamic conception of excellence (*ihsan*).

I would now like to explore in some depth the virtues of moderation and balance, so as to reflect the statement in the Qur'an that Muslims are *a community of the middle way* (2:143). What is meant by moderation? A dull compromise? A state of mediocrity or half-heartedness? A mere avoidance of difficult choices? Certainly not. The Qur'an urges us to use our reason in validating the truth, to 'listen closely to all that is said, and follow the best of it' (39:18). Certainly, the best of it may often be the position which is most balanced and moderate, but it is not arrived at by a kind of quantitative calculation which finds a mathematical average or apparently equitable compromise irrespective of what is actually just, right and fair. The meaning of original Germanic root *(fagraz)* of the word *fair is* 'fitting', that which is the right size, in the correct ratio or proportion. Its two modern meanings, 'just' and 'beautiful' – a combination of connotations which closely parallels the meaning of *'adl* in Arabic – have preserved that connection to its original sense. Moderation and balance are qualitative states which honour what is appropriate and proportionate. The range of meanings of the word *fair* reflects a truly Islamic concept, the idea that to be just is to do what is beautiful (*ihsan*), to act in accordance with our original nature (*fitrah*), which God has shaped in just proportions (Qur'an 82:7) as a fitting reflection of divine order and harmony. Indeed, the Qur'anic statement that 'everything have We created in due measure and proportion' (54: 49) is completely in harmony with the sense of the English word *moderation*. The word *decency* has exactly the same underlying meaning as *fairness*. It comes from Latin *decere*, 'be fitting or suitable', and is closely related to the word *dignity*. To be fair and decent, and hence to act with dignity, is to behave proportionately, to do what is appropriate in the circumstances, to act, above all, with innate balance and common sense.

It is also noteworthy that in the story of Jason and the Argonauts, to pass between the Rocks symbolised the passage through the 'strait gate' or the 'needle's eye' between the contrary pairs of opposites which make up the conditioned world. It is to follow the Middle Way, to find the Truth which, as the sixth century philosopher Boethius put it, is a 'mean between contrary heresies.' Inwardly, it is to be guided by the lamp 'lit from a blessed tree – an olive-tree that is neither of the east nor the west' (Qur'an 24:35). Aristotle's notion of the golden mean was a pivot of Al-Ghazali's exposition of Islamic ethics in his *Revival of the Religious Sciences*. Al-Ghazali concludes Book XXIII (*On Breaking the Two Desires*) with the words of the Prophet that 'the best of all matters is the middle way.' As one of various examples of the golden mean, Al-Ghazali sees the virtue of courage as the mean between its defect in the vice of cowardice and its excess in the vice of recklessness.

There are many reported sayings of the Prophet on the central Islamic virtue of steering between extremes. On one occasion, the Prophet said to Abu Bakr: 'I passed you when you were praying in a low voice.' Abu Bakr said, 'the One with whom I was holding intimate conversation heard me, O Messenger of God!' He then turned to 'Umar and said, 'I passed you when you were raising your voice while praying.' He replied, 'Messenger of God, I was waking the drowsy and driving away the devil.' The Prophet said, 'raise your voice a little, Abu Bakr,' and to 'Umar he said, 'lower your voice a little.'

The English word *moderation* comes from Latin *modus*, 'keeping within due measure', which is related to another word which is also the source of English 'modest'. Etymologically, moderation has the same inherent meaning in English as modesty, a connection which is also truly Islamic. The Prophet himself said that 'true modesty is the source of all virtues.' He said too that 'every religion has a distinctive feature and the distinctive feature of Islam is modesty'.

The late Charles le Gai Eaton, Sufi scholar and diplomat, spoke beautifully on the topic of balance and equilibrium in his *Reflections* and *Words of Faith* for a series of BBC World service broadcasts between 1978 and 1996. Discussing the 'Do's' and 'Don'ts' of religion, he said 'they have, ultimately, one purpose, and that is to establish harmony, balance and order within the individual personality as also in society; the same harmony, balance and order visible in creation as a whole.' And again, 'let me, in conclusion, emphasise one of the most basic principles of Islam. Balance, both in spiritual life and in our human existence as creatures plunged into the light and shade of this world. As the Muslim sees it, there is another word for balance, and that is peace. The very word Islam is derived from the Arabic word for peace. Where balance is lacking there is conflict and disorder, both outward and inward. While it is maintained, men and women are free to turn to God as plants turn to the sun.' This is a strikingly beautiful affirmation of the harmony and equilibrium inherent in the created order. If we can remember who we are and where we are going and by so doing restore in ourselves that balance, we will have access to that inner discernment which will enable us to be true to the Qur'anic injunction to listen closely to all that is said, and follow the best of it.

As a boy given to certain excesses (including a rebellious and outspoken streak of non-conformity) my grandmother, who was born in 1896 when Queen Victoria was still on the throne, habitually intoned the maxim 'moderation in all things'. I can see now that this stemmed from her belief that moderation was a hallowed British virtue along with decency, fairness (a 'deep-rooted British commitment' according to Gordon Brown) and stolid application, and this raises the tricky question as to whether certain virtues are typically represented in a specific national identity. Abdal Hakim Murad (Tim Winter), proponent of neo-traditionalism, appears to believe so, having referred to 'the convergence of Islamic moderation and good sense with the English temper' in a lecture given to a conference of British converts in 1997. He went on to claim that the values of Islam 'are our values. Its moderate, undemonstrative style of piety, still waters running deep; its insistence on modesty and a certain reserve, and its insistence on common sense and on pragmatism.'

The late President Izetbegovic of Bosnia also affirmed the convergence of what he called the 'Anglo-Saxon spirit' with Islam in the idea of the Middle Way. Izetbegovic identified the source of this convergence to an Englishman, the thirteenth century philosopher Roger Bacon, who set the entire structure of English philosophical thought on two separate foundations: inward experience, which leads to spiritual insight, and observation and experimentation, the basis of modern science. According to Izetbegovic, this aspect of Bacon's genius, this striving for balance between the inward and the outward, 'is considered by most Englishmen as the most authentic expression of English thought and feeling.' It goes without saying that the same balance between faith and observation is integral to Islam; indeed, our faith is not a blind faith but a faith strengthened empirically through observing and studying the divine imprint in the world around us. There is another important fact about Roger Bacon that has never been sufficiently studied and recognised: the father of English philosophy and science was a student of Arabic. Indeed, he lectured at Oxford in Arab clothes. He was strongly influenced by Islamic thinkers, especially by Ibn Sina, and to this influence can be attributed the character of Bacon's thought and, through him, perhaps the origin of the middle way as an important guiding principle in English (and British) life. He stressed the need for balance: balance not only between reason and observation on the one hand, and faith on the other, but also balance between individual freedoms and rights, and wider social responsibilities; and balance between a pragmatic concern with everyday needs and an altruistic hunger for transcendence.

I will not attempt here to distinguish between Britishness, Englishness and the 'Anglo-Saxon spirit', even though in his work on British identity, Chris Rojek has contended that in 'the high-water mark of empire' (as he put it) Britishness was regarded as 'the combination of the best and highest that nature and nurture could provide in the British Isles', with each nation within the Union providing 'crucial elements that the others lacked' – a composite identity representing a 'marriage between Scottish invention and discipline, Irish daring and imagination, Welsh decency and pluck, and English application and genius for compromise.'

Is it advisable to assign specific virtues to national identities? Such assignation is clearly problematic, especially when it is exploited to attribute moral superiority to a nation state. We are only too familiar with the 'exceptionalism' claimed by the United States as making it exemplary compared to other nations. In asking what it means to say the United States is exceptional, American historian Walter McDougall points out that 'if exceptionalism means that the United States is exceptionally virtuous given its precocious dedication to civil and religious liberty, equality, justice, prosperity, social mobility, and peace and harmony with all nations, then *ipso facto* the United States is exceptionally vicious for falling so short of those ideals.' As for the American illusion of 'divine dispensation' and exemption from the rules of conduct it makes and enforces upon other nations, McDougall sees in it 'the pride that goeth before a fall' and he rejects the notion of exemption from the 'laws of entropy' to which other nations are subject. If, however, exceptionalism just means unique, 'then the claim is unexceptional because no two countries are exactly alike', and 'if it just means that Americans have *believed* their country is special, then (as the British sceptic, Godfrey Hodgson writes) "there is nothing exceptional about this exceptionalism. All great nations cherish national myths."'And in support of this contention, one need only refer to the national motto of France, 'Liberté, Egalité, Fraternité', or the massed ranks of 'true Brits' ardently singing 'Land of Hope and Glory, Mother of the Free' every year at the Last Night of the Promenade Concerts in the Royal Albert Hall. I should not scoff at this spectacle, for I too feel the emotional pull of these words as set so magnificently to the music of Edward Elgar, even though they are prone to the spectre of jingoism. It is well to bear in mind that while Ibn Khaldun (d.1406) recognised the negative aspect of tribal partisanship (*'asabiyyah*), he also affirmed its positive aspect in promoting solidarity and social cohesion. He understood that co-operation and community spirit are hard wired into humanity, and social organisation and community pride are necessary for an internally coherent civilisation to flourish.

Leaving jingoism aside, let me wind up this essay by returning to Tim Winter's sincere belief in 'the convergence of Islamic moderation and good sense with the English temper.' I am tempted to aver that what the sociologist Krishan Kumar describes as the 'calm fortitude and cheerful stoicism' of the British seems to have much in common with the Islamic virtue of *sabr,* that patient endurance which is constant in both easy and hard times. The distinctively British brand of stoicism, the stiff upper lip, which Tim Winter associates with being modest, reserved and undemonstrative, is represented in the famously laconic exchange between the Duke of Uxbridge and the Duke of Wellington at the Battle of Waterloo. The former announced, 'My God, sir, I have lost my leg!' to which the Duke of Wellington replied, 'My God sir, and so you have!' I recall, however, that the Duchess of Devonshire, in a lamentation a while ago on the death of the British stiff upper lip, disapproved mightily of the deterioration into a 'sloppy-sentimental' culture of 'self-pity and self-esteem.' We might detect more than merely a germ of truth here, but the level seems to be slipping, and it seems to me that it slips dangerously in the association that right-leaning British philosopher Roger Scruton makes between being 'distant, cool, reserved' as a key marker of Englishness and the readiness of the English to deplore what he calls 'the volatile humours of Mediterranean people, and the fickle sentimentality of the Irish.' This distortion of a virtue and its exploitation as a tribal marker is a steep descent from the higher level of convergence of underlying principles which I believe we should be trying to bring to light. Ultimately, it descends merely to mutual derision of repugnant eating habits or perceived cultural eccentricities: Madame de Monplaisir's horror, for example, at the abominable English habit of 'eating meat with jam', or her belief that the 'garden shed is the place where Englishmen want to be.'

The same trivialisation is evident in Stephen Fry's identification of 'joy in ignorance and anti-intellectualism' as a key marker of Britishness, and in Andrew Marr's claim that the British love of moderation makes them 'hostile to taking anything, even the meaning of life, too seriously...If God is still with the British,' he says, 'He will be quiet, understated, embarrassed by enthusiasm.' Marr claims that the same love of moderation and deep-seated distrust of fanaticism and extremism makes them 'hostile to fervour'. Well, we can agree that the principle of moderation is by definition opposed to fanaticism and extremism, but it is then trivialised and reduced by Marr, at worst to a mediocrity incapable of passion or enthusiasm for anything serious. Moderation is surely the well-tempered mean between the opposite extremes of excess and defect, in this case between taking things too seriously and not taking them seriously enough. And how can understatement be an example of moderation when the very word denotes an extreme, the opposite of overstatement?

However we conceive of excellence, whether through the lens of Greek philosophy and mythology, Christianity, Islam, or any other tradition or way of life, or, indeed, through the less expansive lens of idealised national or cultural identity, the essence of it is surely the 'primordial disposition' or 'essential nature' with which each of us has been divinely endowed, and which gives us the potential at every moment to embody as far as is humanly possible the attributes of Divine Perfection, the Ninety-Nine Names of God in Islamic spirituality. That essential nature underlies all variants of human 'identity' and the Qur'an exhorts us to engage openly and respectfully with all nations, tribes, colours, tongues, and ways of life so that we might encourage and vie with one another in striving to live a virtuous life.

MUHAMMADI BEGUM

Aamer Hussein

1.

In 1898, a young woman of twenty, newly married and living in Lahore, wrote a letter to her older sister: 'I have decided to start a journal for women. Would you be willing to help me with the task, and write some essays for me?'. Her sister replied:

> Your brother-in-law gets angry when he sees me writing. I am powerless. If it is ever possible, I will send you an article and sign it 'a well-wishing sister'. I am afraid that with the noise the children make around me, and my many household chores, I will find it hard to divert my attention to writing an article.

The younger sister was Muhammadi Begum. She would go on to establish *Tahzeeb e Niswan*, a pioneering weekly magazine for women. The purpose of the new magazine was not just to promote female writers but also to fight for women's rights. The hesitant response of the elder sister, Ahmadi Begum, couched in stilted prose, illustrated the problem that has to be addressed. Women were conditioned to only serve the needs of the family: first in their father's home, and then in the marital abode. Both sisters helped at a very early age to bring up their brothers when their mother died, until a stepmother took her place.

Muhammadi Begum married Sayyid Mumtaz Ali (1860-1935), a Deobandi scholar who acquired the title *Shams al-Ulama* (Sun of Religious Scholars). A widower twice her age, he expected much more from his wife then to be the mother of his three children from a former marriage. For Mumtaz Ali was a women's right advocate and wrote vigorously about the social situation of Muslim women and the problems of gender inequality in nineteenth century India. In his ground-breaking 1898 book, *Haqooq-i-Niswan* (Rights of Women), Mumtaz Ali rejected the conventional arguments advanced by Muslim scholars for female subjugation. There is no notion of inherent male superiority over women in Islam, he wrote. Neither do men have greater physical or intellectual strength. There is no rational basis for requiring two female witnesses against one man in a court of law. Or for a daughter to have only half the share of the son in inheritance. In the late nineteenth century, these were revolutionary ideas – a declaration of war against the orthodoxy. It is said that when Mumtaz Ali read the first draft of the book to Sir Seyyed Ahmad Khan (1817-1898), the modernist reformer and founder of the Aligarh Muslim University, Sir Seyyed was so enraged that he tore up the manuscript. In the young Muhammadi Begum, Mumtaz Ali saw a similar spirit. He married her because she was highly literate and had the potential to be a journalist. He wanted his young wife to be the sole editor of his dream project – a magazine for women largely by women.

The first issue of *Tahzeeb-e-Niswan* came out on 1 July 1898. It consisted of eight pages, later to be increased to ten and then sixteen. The masthead announced that it was edited by a 'sharif bibi' - a gentle, noble, or virtuous woman – cloaking the name of the editor in pious nobility. Muhammadi Begum's own name would soon appear on the covers of all her books, published by Darul Ishaat Punjab, her husband's press. The earliest of these is *Rafiq e Arus* (The Bride's Companion) a selection of her early pieces from *Tehzeeb*, which she compiled in 1901. This was followed by a work of full-length fiction, *Safia Begum* (1902). Using her given name, she would dispense with the appended respectability of father or husband's name with which many women writers, then and much later, cloaked their individual identity. The honourific appellation, Sayyada, denoting her high birth, which she never used in her books, has been added recently.

Her life was short. She died in 1908 at the tender age of thirty. Her career as editor of *Tahzeeb-e-Niswan* and as storyteller, journalist, and tireless campaigner for women's rights lasted only ten years. Living in a form of purdah and rearing stepchildren and a son of her own, she achieved more in this brief span than many writers in a lifetime. After her death, *Tahzeeb-e-Niswan* was edited by her stepdaughter Waheeda Begum, who eventually handed over to her brother, Imtiaz Ali Taj, who by now had established himself as a notable scholar. Later, it was edited by a number of male scholarly figures.

The elder sister, Ahmadi Begum, did eventually respond to her sister's request. It came in the form of a biography of her sister: *Halaat e zindagi e Muhammadi Begum* (An Account of the Life of Muhammadi Begum). The manuscript lay unpublished for many years. It was finally published in 2018, edited by her grandson-in-law Naim Tahir. It is the basis of most of what we know about Muhammadi Begum.

Her prodigious output – some thirty books, including novellas, poems, short stories, fables and tales for children, and manuals of cooking and housekeeping (for which she was best remembered), lay in oblivion for decades. They have only been rediscovered recently, most notably in *Majmua Muhammadi Begum*, an anthology of her work edited by Humaira Ashfaq and published in 2018. Ahmadi Begum's biography has provided information to many scholars, including Gail Minault, author of *Secluded Scholars:Women's Education and Muslim Social Reform in Colonial India*, and C.M Naim who translated *Hayat e Ashraf*, Muhammadi Begum's biography of her role model Ashrafunissa Begum as *A Most Noble Life*. Ashrafunissa Begum (1840-1903), was another nineteenth century pioneer of women's rights who the first girl's school in Lahore.

I first came upon Muhammadi Begum's work in 1994 in the archives of the SOAS library. I had also caught glimpses of her in the influential novelist and short story writer Qurratulain Hyder's (1927-2007) accounts of her parents' lives. I was deeply intrigued by the writings of this woman, who changed my conception of the history of women's writing in Urdu. It led me to write an article on *Sharif Beti* –Virtuous Daughter – one of her most significant stories, published under the title 'Forcing Silence to Speak' in the *Journal of Urdu Literature* in 1996. But it is only recently that I have discovered the true scope of her remarkable output.

2.

Muhammadi Begum sees enterprise, even more than education, as the major tool of advancement for women.We find her, repeatedly, juxtaposing stories of women trapped in the misery of unsuitable arranged marriages with the few success stories of women who break through socially imposed sanctions and barriers with the resources they gain from faith, courage, and patience. There is, in her writings, a marked contrast between her inherent understanding of the boundaries imposed by *sharafat* – literally nobility, the term encompasses goodness, virtue and family honour – and the freedom to examine and extend these limits through education, writing, and paid work, considered dishonourable in her time and even much later. It is in her fictions, parables and biographies, more than in her essays and articles, that her voice of protest can most clearly be heard. To appreciate how she refigured the definition of 'sharafat' to guide the virtuous women confined by strictures towards pathways of industry and productivity, I have translated 'A Tale of Two Shells', a story hidden away among various articles in a manual of etiquette in which she appropriates the stark oral manner of a traditional tale for her own moral purpose.

A TALE OF TWO SHELLS

A young woman, well-known for her intelligence and wisdom, who married a young man from a wealthy family. Her husband was a spendthrift. They lived for a while in luxury, but because of his extravagance they were soon left with nothing. His wife would counsel him: If one has only two cowrie shells, even those must be kept most carefully. You don't even take care of your cash!

One day, the young wife said to her husband: as a girl, I was playing with three friends when two shells emerged from the mud. My companions disdained them, but I put them away and said: Someday these shells, too, may come to be of use. I still don't have the heart to get rid of them. That's the way I am, while you throw away large sums of money without a care.

The husband was distressed by his pennilessness; her advice annoyed him even further. One evening, he drugged his wife with a sleeping liquid. As she lay unconscious, he swept their home clean of all the furniture and clothes that were left to them, and leaving the two shells under his wife's pillows, he took off to another region.

The poor woman was astonished when she awoke in the morning and found herself devoid of all their possessions. As she looked around the house, she could only see its freshly swept floors. She found the two shells under her pillow and understood how her husband had treated her.

Wandering here and there around the house, she saw nothing more than a broken straw broom in the fuel shed. She picked it up and took it away. When the neighbourhood cleaning woman came to clean the lavatories, she asked her to call the woman next door who was herself reduced to penury and didn't eat for two days at a time. How could she depend on her for help? She gave the neighbour the two shells and said: could you take these to the market and bring me some cotton thread?

Times were cheap then; you could even exchange shells for some goods. The neighbour went to the pawn shop and placed the shells in the broker's palm. In exchange for them, he gave her some string of the sort that is used to bind paper parcels. The neighbour brought these back to her friend, who unbound the broom, picked out some straws, and made two fans which she bound with a piece of string. She took these to her neighbour and asked her to sell them.

The neighbour sold them both for a penny, but that day shame and sorrow had robbed the woman of her appetite. How could someone whose comfortable home had been plundered in the blink of an eyelid even be aware of hunger's pangs? She spent the day without eating; she sent for more string with the penny she had, and the next day she made two very fine fans which sold for sixteen pennies. She sent for some chickpeas for a penny, which she ate, and spent the rest on more string which she regularly used to make four or five fans a day to sell.

As time went by, she became renowned for her craftsmanship. People brought her their sewing; she began to make clothes for them. Bothered by the thought of her solitary condition, she called her neighbour over to share her home and the sparse simple food she ate. To amuse herself and to make some profit, she kept some hens and began to sell their eggs. Slowly she saved so much money with her competence and thrift that she began to trade on a larger scale. Now she was able to set her house in order, send for fixtures and fittings that she could afford, and live a life of ease.

After an absence of twelve years, her husband returned. A guard was at the gate. The husband wanted to enter, but the guard stopped him. The man said: please inform the mistress of the house that her husband is here. The doorman informed the woman, who asked her neighbour: Go out see if it really is him? If it is, let him in.

The story ends with the wife forgiving the errant husband, a reconciliation which seems somewhat spurious but also reflects the oral nature of its narrative mode. The last line points out that talent and good fortune are closely aligned, which is of course the moral of our tale.

3.

The story foregrounds women's resilience, their virtuosity with craftmanship, and the necessity of turning talent into trade. These motifs will be picked up in *Sharif Beti*. But it is with her biography of Ashrafunissa Begum, published in 1904, that she turns from parable to fact to tell the story of a woman who started her career as a teacher and rose to unprecedented heights. It is also worth noting that Ashrafunissa was a Shia Sayyad woman.

Widowed at an early age, Bibi Ashraf – as she was affectionately known to her circle of acquaintances – found employment teaching at a girls' school in Lahore, partly funded by the bourgeoise of the city for the education of their daughters, under the aegis of the colonial administration. *Hayat e Ashraf*, which can also be termed a eulogy as it appeared in the year after the death of its subject, interweaves 'Bibi Ashraf's' own words about how she learned to read and Muhammadi Begum's accounts of her protagonist's tragic life as a young widow who also lost her children at an early age, her progress in the public sphere as an educator, and her later role as the principal of the semi-colonial, semi-feudal Victoria Girls school in Lahore. It also includes the author's own intimate memories of Ashraf's later years. In contrast to Muhammadi Begum's fictions which are located in unnamed cities, this memoir gives us a vivid picture of Lahore life, religious and other gatherings, and transactions between communities including colonial British women.

Compared to the struggles of Bibi Ashraf, Muhammadi Begum's own education, a generation later, was privileged: she was tutored at home by her progressive father, brother, and later Mumtaz Ali. She memorised the Qur'an at an early age. She does not, however, dwell on this, instead effacing her own achievements to canonise her role model and illustrate how Muslim women such as Ashraf had overcome numerous barriers to achieve even the simplest goals of emancipation. Nevertheless, the biography is also, in a subtle way, a compelling self-portrait of its kind, of the enterprising author and her abiding concerns.

Despite the barrier of age, these two women had an almost familial regard for one another, which seems to have been nurtured by the younger and more dynamic Muhammadi Begum. Bibi Ashraf had been brought up to avoid the company of women outside the strict Shia Sayyad family to which she belonged. Unusually, after a misunderstanding, Muhammadi

Begum addresses this difference in a letter, forcing her older friend to examine any remaining prejudices she may have had for the Sunni community.

Along with incomparable value of education, Ashraf's life storyunderlines two of Muhammadi Begum's major ethical concerns: virtue, in the sense of an honourable, upright existence; and industriousness, in one of its many forms from handicrafts through teaching to writing in various genres. By telling the story of a woman who manages to uphold the values of a traditional household while moving beyond its boundaries, Muhammadi Begum is not upholding conservative norms but also depicting how small steps outside the confines of the women's quarters can clear a path for the women of the future.

4.

It is impossible to avoid the thought that *Sharif Beti*, published shortly before its author's untimely death in 1908, is not, at least in part, a tribute to her mentor. Even the names of the heroines of the books are similar: each work describes the triumph of resilience over adversity; both titles play on the symbolic connections of their protagonists' names with the titles of the books. In his poignant introduction to the third edition of the book, Mumtaz Ali bewails the fact that most stories for girls are about affluent families. Muhammadi Begum's intention here is to remedy this by writing about hardship and financial need. The fact that even this account of poverty is enclosed in a frame of gentility makes it even more poignant as the author does not attempt to chronicle the lowest depths of the kind of deprivation she has never experienced. (This would be left to Rashid Jahan, the fiery communist woman writer who emerged in the 1930s, and her even more successful follower Ismat Chughtai, and her male contemporaries such as Manto.)

In her pioneering study of modern Urdu fiction, Shaista Suhrawardi Ikramullah (1915-2000) sees *Sharif Beti* as derivative of Deputy Nazir Ahmad's (1836-1912) Dehli's classic didactic novel *Mirat ul urus* – The Bride's Mirror. Published in 1869, it is the story of two sisters of opposite characteristics set in the milieu of affluent bourgeois Delhi. Ikramullah was also a contributor to *Tehzeeb-e-Niswan*; her collection of stories from the journal were published as *Koshish-e-Natamaam* in 1950. Later, she became a politician and diplomat and published her autobiography *From Pardah to Parliament* in 1963. But her most known book is *Letters to Neena* (1951), which consists of ten letters to different types of Indian all personified as a woman called Neena. Despite her background and knowledge, Ikramullah was mistaken in suggesting that *Sharif Beti* was derived from *Mirat ul urus*. As I pointed out in my 'Forcing Silence to Speak' article, there is no evidence to suggest this. Ikramullah fails to recognise the entirely original structure of a polished and technically mature work, described by its author not as a novel but as a *qissa* or story designed for younger readers.

Sharifunissa is the adolescent daughter of Abdul Ghani, a struggling clerk, an upright man who refuses to accept bribes and blandishments. When he asks his wife to save a little money every month to send their older son to school, she retails her monthly household accounts before voicing the prejudices and constraints of 'sharafat', in a passage that seems harshly snobbish to a contemporary reader: plebeians and people of the lower classes, she says, earn their living in any possible way, sending their women out to work as housemaids or nurses and their sons to become porters and labourers. Gentlefolk, on the other hand, are restricted to the earnings of the male wage earner until their sons reach adulthood, unless the women of the family turn to embroidery and other skilled crafts to make money in the privacy of their homes.

Necessity, however, forces her to persuade her daughter to learn from her brothers and to try to find a way to add to the family's income. It is, however, a very colourful, articulate working class figure, a *nayan* or hairdresser – a 'common' woman allowed by society to roam freely from house to house to earn a meagre living, and well aware through need and necessity of the importance of labour - who she approaches for help. The *nayan* teaches her protégée to combine the refinements of her gentle upbringing with the entrepreneurship of a working class woman. The *nayan* counsels her respectable friend to start sewing and stitching garments for an income and to pass on her skills to her daughter. Almost by magic, she acquires a sewing machine discarded by an affluent family, which enables Sharifunissa's mother to set up a small but thriving cottage industry supplying garments to women in various parts of the city. The *nayan*, now addressed as Bari Bi (a term of slightly patronising respect usually used to address older women of a lower stature) in spite of her almost familial role, brings her commissions and delivers the garments.

When Abdul Ghani dies of a sudden illness, his wife descends into despair and mental illness, leaving the cares of the house to their daughter. Once again, Bari Bi comes to her aid, by suggesting that the little family plant vegetables and fruits, and rear goats, sheep, and chickens to sell milk and eggs, in a manner first sketched out in 'A Tale of Two Shells'. There is an exuberance to the narrative of the family's progress which replaces the bleak account of their earlier travails, imbuing what may appear as a list of humdrum daily tasks with a spirit of adventure.

Sharifanissa's thrift and resourcefulness gains her a reputation among the privileged ladies of the neighbourhood, who want her to come and tutor their daughters in their homes. Bari bi brings her their messages and advises her to share her gift of knowledge with others: this will not only gain her heavenly rewards, but also become a source of income. Pride and propriety forbid Sharifanissa from frequenting the homes of the rich and privileged. She responds that she wants to lead a quiet life which will be disrupted by interactions with privileged young women and may also cause people to gossip and spread rumours about her. Let the girls visit you in your own home, Bari Bi says, and pay you for your tuitions. Sharifanissa finds the thought embarrassing; she does not want to be known as a *mullani* or teacher of religious studies who accepts money for her services. Bari Bi approaches a woman who wants her daughter to learn Urdu, Farsi, and embroidery, for which she is willing to offer a sum of ten rupees a month, and transport to bring her over. Bari Bi explains that Sharifa will agree only if she can tutor her within the walls of her own home, where purdah will be observed; her younger brothers are at the madrassa all day, and there are no grown men in the household.

Bari bi is thus able to gather several more girls of the neighbourhood, each of whose mothers agree to pay a certain sum. Arrangements are made for the girl's *maktab* or school to be set up in the courtyard of Sharifanissa's home. The gently nurtured girls arrive, bringing boxes of sweets and gifts. They are put off by the simple surroundings and the straw matting on the floor of the courtyard. But Sharifanissa's warm welcome and sincere manner soon set them at their ease. She spends the first session merely conversing with them instead of teaching and, as they leave, she passes on boxes of sweets, which she has cleverly exchanged, to each one of them.

In the concluding chapters, we see Sharifanissa move to a new home; the school becomes a thriving concern, and she adds to her income by producing fine embroidery which Bari Bi sells. Comfort allows her to plan a future for her brother, whom she sends abroad for further education. In the manner of a fairy tale, the author adds a marriage into a noble family to Sharifanissa's store of luck, before she ends on a traditional note, praising her goodness, kindness and virtuosity for which she is amply rewarded by providence and God.

5.

Mostly forgotten by readers for nearly half a century even in the city of her birth which became the literary capital of Pakistan after Independence, Muhammadi Begum's legacy nevertheless lived on in the renown achieved by her son, Imtiaz Ali Taj (1900-1970), and his wife Hijab Imtiaz Ali (1908-1909). Imtiaz was a playwright whose most famous play, *Anarkali,* was turned into *Mughal-e-Azam,* the most celebrated and renowned film of Bollywood. Hijab was the trailblazing and very original modernist author of dark romance and fantasy, who was also South Asia's first woman pilot, and brought the colours of her South Indian heritage and a knowledge of Freudian psychoanalysis to Pakistani literature. The marriage of Hijab and Taj was arranged by another literary couple, Sajjad Hyder Yildarim (1880-1943) and his wife Nazar Sajjad Hyder (1894-1967). The first woman of letters in Urdu literature, Muhammadi Begum opened the gates for younger contemporaries including the prolific poet and writer, the Hyderabadi Sughra Humayan Mirza (1884-1958), whose *Zahra ya Mushir e Niswan* was a novel-length story of a marriage made successful by the eponymous protagonist's education, enterprise and thrift. *Hajira ki Sarguzasht*, another of Mirza's novels, recasts the traditional classic narrative form of The Four Dervishes in the voices of four women discussing the vicissitudes of their lives. *Mohini and Bibi Turi ka Khwab* use the techniques of fantasy fiction to foreground the author's feminist preoccupations.

Muhammadi Begum introduced a string of prominent writers in the pages of *Tehzeeb-e-Niswan*, including Nazar Sajjad Hyder, several of whose early novels were published by Mumtaz Ali's press. She was to become the most popular novelist of her time. Her daughter, Qurratulain Hyder (1927-2007), is probably unsurpassed in her position as Urdu fiction's greatest writer of the twentieth century. Hijab Imtiaz Ali, then known as Hijab Ismail, was also published in *Tehzeeb*; her first novella *Meri natamam muhabbat*, also published in Lahore, is a technically accomplished depiction of the superficially westernised but deeply conservative Sayyad aristocratic society. In Lahore, Jahanara Shah Nawaz (1947-1954) also contributed to *Tehzeeb* for many years, though after publishing a single novel, she joined the Muslim League and moved to a long career as a parliamentarian. In her English-language memoir, *Father and Daughter*, she mentions with great affection her meetings with Muhammadi Begum.

Muhammadi Begum's subdued cry of protest may today, in contrast to the poetry of Fahmida Riaz and the novels of Ismat Chughtai, Khadija Mastur and others, seem muted. But when in a recent conversation about Bibi Ashraf's biography, Shazaf Fatima, a young novelist from Pakistan, I brought up the question of the rules of *sharafat,* she not only recognised them from her own background but also charted the abiding constraints that continue to tie down both men and women. I know other women, such as my older sister, who grew up on novels such as *Heidi* and *Little Women* and wonder what impact Sharifa's story, firmly rooted in a culture we can recognise, might have had on their developing minds and imagination. Thus, Muhammadi Begum enabled, by forcing silence to speak, not only the voices of her own generation, but those of so many other writers to come to the fore. We can debate the value of some her work. Some may even dismiss them as dated with bygone values. But *Sharif Beti*, for the sparkle and wit of its dialogues, or its successful attempt to foreground education as a tool of empowerment for younger readers, and *Hayat e Ashraf*, as a highly original recreation of time, place, and the intertwined lives of two brave exemplary women, should be read by all.

SHUHADA'/SINÉAD

Naomi Foyle

'They tried to bury me. They didn't realise I was a seed.'
Shuhada' Sadaqat/Sinéad O'Connor
after Dinos Christianopoulos

In the dream factory farm of the Western pop music industry, women singer-songwriters with siren voices who are also anti-racist activists, gender non-conformists, emotional lightning rods and fountains of love are golden needles in a haystack. Such a precious needleworker was the Irish musical artist Shuhada' Sadaqat/Sinéad O'Connor, who reverted to Islam in 2018 but continued to record, publish, and perform under her birth name until her premature death at the age of 56 in July 2023. A global superstar in her early twenties, Sinéad/Shuhada' (as she was known to sign emails) was never forgiven in some quarters for dramatically rejecting this conventional success, and tributes in the British mainstream media were either lacking or insulting to her memory. But she knew that her true fans were not starstruck by her phenomenal voice or captivating looks but were 'on my level', as she put it in an early interview, people who related to the vulnerability, passion, and political anger she expressed in her work. These fans are legion: on social media her loss provoked an outpouring of grief and a slate of insightful eulogies, mourning the loss of a riveting artist, a powerful voice of protest, a modest and private benefactor to many, a proud single mother, and a courageous role model who spoke openly about her many physical and mental health difficulties. But while much has been said lately about how Shuhada' Sadaqat used her high profile to shine a light on social and political ills, often well ahead of her time, she has not yet been given enough credit as a theologian.

That neglect is no doubt partly because mainstream journalists do not want or know how to engage with her Muslim beliefs. But also because in a secular, individualist society, a celebrity's political views and psychological condition are of far more interest than her spiritual beliefs. Sinéad/Shuhada' spoke out about the vicious abuse she suffered as a child at the hands of her mother, who died in a car accident when the singer was eighteen. At the age of twenty-four, at the height of global fame, she was overnight shunned by the music industry for protesting, on live American television, systemic child abuse in the Catholic church. Having also earlier refused a Grammy, on the grounds that the award was for 'shifting units' not artistic merit, she forged a career outside the mainstream, producing eight more highly regarded, if not commercially supersonic albums, enabling her to raise her four children on her own. But it was not an easy road.

Over the last twenty years Sister Shuhada'/Sinéad also lost a protracted custody battle and suffered poor physical and mental health, contending with fibromyalgia and a radical hysterectomy for which she was not given the necessary hormone treatment, flinging her into surgical menopause on which she blamed her suicidal feelings of the time. She *was* given medication for a misdiagnosis of bipolar condition – for symptoms that may have been related to her childhood abuse and/or a head injury she sustained as a teenager, when she was hit by a train door, opened seemingly as a lark by a boy on a passing train as she stood on a station platform. In recent years, she fluctuated between spells of immense creativity and long periods in rehab for a three-decade marijuana habit and in mental health asylums, treating what was also diagnosed as complex post-traumatic stress condition or borderline personality disorder.

Her unsettled state was reflected in her name, which she changed in 2017 to Magda Davitt, rejecting the patriarchal origins of 'Sinéad O'Connor', though continuing to use it professionally. When she reverted, as she termed it, to Islam, she became first Shuhada' Davitt, and then Shuhada' Sadaqat. In 2021, just as she was making yet another comeback with the publication of her bestselling memoir *Rememberings*, her third child, Shane, committed suicide at the age of seventeen. She struggled intensely and often publicly to accept this devastating loss, and while at time of writing the cause of her death has not been announced, it is hard to avoid the impression that Sister Shuhada'/Sinéad died, one way or another, of a shattered heart.

One might also – but I think superficially – describe her death as a tragic irony. In *Rememberings*, Sinéad/Shuhada' called her life a healing journey – since 2018 she had been working on an album of songs on the theme of healing, and it is deeply sad to consider how that journey may have been cut short by unbearable grief. But while her death is undeniably a tragedy, it does not undermine her soul purpose, which, clearly, was to communicate to the world, not just her pain and troubles, but her passion for justice and faith in God's love. If Shudaha' Sadaqat was a wounded healer who succumbed to her wounds, nevertheless, her loss reminds us that the kind of healing we need to do as a global society is collective, intergenerational, ongoing. And if anyone ever tells you that such healing will be painless, don't believe them. The medicine Sister Shuhada' offered us is more bitter for her death, yet perhaps also more potent. As is often the case with those ahead of their time, her loss has prompted a re-reckoning of the value of her songs and her personal virtues, and is already spurring people to raise their own voices against abuses of power: a task Sinéad/Shuhada' saw as central to her work on Earth, and for which in her lifetime she was derided and ignored.

At the core of that activist work, and to Shuhada'/Sinéad's creativity, was a profound relationship with God, declared and reaffirmed over and over during her dynamic career. In later years a proud *hijabi* and self-described Sufi, her lifelong campaigns as an artist-activist against child abuse, misogyny, colonialism, and racism were deeply rooted in her evolving spiritual and religious beliefs, which can be charted in her interviews, memoir, and songs. In a short essay it is not possible to do full justice to her theological journey, but in tribute to an artist I came of age with politically, and who has accompanied me at times of hope and heartbreak, I would like to offer here, in the pages of *Critical Muslim*, some initial thoughts on her immense and unique contribution as a punk liberation theologist.

The Wounded Healer

One might find it remarkable that Sister Shuhada'/Sinéad had any kind of belief in God at all. Brought up in the Catholic church, after her parents' divorce when she was eight – rare for Ireland at the time – she was, for years, monstrously abused by her mother. Little Sinéad/Shuhada' was regularly punched and kicked in the stomach and genitals, forced to say 'I am nothing' over and over again, locked out in the garden for days, imprisoned in her room or the cupboard under the stairs, even made to steal from the Church collection plate and charity tins. 'Sexual and physical. Psychological. Spiritual. Emotional. Verbal. I went to school every day covered in bruises, boils, sties and face welts, you name it. Nobody ever said a bloody word or did a thing,' she once said in an interview. Over her life, her condemnation was primarily directed at the Church she blamed for her mother's mental condition, and for creating a culture of silence around its own abuse of children. Long before the *Boston Globe* exposed the scandal, Sadaqat/O'Connor was well-aware of the rampant sexual abuse of children committed by Irish priests, protected by the highest levels of the Catholic Church, for decades simply moved from parish to parish, or to the Vatican, when their crimes were suspected or discovered.

When at last, in a landmark Irish legal case, her father regained custody of his children, Shuhada'/Sinéad was thirteen and running wild, shoplifting and playing truant from school. At fifteen she was sent to a Magdalene asylum, one of the infamous Magdalene laundries set up across Ireland in the late eighteenth century as homes for 'fallen women', where sex workers and unmarried pregnant women were incarcerated and forced to endure cruelties including gruelling shifts in steaming hot laundries, an imposed monastic code of silence, and the theft of their children – their babies being given up for adoption, often overseas. By the latter half of the twentieth century, the Magdalene asylums were an integral part of Irish social welfare system. While unwed mothers were mainly now housed in the country's also notorious Mother and Baby Homes, the asylums admitted a wide range of mostly unpregnant women via the criminal justice system, reformatory schools and social services. They still functioned as moral prisons. Although O'Connor was mentored by a kind music teacher, and eventually allowed to attend an outside school, she did not escape the grim lessons of the asylum: if she broke the rules, she was sent to spend the night in the asylum hospice, where old women who had spent their entire lives in the laundry lay dying, unattended. The horror of that room never left her, and neither did she forget the anguish of a fellow student, whose baby was stolen from her and its father, leaving the young mother bereft, unrecognisable, her former vivacity destroyed.

From early in her career, Sinéad/Shuhada' denounced Ireland as a theocracy, a critique of the Catholic Church that reached its apex on 3 October 1992. That night, her smash hit cover of the Prince song 'Nothing Compares 2 U' having catapulted her into global stardom, Sadaqat/O'Connor appeared as a guest on the NBC programme *Saturday Night Live (SNL)* where she famously concluded an *a capella* rendition of Bob Marley's 'War' by holding up a colour photograph of Pope John Paul II to the final drawn-out word 'evil'; then, in three sharp movements, ripping the picture to pieces. Staring stony-faced into the camera, she declared 'Fight the real enemy' and dropped the fragments of the photo on the floor. In the silence that followed the singer, clad in a long white dress, removed her earpieces and bent to blow out the church candles on the small table beside her. For this act on live American television, watched by millions, she was reviled by the music industry – and thoroughly earned her later name Shuhada', meaning 'martyrs' or 'witnesses'. She was banned from NBC for life; mocked and castigated by media personalities including Madonna. Two weeks later, booed and cheered in a deafening roar at a Bob Dylan concert at Madison Square Gardens, she abandoned the intimate song she had planned and declaimed 'War' again. Her records never again topped the charts and for years she was ostracised by fellow musicians, who would pointedly ignore her in dressing rooms. In a single act, she had destroyed her managers' hand-rubbing plans for her mega-stardom.

She had also performed an immense act of healing. Unknown to viewers at the time, the photo was from her late mother's bedroom wall. In *Rememberings*, O'Connor explains that it pictured the Pope on his 1979 visit to Ireland, where he had kissed the ground at Dublin Airport and declared 'Young people of Ireland, I love you'. On the day of her mother's death, O'Connor took the photo, determined to destroy it when the time was right – because, as she said, 'nobody ever gave a shit about the children of

Ireland'. Watching the *SNL* protest were members of the newly formed Survivors Network of those Abused by Priests (SNAP). Quoted after her death, founding member Brian Clohessy, at the time in his thirties, said, 'We were all just deeply convinced that we would go to our graves without ever seeing any public acknowledgment of the horror and without any kind of validation whatsoever. That's what made her words so very powerful.' His feelings were echoed by Michael McDonnell, interim executive director of SNAP, who said O'Connor 'wore the anguish of victims of clergy abuse and it seems as though she knew in 1992 the horrors that hadn't yet been revealed ... Ultimately, she relieved the pain for tens of thousands of victims with rebellion.' Nine years after the *SNL*. protest, Pope John Paul II issued a Vatican apology for the sexual abuse of children by Catholic priests, though no apology was ever made to Sinéad / Shuhada' by him or anyone who had condemned her protest at the time.

Her detractors declared that O'Connor was a crazy, godless hater of religion, and even sympathetic observers might well have assumed she was an atheist. Nothing, though, could be further from the truth.

The Seeker

From childhood Sinéad / Shuhada' had a deeply personal relationship with God, Christ, and the Holy Ghost, whose loving presence helped her survive her mother's abuse. Just as some torture victims report sensing the presence of angels during their excruciating ordeals, O'Connor / Sadaqat relates in *Rememberings* how Jesus once appeared to her as she was on the kitchen floor, naked and covered in coffee grounds and cereal, her mother kicking her bottom:

> Suddenly, there Jesus was in my mind, on a little stony hill, on His cross. I never asked Him to come; He just arrived. He had on a long white robe and blood was flowing from his heart all the way down His robe and down the hill and onto the ground and then onto the kitchen floor and into my heart. He said He would give me back any blood my mother took and that His blood would make my heart strong. So I just focused on Him.

On another occasion, when her mother had taken her siblings to visit her family overnight and left a beaten Sinéad/Shuhada' locked up in the dark in her room, she asked for help from God and a 'small, white, very misty cloud' she understood to be the Holy Spirit appeared and kept her company all night. But not all her childhood religious experiences stemmed from trauma. Her memoir also recounts the case of a stubborn verruca that disappeared the night before she was due to go to hospital to have it removed, after being rubbed with Holy Water from Lourdes – a place little Sinéad/Shuhada' obsessed over and was thrilled to visit on a family pilgrimage.

Many people, of course, try to explain away such 'mystic' experiences as coincidence or brain chemistry, but consciousness studies remain resistant to materialist reductionism, and any believer knows that a personal relationship with God is the living heart of faith. Scripture, in this analogy, is faith's lifeblood, carrying the divine message through the veins of the body politic. Religious institutions might be likened to clothing: at best, beautiful, protective and expressive of our nature as social, cultural, and spiritual beings; at worst, ostentatious and hierarchical, restrictive and militaristic. Though Sadaqat/Sinéad was a lifelong scholar and lover of scripture, her relationship with religion was more ambivalent. As a child she took up the study of scripture independently because, as she explained in a 2019 interview for RTÉ's *The Late Late Show*:

> in those days everybody was miserable, nobody was getting joy in God and whatever the church were teaching – and they weren't happy either – whatever they were telling you God said, I thought well, it makes no sense, everybody's miserable, so I started reading the scriptures as a very young child.

But her interest in scripture went beyond intellectual curiosity. It also transcended poetic appreciation of the beauty of the verses. She was a believer, on a quest for knowledge that later took her to study Judaism and Rastafarianism, to become a Catholic priest and seminary student, and ultimately to embrace Islam.

Her conversion was surprising to many, not just due to widespread Islamophobia, but because for many decades Sinéad O'Connor had a deeply ambivalent relationship to religion. Seeking to crack open the armour of corrupt religiosity, in word and deed she challenged the patriarchal, abusive and hypocritical institution of the Catholic Church. As well as in the *SNL* protest, she challenged the Catholic church in interviews on Irish television and op eds for international newspapers. She did so, however, from a position of faith and love. In 1999, she was ordained as a priest by Michael Cox, Bishop of an Independent Catholic Church, appearing in dog collar on Irish television and raising the issue of women priests to a national debate. At the time she declared she was considering celibacy, would always appear in priest's garb, and was planning to auction off all her old clothes and make-up. Later, she sought to be excommunicated. Promoting her album *Theology* in a 2007 radio interview for Fordham University, America, she claimed she was trying to 'rescue God from religion'. In 2013, speaking in response to the election of Pope Francis, she told Channel 4 news:

> Religion is a smokescreen, it has everybody talking to the wall. There is a Holy Spirit who can't intervene on our behalf unless we ask it. Religion has us talking to the wall. The Christ character tells us himself: you must only talk directly to the Father; you don't need intermediaries. We all thought we did, and that's ok, we're not bad people, but let's wake up [...] God was there before religion; it's there [today] despite religion; it'll be there when religion is gone.

And when asked by *Time Magazine* the same year about her religious views, she said, her tattoo of Jesus peeking up from her shirt neck, that she preferred to use the term 'Holy Spirit', as it lifted God from the possession of any particular religion.

While the *Time* interviewer was respectful, by this time many people undoubtedly saw O'Connor's views on religion as an element of her 'craziness', part of the volatile sideshow the media made of her mental health difficulties, at best a crutch or distraction from her undeniable musical and poetic gifts, rather than her creative fuel. Her conversion to Islam and change of name were superficially reported in *The Irish Times*, the journalist mainly relying on quoting her own Tweets; but for her, as she reported in the *Late Late Show* interview, dressed in a red abaya and hijab, it was the fulfilment of a life's quest:

> I started studying scriptures from different religions, trying to find you know the truth about God and such, and I left Islam to last — and I never thought I would join the religion — I left Islam to last because *I* had so much prejudice

about Islam, you know, and then when I started reading, I read just chapter two alone of the Qur'an, I realised oh my god I'm home, I've been here a Muslim all my life and I didn't realise it.

In other interviews, Shuhada' explained that she saw herself as a Sufi, was grateful to belong to the Ummah, and wore the hijab when she chose, as a sign of identification with other Muslims. In *Rememberings* she wrote that she felt 'naked' without her headscarf. Tweeting that it was 'the natural conclusion of an intelligent theologian's journey', she was clear in the RTÉ interview about her reasons for embracing Islam:

> and it does say [in the Qur'an], the reason why I liked it too, its reason for existing is to confirm all previous scripture and to complain that scripture has been tampered with and that's when I was like holy God I'm home because when I was a kid they were tampering with the scriptures, they were telling you God hates you, they were telling you to be a good person you have to think you're a bad person, the worse you think you are, the better a Catholic you were in those days ...

Turning to Sūrah Two in Muhamad Asad's translation, one can see how the scales would have fallen from O'Connor's eyes. Far from being the fundamentalist text Islamophobes assume, the Qur'an, as all Muslims know, clearly states:

> Verily, those who have attained to faith [in this divine writ], as well as those who follow the Jewish faith, and the Christians, and the Sabians, all who believe in God and the Last Day and do righteous deeds – shall have their reward with their Sustainer. (2:62)

In light of this and other similar verses, the verses concerning the danger of 'tampered' scriptures (2:77-79) should not be misconstrued as suggesting that the Torah and the Bible only survive in corrupted forms. The verses are, rather, a historical allusion to groups of 'unlettered people' who write their own scripture for 'trifling gain' – additions to, not alterations of the Gospels. O'Connor/Sadaqat seemingly read Sūrah Two in her own context as a reference to Irish priests who in their sermons would distort the message of God in order to control a whole country through fear. I imagine that Sūrah Two's warning not to worship the 'golden cow' (2:92-93) resonated with her own rejection of pop

stardom. I can also see how its appeals to reason (2:164) and call for
Muslims to actively work toward social justice (2:177) would have been
welcome to her. At heart, though, for O'Connor, the message of the Holy
Qur'an was simple, and one she had been espousing her entire life:

> it's a way of thinking, Islam, you could almost be Muslim without actually
> officially being a Muslim, it's a headset, a Muslim is only a person who believes
> that nothing in the universe should be worshipped except God...

'The Priesthood of Music'

A person's spirituality is beyond words or rational explanation, and there
is a limit to the insight to be gained from reading media statements about
it. In *Rememberings*, Shuhada'/Sinéad writes that to understand her more
deeply, one must turn to her songs. The same holds true for her
relationship to God and religion. In her 2013 *Time Magazine* interview, she
declared that she saw 'music as a priesthood', and in her songs and albums
– as well as her many acts of charity, which she did not boast about – her
spiritual and religious journey finds its fullest and deepest expression.
From her first album, *The Lion and the Cobra* (1987) to her tenth, *I'm Not
Bossy, I'm the Boss* (2014), she shared with the world her love of God and
the succour she found in scripture. Due to the constraints of copyright
law, I am unable to quote from her lyrics, but from the titles of her albums
and songs alone, one can tell that her distinctive oeuvre is a musical
tapestry woven on the loom of faith.

The Lion and the Cobra is a reference to Psalm 91, quoted in full in
Remembering, verses Sinéad/Shuhada' was instructed to recite by her first
spiritual teacher in London. The psalm's long dramatic declaration of the
power of faith includes the following lines, which were chanted in Irish by
Enya as a guest on the album's song 'Never Get Old':

> If you say 'The Lord is my refuge,'
> and you make the Most High your dwelling,
> no harm will overtake you,
> no disaster will come near your tent.
> For He will command His angels concerning you
> to guard you in all your ways;

they will lift you up in their hands,
so that you will not strike your foot against a stone.
You will tread on the lion and the cobra;
you will trample the great lion and the serpent.

In songs like 'Mandinka', 'Jerusalem' and 'Just Like U Said It Would B', and a voice that could slide in a heart-wrench from a pure sheer whisper to sinuous lament to raging *cri de coeur*, the album expresses the invincible vision of a young woman determined to take on the world on her own terms, right historical wrongs, enjoy sex, reject sexism, and walk in a Blakean garden of God. The album was followed by *I Do Not Want What I Haven't Got* (1990) which contains the Prince song she made a global hit, but opens with the words of the Serenity Prayer said at the start of Alcoholics Anonymous meetings, casting the song 'Feel So Different' as a Sufi ode to God's blessings. The album also features the protest song 'Black Boys on Mopeds', written in response to the deaths of Colin Roach, who died in police custody in 1983, and Nicholas Bramble, who was killed in a crash in 1989 while being chased by police on his own moped, which the officers had assumed he had stolen. With its references to Thatcher and Beijing, racism, and poverty, the song signals a key element of Shuhada' / Sinéad's ministry, a commitment to stand up politically and tell it like it is. The last and title song references a dream she had about her mother accepting that Sinéad's sister could not forgive her. It has a hypnotic, psalm-like quality, the a cappella speaker wandering fearlessly through the desert, taking all the time in the world with her low, hushed notes, cloaked in the serenity evoked in the opening track. Both her first two albums, as she notes in *Rememberings*, also contain songs about the dead: for her, a stated believer in the eternal soul, the study of scripture was a way of losing one's fear of death.

Songs are not just words, of course: the musical choices Shuhada' / Sinéad made are also ways of expressing faith. In *Rememberings* she explained that, far from the *SNL* protest derailing her career, 'having a number one record derailed my career and my tearing the photo put me back on the right track,' forcing her to make a living performing, which she loved. Freed from the constraints of pop stardom, she was able to create albums in a variety of genres. Punk in spirit, musically she was highly sophisticated and versatile. The jazz cover album *Am I Not Your Girl*, which she describes in *Rememberings* as a way to catch her breath after the meltdown of the *SNL* protest, was followed by albums of protest and love songs, spoken word, indie rock, reggae, Irish folk'n'roll and liturgical music. *Universal Mother* (1994), a pulsating exploration of the dark and light sides of motherhood in all its personal, national and theological dimensions, signalled O'Connor's intention to be as far from a stadium pop singer as it is possible to be. Here God is a woman, but women are not always kind and loving: in the blazing torch song 'Fire in Babylon' and defiant 'Red Football' Sadaqat roars back in anger to her childhood abuser. Feminist and decolonial, the album also features a speech from Germaine Greer, a song from Sinéad's little son Jake, and the unclassifiable 'Famine', part rap song, part lecture, in which O'Connor/Sadaqat displays an acute understanding of the intergenerational psychological effects of the trauma of colonial occupation. Further showcasing the range of O'Connor's voice and creative ambitions, 'All Babies' is a gentle hymn but also elegy to our inherent divinity, forgotten in our secular world.

The eclectic, syncretic albums kept coming. The themes of motherhood, political awareness and spiritual immanence are picked up in the EP *Gospel Oak* (1997), written while Sinéad/Shuhada' was having therapy with a Jewish psychiatrist, carrying messages of comfort including the enchanting 'This is to Mother You', the mesmerising 'I am Enough for Myself', with its plaintive Irish whistle, and the philosophical, confident 'Petit Poulet', written as if in the voice of the cosmos for the people of Rwanda. *Faith and Courage* (2000), dedicated to 'all Rastafari people, with thanks for their great faith, courage and above all, inspiration', opens with the delicate, half-whispered 'The Healing Room', an invitation to the listener to hear the divine spirit within us all, and includes the staccato reggae Irish folk fusion chant 'The Lamb's Book of Life', made with African-American producer Kevin 'She'kspere' Briggs, in which O'Connor/Sadaqat calls on the world to heed the wisdom of Rasta men and women, seek God and work toward human unity in all that we do. The Rasta influence ran deep. In *Sean-Nós Nua* (2002), a collection of traditional folk songs that became a bestseller in Ireland, Sinéad/Shuhada' interpreted 'The Singing Bird' as a Rasta prayer in praise of Jah, and on *Throw Down Your Arms* (2005), produced by Sly and Robbie, she covers reggae classics from 'Jah Nuh Dead' and 'Marcus Garvey' to 'Downpressor Man', her voice variously haunting, piercing, velvet, and cavernous as it communicates the songs' political, spiritual, and emotional truths. She also creatively explored her own interpretation of the Bible: *Theology* (2007), made at the suggestion of her seminary teacher, is an album of songs inspired by or drawn directly from scripture including renditions of Psalm 91 and the Song of Solomon, titled with its problematic line 'Dark I Am But Lovely', which sadly speaks to the historical depth of racism and its internalisation. The album also sings 'The Glory of Jah', twice, all songs being released in two versions, acoustic and full band, each stirring and meditative in their own way. O'Connor / Sadaqat cared about these last two albums so much she self-funded them to the tune of hundreds of thousands of pounds. She said in *Rememberings* she wanted to take *Theology* into her grave. In a measure of just how badly she was misunderstood by the mainstream press, they were described by the *Guardian* in her obituary as 'perplexing curios'. But while the rawer energy and more conventional love songs of her last two studio albums, *How About I Be Me (and You Be You)?* (2012) and, especially, *I'm Not Bossy, I'm the Boss* (2014), brought her back into the fold of music magazines, religion and spirituality are not absent from their songs, which quote the Proverbs, shun MTV, seek holy love even if they do not find it, demand 'Take Me to Church', and honour the Hindu God Vishnu in a lover's chest.

All her albums are golden testaments to Shuhada''s faith in a higher power, and the ability of God to uplift and sustain us through the darkest of times. One does not have to share that faith to appreciate its power. We all to one degree or another suffer the vicissitudes of life, and that she could endure so much, and yet consistently produce music that is empathic, inspirational, visionary is profoundly life-affirming. Painful as its title is, and premature as the wish might be, I am sure I am not the only person to devoutly hope that Shuhada' / Sinéad's final album, *No Veteran Dies Alone*, a collection of healing songs based on her work with war veterans, which was virtually complete at the time of her death, will one day be released. She also left a host of drawings of scriptural verse she would give to friends – stopping, she said in *Rememberings*, when she realised that she would often fall out with people after doing so. Whatever the truth of that, she expressed a wish for the recipients of those gifts to come together after she had died to create an exhibition of those works, and whether or not this is open to the public, it would be wonderful if that wish could be honoured.

A Punk Liberation Theologian

Sadly, Sinéad/Shuhada' was not a professed Muslim for long enough to integrate her understanding of Islam into her work, but it can be read retrospectively into her constant searching for a merciful and unifying God. For all the evidence, though, of her love of the faith, and lifelong commitment as a seeker, some might call her a spiritual loose cannon, her various changes of religion and name symptoms of a deep psychological instability. Theologian Brenna Moore, argues that this would be a mistake, writing in an eloquent and perceptive eulogy that 'O'Connor defied religious labels, exploring multiple faiths. The exquisite freedom in her music cannot be disentangled from that something transcendent she was always after'. For Moore, O'Connor/Sadaqat stood in the line of the provocative Judeo-Christian prophets of old, never afraid to raise their voices in defence of holy truths. For the academic Tatiana Kalveks, Sinéad/ Shuhada' was an 'unorthodox theologian', excluded from the institutional church due to her gender, but engaged in active ministry outside it – a ministry more effective for her own social exclusion, which, Kalveks maintains, can enable a 'radical openness to difference' that 'facilitates inclusivity, even within complex, intersectional communities'.

For as more tributes flowed in after Shuhada'/Sinéad's death, it was revealed how actively she worked to support vulnerable and marginalised members of society. She not only called out clerical sexual abuse and willingly took the hit for it, but gave compassionately of herself and her material fortune to those in need, without ever seeking recognition for her generosity. It has emerged that she privately funded therapy for a single mother who called a radio talk show to confide that she was victim of domestic abuse; she sought out and befriended a young woman with terminal cancer; she donated her house in LA to the Red Cross. But she was not just a philanthropist. She was an outspoken ally of the LGBT+ community; she supported Irish travellers; throughout her life she empathised with the oppression of people of African origin, and in her songs and public statements stood in solidarity with their decolonial struggles for justice. While she has been criticised for a handful of off-the-cuff remarks or ill-considered Tweets concerning race (for stereotyping both Black and white people), it is clear from *Rememberings* and her life's work how deeply she respected her Rastafarian and Muslim teachers, and to anyone with basic knowledge of the history of English conquest and occupation of Ireland, her empathy as an Irish person with global decolonial struggles is fully understandable. To me, her political activism aligns her 'priesthood of music' with liberation theology, which, while strongly associated with a Christian movement in Latin America focused on challenging injustice and alleviating socio-economic oppression, also has an Islamic dimension in the African-American Nation of Islam. The fact that the major British TV channels did not mount tributes to Sinéad O'Connor / Shuhada' Sadaqat after her death is contemptible – but also shows just how threatening her values and beliefs were and are to conventional ideas of success. Thanks, though, to social media her many acts of virtue are now well-known. Now we know just how hard she tried to heal the wounds of others, her ministry stands as an inextricable part of her legacy, and a powerful example of faith in action for others to follow.

Sceptics and atheists may also ask why her faith did not support her through the death of her son, or why a loving God would have allowed her to suffer all that she did. But that is to assume she killed herself; and also to display a shallow understanding of God. The idea of God as an uncaring puppet master who controls our destinies and chooses not to help us when He could, or a judgemental Father who rewards good behaviour and punishes evil, are simplistic theological notions rooted in patriarchal social systems. It might also seem simple, perhaps, to claim, in contrast, that God is One, or God is Love. But the Oneness of God lies in the paradox of the Oneness of the Many; and in Love there is not only complexity but a strong claim on us.

God's love does not entail preserving us from all harm: rather it means being with us, comforting and strengthening us when we experience pain. It also suggests a radical empathy. In *Rememberings*, O'Connor says that God sometimes does not answer our prayers because He is weeping over our suffering, and no-one can talk when they are crying. The notion of God as love also suggests that to fully experience God's presence, we ourselves have to be at least open to that love, and ideally, be loving to God and our fellow living creatures in return. As human beings, inherently flawed, and damaged by a world that is not governed by the laws of love, such a state of grace is not always possible for us. Shuhada'/Sinéad was remarkably open about her life, and from what she herself said, it seems that her mental health was a pendulum swinging wildly at times. Abused as a child in unthinkable ways, as an adult she found it hard to make stable relationships and experienced known periods of suicidal distress. But in her life and work she was also determined to reveal and return to God's love – which she did not view as a destination but a natural state within us she wished everyone could experience. In at least two of her songs, 'All Babies' and 'The Lamb's Book of Life', she laments the loss or corruption of faith in a world in which belief in God is seen as 'crazy'. In a saner world, one imbued with a sense of awe and governed by wisdom, Shuhada'/Sinéad's life would no doubt have taken a very different path.

Whatever the circumstances of her death, it is tragic that we won't hear again from Sister Sinéad/Shuhada', with her compassion and heart-fire, breathing in the world's pain and breathing out alchemical flame. As others carry on her vital work of ministry, in music, poetry and on the streets, may her whirling spirit find the universal peace and love she craved and wished for us all.

THE VIRTUE OF AGEING

Liam Mayo

I recently got a haircut. I don't have a regular hairdresser, instead I will often go to the place that is most convenient rather than find myself in a routine of visiting the same spot. This is probably why some of the biggest mistakes I have made have been haircuts. On this particular day, I wandered into a salon that I had visited over twelve months ago. I hadn't been back, not because of a bad haircut, but because life and work had me in different parts of the world for some time. I hadn't met Mandy at this salon before, but when she came out to greet me, her demeanor gave me an immediate sense of warmth and welcome. And we got chatting.

Mandy had owned her own salon for over thirty-five years. It is closer to the city, near the university campus. It was a large salon, and very successful. She was proud to boast that some of the country's most well-regarded business leaders were her clients, and that her reputation for giving fantastic haircuts meant people would often travel long distances to see her. She had built the business herself, and at one time had ten hairdressers working for her. She even had an offer to franchise the business at one time but turned it down because she wanted to focus on her passion for customer service. When Mandy and her husband decided to retire, they purchased a small farm in the hinterland, with plenty of space for their grandchildren to run around and room to grow produce.

But after a year of retirement Mandy started to feel at a loose end. 'I don't think retirement is really for me,' Mandy said, catching my eye in the mirror. 'I started to feel like there was no purpose in my days. And I want to feel like I am doing something meaningful. I could especially feel it when my friends would tell me that I didn't seem happy in retirement. They couldn't understand it!' So, she decided to return to work and picked up two days a week at the local salon near her hobby farm. She'd been here for three months now, she told me, and can't imagine ever retiring full time. 'I was just sort of moving from one thing to the next, and not really feeling as though I was achieving much in my life. And there is no virtue in that.'

Virtue is an interesting word for Mandy to have used. It struck me as unusual for her to frame her experience in this way. It could have come across as quaint, but coming from Mandy, in that context, it felt pointed and meaningful. And I couldn't stop thinking about that word - virtue.

Not long before I met Mandy, a dear friend had handed me a copy of Jean-Paul Ricœur's *Memory, History, Forgetting*. It is a profound exploration of the relationship between remembering and forgetting, and how these influence both our perception of historical experience and the production of historical narrative.

I hadn't encountered Ricœur's work before. I read further and found myself drawn to his notion of narrative identity, the concept that our identity is an internalised and evolving story of self that we construct and use to make sense and meaning of our life. The life narrative integrates one's reconstructed past, perceived present, and imagined future. It's a story with characters, episodes, imagery, a setting, plots, and themes that often follows the traditional model of a story, having a beginning (initiating event), middle (an attempt and a consequence), and an end (denouement). In this sense, narrative refers to the way that humans experience time, in terms of the way we understand our future potentialities, as well as the way we mentally organise our sense of the past.

I could see from my conversation with Mandy how, by reflecting on her experiences, she had reconstructed her past, akin to narrative identity. Her present is marked by her return to work after retirement, aligning with Ricœur's concept of the perceived present. And her expressed discomfort with the notion of retirement indicates to me her vision for her future, or Ricœur's notion of an imagined future. Her life story, for her, has a clear beginning with her successful career, a middle marked by retirement and a feeling of purposelessness, and an end characterised by her return to work.

But why 'virtue'? Why that word? What does virtue have to do with Mandy's narrative identity? Language is important. It is the primary tool for expression and communication, and it's through language that stories are crafted and shared. Stories, in turn, provide a context in which language can be used creatively and meaningfully. It's a relationship that is symbiotic. So, what is it in Mandy's reconstructed past, perceived present, or imagined future that led her to use the word virtue? And, more interestingly, in Mandy's internalised and evolving story of self, which character, episode, imagery, setting, plot, or theme influenced her conceptualisation of virtue.

Wikipedia tells me that virtue is a trait of excellence, including attributes that are moral, social, or intellectual. It is often associated with behavior showing high moral standards and can also refer to a quality considered morally good or desirable in a person. For example, humility is often cited as a virtue. The cultivation and refinement of virtue is held to be the 'good of humanity'; and thus is valued as an end purpose of life or a foundational principle of being. The opposite of virtue is, of course, vice.

For Mandy, it was not simply that her retirement was unenjoyable. It would appear, I deduced, that Mandy also felt that in some way her retirement had brought forth traits in her that are counter to what she deems as excellence, of high moral standard. Because whilst it may seem obvious that the experience of retirement is not enjoyable for everyone, in linking her experience to that which she deems as virtuous, Mandy signals a philosophical disconnect between how she wants to be in the world, and how she was able to be in the world as a retired person. So, it is not correct to say that Mandy thinks retirement is not virtuous. Rather, Mandy thinks that living through the age of retirement she enacts a lack of virtue. Is that right?

I wondered how much of Mandy's sentiments about virtues have to do with the way ageing is perceived by society, rather than her own internal framework for understanding virtue.

Ageing and Choice

This is a fascinating notion to ruminate on. Aristotle thought that virtue was crucial for a well-lived life. To him virtue was skill at living. And as we go through life, as we age, surely our ability to hone these skills becomes more acute. Perhaps Mandy is demonstrating a well-honed life-skill. Because ageing is not a vice, is it? But is there virtue in ageing?

I lead an organisation whose purpose is to change the way we age in our communities. Part of this work is to provide services so people can live in their homes and their communities longer. Services like transport, home cleaning, health and mobility classes, and connection to health care services. We try hard to avoid words like 'empower', 'support', and 'enable.' Aged people do not need to be empowered, supported, or enabled. They have well and truly earned their place in our communities and language that suggests otherwise can, often unconsciously, become patronising. And words like 'independence', and 'care', can also have the same undertones; grounded in problematic assumptions, like something is lacking and needs to be replenished. Or that something now needs to be outsourced, because the original is at sub-optimal performance, and greater efficiency can be achieved through a third-party provider. That to age is to lose, rather than gain. To wither, instead of flourish. Indeed, the language of ageing, when you really start to engage with it, is surprisingly impeding.

Thus, the story we tell of ageing is equally encumbered. Ours is a society that preferences progress and productivity over immobility; where ageing is pathologised and regulated. And as a result, heavily bureaucratised. There is a profound disconnect globally; as populations everywhere are ageing, we haven't quite worked out what to do with old people. The aged care sector has emerged, but the workforce remains comparatively undervalued and underpaid. Healthcare providers are sandwiched between need and resource, and large corporates innovate in ways where profit trumps community benefit. Both espouse medical interventions, whilst people ageing in our communities are bereft of the wherewithal to make sense of any of it. And as we have established, who is to say they want or need to be cared for anyway?

To start to overcome this I encourage my team to think and talk about the work we do as 'walking the journey of ageing' with our clients and our communities. The intent here is that we remove our assumptions from our language but remain forthright in purpose; our role is to walk alongside people and communities as they age. To *do with*, not *do to*! To act as a trusted companion and ally through the process of ageing. It's also an open-ended statement, because one person's journey in ageing is very different to another's. Everyone is different, each journey is unique, and our relationship with those we journey with is in turn exceptional. This is about choice. And dignity.

Choice and Dignity

I was in Bundaberg recently, visiting our office there. Whenever I am visiting our offices, I like to take the time to get out and visit some of our clients. Bundaberg is a charming city of around 100,000 people, located in Queensland, Australia. It is known for red dirt, sugar cane, and rum. It can also get very hot there. And it was an exceptionally hot September day when I was visiting. So, when I find myself at Eric's house, I'm pleased to accept the offer of a glass of cold water. Eric drinks a cup of tea, with no sugar.

He is ninety-three and has lived in Bundaberg for just over thirty years. His living room is full of signposts of his life's journey: a large black and white photograph of a young Eric, holding a long rifle, crouched next to a lions carcass on the desert floor; elephant tusks mounted above a long book shelf; an African war shield; a picture of a group of around fifty men in turbans standing in a staircase pose, cascading down to a row of seated men, clenched fists on their knees, in British military uniforms. 'My father was a member of the masonic lodge in Calcutta', Eric tells me. 'I come from a long line of Empire builders.' Muted coverage of Queen Elizabeth's funeral is on the television in the background.

Eric was born in the UK, but spent his formative years in India, before his time with the British services took him to what was then known as Rhodesia. He fell in love with the African continent and stayed there for over forty years until his second wife fell ill with cancer. He moved to Bundaberg to be closer to medical support and because he had heard that the game fishing was good (in Australia he traded his hunting rifle for a fishing rod). He now spends his days close to home, on his oversized recliner chair. He says his body is bruised and broken from years of physical activity. But he does make a habit of making his way to the front porch at dusk each afternoon, to throw bird seed to the local rosellas that flock at last light. Here he swaps his tea for a neat Scotch.

Two hours later, I am in Mike's back garden. We're discussing Mike's daily routine. Up before the sun, push-ups and a brisk walk. Fruit and nuts for breakfast, and then he joins one of the many social clubs he's engaged with across the city. This morning he was at the bowls club. Mike was born in Bundaberg, grew up in Bundaberg, owned the local motor mechanics for the entirety of his working life, and has retired in the house he and his wife built to raise their family in. At eighty-seven, Mike is an oddity to his friends because he is a devoted vegetarian and refuses to buy a caravan. 'Why would I want to leave Bundy?' he asks me. 'I have everything I need right here.' In his eighty-seven years on earth, Mike has never left Bundaberg, not even to holiday. He has never travelled the four and a half hours south to the states' capital Brisbane. Nor has he ever felt the urge to take a cruise like many of his friends have done in their retirement. He has no interest in leaving Bundaberg and has no regrets about making that decision when he was young, and nearly every day since.

Choice is almost the only thing Eric and Mike have in common. Whilst choice in and of itself is not considered a virtue in the traditional sense, in the context of ageing, the concept of choice holds significant importance. As we grow older, we encounter a multitude of decisions that profoundly affect our well-being and quality of life. These decisions encompass various aspects of life, from healthcare choices and lifestyle decisions to housing arrangements and financial planning. The ability to make informed and autonomous choices in these areas becomes a hallmark of maintaining dignity and autonomy on our journey of ageing. Choice is also a fundamental aspect of human agency and autonomy. It is through the exercise of our choices that we can express and embody virtues. For example, the choice to act with honesty or kindness in any given situation is what demonstrates those virtues. So, while choice as a concept is not a virtue on its own, it plays a significant role in the expression and practice of virtues. The moral value of a choice depends on the virtues or principles that guide that choice and the consequences it leads to.

I'm thinking about Ricœur here again. Perhaps the way we give meaning to our life through that internalised and evolving story of self, informs the choices we make about how we live our life. So, whilst choice itself isn't a virtue, is it the virtue itself that informs the choice?

It must be said choice and dignity are intricately interwoven facets of the aging experience. The ability for older people to make choices that impact their lives directly contributes to the preservation of their dignity. Dignity may be considered a virtue, although it is more accurately described as a concept or quality associated with virtuous behaviour and ethical principles. Dignity is the state or quality of being worthy of respect, honour, and esteem. It is closely related to virtues like respect, integrity, empathy, and compassion. And whilst dignity itself may not be listed as one of the classical cardinal virtues, it is a fundamental aspect of ethical and virtuous behaviour. Because virtues like respect and empathy lead people to treat others with dignity, recognising their intrinsic worth and treating them with fairness and kindness. In ethical and moral frameworks, upholding the dignity of others is often seen as a virtuous and noble pursuit, reflecting a commitment to treating people with fairness, respect, and empathy. So, while dignity may not be a virtue in the traditional sense, it is closely intertwined with virtuous behaviour and ethical principles.

But what does this mean about the choices we make about how we live our own lives? I'm searching for a link between Mandy and Aristotle's notion of virtue and the well-lived life and Ricœur's concept for how we make sense and meaning of our life. Particularly if, as Aristotle says, virtue is a skill at living. Does age propel virtue? Or virtue propel age?

Dignity and Wisdom

I was listening to a podcast about Bryan Johnson, the American technology entrepreneur and venture capitalist, his personal enterprise to live longer. Bryan is an extremely rich tech entrepreneur from California, who, at the age of forty-five, strives for the biological age of eighteen. And Bryan is both so disciplined in his lifestyle choices and willing to spend as much money as it requires that he believes he will fulfill his goal. Bryan follows a strict diet, ritualised sleep practices, exercise regimen, takes daily supplements, and undergoes countless medical tests that track his health and wellbeing. He has even had plasma donations from teenagers – including his seventeen-year-old son. Bryan estimates that to date he has spent over two million US dollars on his venture and works with a team of thirty doctors and health experts that are supporting him to refresh his body and track his results.

Longevity is the aim of this game. And Bryan claims he's winning. Tests indicate that his biological age is five years younger than it should be, meaning that he is currently ageing the equivalent of nine months for every calendar year. In the world of biohacking, Bryan is both a celebrity and a forerunner, and promotes his work, *Project Blueprint*, as the future of health and wellbeing. He says he is developing the guidebook for prolonging your future. This is the anti-ageing ageing journey! And with the claim that all the science indicates that he is onto something, Bryan wants us all to buy in. ✕

Biohacking is a technical approach to engineering the body. It involves collecting data from your body to help inform the choices you make about everything you do, from what you eat, how you exercise, and when you sleep. Think computer hacking logic applied to the human body; how can I hack the system to get the outcome I want? This is a world where data is king! None of this is new of course. Dieting, meditation, and intermittent fasting are examples of more traditional forms of biohacking and have been used for decades to overcome weight problems, combat stress levels or improve focus. But in a society saturated by technology, where data is omnipotent and readily available, the challenge of overcoming the impacts of ageing is the holy grail of body hacks, and one that is gaining increasing popularity.

Let's put aside for a moment the fact that Bryan's lifestyle is grossly (and materially) unattainable for most people on the planet: what exactly is Bryan doing here? And is there any virtue in it? Certainly, we can see choice – it is after all Bryan's choice to live and age in this way. And we, in some way shape or form, afford him the dignity to do so. But is he behaving with any dignity himself? Has Bryan performed the ultimate virtue hack and attained the Aristotelian skill of a well lived life without needing to age? Is there any dignity in data?

The concept of dignity was prominent in the work of Immanuel Kant, who argued that objects can have a price or dignity. If something has a price, it is valuable only because it is useful to us. By contrast, things with dignity are valued for their own sake. This is an interesting intersection to have arrived at with Bryan Johnson and his biohacking adventures. Today data is treated as an extension of one's identity. It is viewed as something that deserves respect and protection from misuse or exploitation. But data is also seen as a resource that can be used to improve one's well-being, and therefore deserves access and empowerment from data providers and users. Because of this, personal data is commodified, commercialised, and industrialised. And we see a continued emphasis on the importance of data literacy, transparency, and quality, as well as the equitable distribution of data benefits and opportunities. But to what end? Where is all this taking us? Does data, our data, age with us? Does it even matter?

These are profound questions that are going to require some deep reflection.

Thankfully there is a link between dignity and wisdom. Both relate to the understanding and appreciation of the inherent value of life and human experiences. While dignity is about recognising and respecting the inherent worth of people, wisdom, on the other hand, is often associated with a deep understanding of life, and the ability to make sound judgments based on knowledge and experience. In this sense, upholding dignity can lead to wisdom, and wisdom can enhance our understanding and practice of dignity. They also reinforce each other in a virtuous cycle. The practice of one often leads to the enhancement of the other, contributing to an individual's moral and personal development.

We may conceptualise this through the model made popular by Russell Ackoff in the late 1980s, the DIKW pyramid: data (D) is interpreted to become information (I), which when further interpreted becomes knowledge (K), and finally, through time and experience, becomes wisdom (W). In DIKW pyramid, dignity might be seen as inherent in the process of moving from data to wisdom. As we interpret data to create information and knowledge, and as we apply this knowledge over time to gain wisdom, we are guided by a respect for the inherent worth of the individuals or communities that the data represents. This respect for dignity can guide us to use data in ways that are ethical, fair, and beneficial.

This is contrasted against Ziauddin Sardar's concept that we're now living in a 'smog of ignorance', where big data leads us to trigoxic information, and gargantuan knowledge means knowledge is always emergent, and we never meaningfully attain wisdom. Sardar's model observes an absence of dignity in the treatment of data. He thinks that data is not just a collection of symbols, facts, and signals, but also a source of behaviour, emotions, attitudes, and ignorances. He argues that big data, which captures and commodifies the essence of individuals and communities, is a phenomenon that challenges the conventional notion of data. And, because big data doesn't differentiate between truth and lies, knowledge and bullshit, news, and fake news, it makes it difficult for us to climb the pyramid and attain wisdom. Thus, Sardar argues, a new order of wisdom, more appropriate for today, involves recognising the dignity of others and a critical questioning of our current assumptions and paradigms.

He takes this line of thinking further, and questions whether artificial intelligence (AI) can ever possess or exercise wisdom. He says that wisdom requires certain human virtues, such as empathy, compassion, love, forgiveness, sincerity, humility, patience, gratitude, courage, modesty, introspection, and contemplation. These characteristics are difficult to create data points for, let alone generate meaningful facts from. And they require a uniquely human approach to time; time that is epistemological, ontological, and phenomenological all at once.

Others agree with this sentiment. Researchers in the field of dignity therapy examined generativity documents - the documents that capture one's life story as one approaches death. Their research foregrounded how dignity, like wisdom, is a virtue that involves a strong sense of self-worth. Approaching dignity in this way suggests that it may be seen as a form of wisdom, as it requires understanding, empathy, and moral judgment. This further affirms that dignity and wisdom are not static, but dynamic and evolving throughout one's life. They are influenced by one's choices, actions, and relationships, which reflect one's values and beliefs. As such, time is a dimension that shapes and reveals one's dignity and wisdom. Therefore, time is a medium that connects and communicates one's dignity and wisdom to others. We may also consider the notion that dignity and wisdom are not only temporal, but also transcendental. They are linked to one's spirituality and faith, which may provide a source of hope and meaning. Particularly for those at the end of their life.

Therefore, time is a perspective that challenges and transforms one's dignity and wisdom in the light of the finitude of life, not for the sake of it. Time is the construct that we use to measure the world, a fundamental aspect of reality, and a conscious experience of our journey through life, that consistently confronts and informs the nature of our virtuous wisdom/ dignity cycle. By this reckoning, our friend Bryan Johnson the biohacker may be seeking transformations in all the wrong places; his fixation on time (slowing it down, reversing it, or otherwise) is simply a distraction from the more dignified pursuit of transforming wisdom. Sardar might say that Bryan, his biohacker colleagues, and those buying into this vision, are struggling to navigate through the smog of ignorance, groping around at emergent knowledge, and never quite attaining wisdom.

Wisdom and Time

'Everyday is a new day.' Hemingway's Santiago tells us in *Old Man and the Sea*. 'It is better to be lucky. But I would rather be exact. Then when luck comes you are ready.' It is a poignant line from a story that is laced with metaphor and allegory. Even with his vast experience, Santiago has not managed to catch a fish in eighty-four days. He endeavors to carry himself with humility, and there is a rightful sense of pride in his skills. His deep understanding of the ocean, its inhabitants, and his profession is unmatched. These fuel his optimism. With age comes wisdom, and age is a product of time. Santiago's life has been a series of trials that have tested his fortitude and resilience. The marlin that he battles for three days, as his young deckhand Manolin watches on, symbolises his most formidable challenge. And although Santiago eventually loses the fish, the marlin signifies his most significant triumph. Despite his advanced age he still anticipates that there is something to look forward to; 'It's silly not to hope.' Hemingway writes of Santiago, 'It's a sin he thought.'

We're not far from Ricœur here, who said that narrative signifies how we perceive time. Thus, the future also possesses an inherent 'narrative potentiality' - it is always perceived as a collection of possible narratives in which we might participate. Like Martin Heidegger's concept of understanding, or '*verstehen*', which intuitively reveals the world to us in terms of a future-oriented sense of the multitude of potential actions available to us, Ricoeur posits that this pre-understanding is always presented through a 'semantics of action'. In other words, the stories of potential we tell ourselves are an ever-present, meaningful sense of potential choices, actions, and their outcomes, as they might fit into our wider frameworks of significance.

This is all about anticipation, the very human emotion that senses the future and informs our decision-making. It fuels our motivation and helps us find excitement and purpose, keeping us engaged and inspired as we navigate the passage of time. However, like choice and dignity, anticipation alone is not enough. It is wisdom that guides us in understanding how to best use our anticipation. Wisdom with anticipation is the ability to discern between short-term desires and long-term benefits, considering the consequences of our actions. Wisdom with anticipation allows us to prioritise and make choices that align with our core values and goals, enhancing our overall well-being and satisfaction. And whilst we've discovered that wisdom requires certain human virtues, wisdom is also time bound.

This means that we are not just the product of our past experiences, but also the authors of our own lives, actively shaping our identities through the narratives we construct. This process allows for growth and change, as our stories can be revised and rewritten over time. It's a dynamic and flexible view of identity that acknowledges the complexity and richness of human life. Further, while there's a possibility for an individual to identify with a narrative, such as a tale of a hero or princess, and thereby form a somewhat illusory self-concept, Ricoeur maintains that the subject can meaningfully integrate existing narratives into their own. This is achieved via interpretation and 'emplotment', and through this process, new and meaningful possibilities for the subject's existence in the world are unveiled. This – you may have picked up - sounds a lot like how we inform choice. Moreover, these attributions of causation, where other human subjects are involved, necessarily entail implications of moral responsibility, and so the narrative self is ineluctably established in a moral universe. And here we're reminded of dignity.

Time, then, is also the canvas on which anticipation and wisdom unfold. It is a finite resource that continuously moves, inviting us to make the most of each passing moment. Understanding the value and limitations of time is essential for understanding virtue. The awareness that time is limited fosters a sense of urgency to optimise our anticipations and act wisely. Time also grants us opportunities for reflection and introspection, enabling personal growth and the cultivation of wisdom. When anticipation, wisdom, and time intertwine, virtuous attitudes and behaviours emerge. The ability to anticipate future outcomes allows us to seize opportunities, plan for challenges, and strive for self-improvement. Wisdom acts as a compass, guiding our anticipations towards choices and actions that are morally upright, responsible, and aligned with our values. Time, providing the space for anticipation and wisdom to unfold, places value on present moments and encourages us to make intentional, meaningful choices that serve both the present and future. As such, the interplay between anticipation, wisdom, and time creates a path towards virtuous living. It ignites our aspirations, enables wise decision-making, whilst adhering to the passage of time. By harnessing anticipation, cultivating wisdom, and appreciating the finite nature of life, we are better equipped to meet challenges, make purposeful choices, and live a fulfilling existence.

'Perhaps I should not have been a fisherman, he thought. But that was the thing that I was born for.' Hemingway writes of Santiago, reflecting on his own existence. 'Fish,' he said softly, aloud, 'I'll stay with you until I am dead.'

Time & Meaning

Back at the salon, Mandy has finished, and I can genuinely say it is the best haircuts I have had in a long time. We move to the reception so I can pay.

'I'm glad I came in to see you today. I really like this haircut.' I tell Mandy enthusiastically.

'Well, thank you. I'm pleased you like it.'

'You know – some of the biggest mistakes I have made have been haircuts' I say. I am being charming.

She looks at me, a flash of confusion and then a furrow of disappointment. 'You know, there are so many more meaningful things in life than haircuts.' She tells me. And then smiles sympathetically. And I feel like I'm eight years old.

I get in my car to leave, but cannot resist finishing this thought, and go back inside and find Mandy sweeping my hair from around the chair I was sitting in just a few moments ago.

'What did you mean by virtue?'

'I beg your pardon?'

'Virtue. You used the word virtue. You said that when you were retired you felt like you were moving from one thing to the next, as though you were not achieving much. You said that there is no *virtue* in that. Why did you say virtue?'

Mandy looked baffled at my confrontation. 'Oh, did I?' She said. 'That seems like an odd thing to say.'

'Yes!' I said, 'That's what I thought too. Why would you use that word. It's curious to me.'

'I don't think I said virtue. I think what I said was that I felt like I was not achieving much in my life, but that there is no *issue* with that.' Mandy emphasised 'issue.'

'Ah.'

'I think you misheard me. I was showing you humility. I realise that retirement is a privilege, a luxury. Some people enjoy it – enjoy not having anything in particular to do. I have no issue with that. I really don't.'

'Ah, yes. I see.' I chuckled a little.

'Besides,' Mandy added. 'It has been a very long time since I was in school, but if I remember correctly, *virtue* is a noun, not a verb. It would be *very* unusual for me to use that word in that way.'

Yes, I thought. There is wisdom in that too.

MY DINNER WITH SALIHA

C Scott Jordan

What delivered me to the dinner table of Saliha Sardar is the sort of thing that vilifies the timeless cliché that 'things happen for a reason'. And God has a keen sense of poetic irony and justice, crafting the whole story and not necessarily catering to your liking. So, the Grand Narrator would deem that Saliha's husband, Zia, would have no small role to play in our world's colliding. Curiously, it was actually thanks to cancer that I would be dining with Saliha on this particular evening – the prostate cancer plaguing Zia at the time – and it would be cancer, yet of a different kind, that would be to blame for my not being able to dine again with her, at least on this plane, in the near future. I was at a bit of a crossroads in my own life; and to progress certain other events needed to take place. So, when you find yourself with time to kill, why not relax and have a quick bite or a nice cup of tea.

I am in a home. Taking that much needed break *à la* the British institution of the Four O'Clock Tea. The steam of my own piping hot cup fogs the images in front of me. The images are mostly dismal. Suburban London on an average day. Glum is a word. Rainy is another. I have to admit I love it. Heaven is a rainy day with a pile of books and good coffee. My fascination is set upon the rapidly setting sun, which I haven't seen for days, but the gradual dimming of lightness gives way to the assumption that the sun must be going somewhere. I am not surprised. I have a surface level understanding of the Earth's rotation axis and seasonal change. 'Daytime' from place to place will not necessarily be the same. But to experience the sun setting at four in the afternoon is a bit jarring when you are not used to it. Sitting in the Sardar living room, surrounded by the artifacts and *objets* of lives lived – of a living family – I could just as easily have arrived from Mars, let alone the opposite side of the Atlantic. I was certainly a stranger in a strange land. Although that trope is evaporating in our contemporary age. One could easily seek out strange new worlds, seek out new life and new civilisations, to boldly go where no man had gone before by simply taking a walk down the street, much less charting a voyage to the far side of the globe or solar system.

But for an American, the United Kingdom is another category. Dishearteningly familiar, yet strictly foreign. An old friend put it well by saying its 'Bizarro World'. What's up is down and what's right is left. The language itself has a certain madness, at times one side holds all the logic, to only lose it in the next moment. Z is not 'zee' it is 'zed'. Full stop, not a period, but a period is a period and so the women who hear me talk about grammar begin blushing for some strange reason. Even the roads and thus the mobility of society are inversed. Right of way is rights of way and the direction does not carry on so intuitively. Honestly, I could not afford to be surprised if it was asked to put hats on my feet and shoes on my hands.

Out the window I looked on. Sipping my tea, which was much more delightful than I had thought, coming from the land of black sludge coffee and its usurping bastard of a brother, iced tea. I bit from my biscuit, which was not the dinner biscuit you'd get in the US, and certainly not a cookie – whatever that is. Though I give credit to those who try to expand the categories of things to include both the American cookie, something of a monstrous biscuit, and a British biscuit in the same continuum. French fries were chips and chips were crisps, but what of crispy things? Never mind. Aluminium, not alumin-um, herbs with a hard 'h' because it has an 'h' in it. Who'd have thought! My mind was a three-ring circus, complete with matinée showings.

Zia sat across from me on the couch. Oblivious to my inner toil with cultural conjugation, he placed his empty tea mug on the coffee table in front of him. He shot me a glance that would almost have me believe he was, in fact, quite aware of my turmoil, or at least questioning why I would expend so much mental energy on silly matters. Also noting the diminishing light, he proceeded to shutting all the front blinds and igniting every lamp and overhead light in the living room and along the stairway to the upper rooms. Zia's efforts to seek continuity of illumination into the darkness of night was a ritual of sorts. He continued to repeat these steps everyday he was at home as he had for many decades. Even as the furniture in the living room changed. Even as the lamps changed. Through the seasons, as the world continued to ignore the reality of climate change. *Swish* and *click* while wars were fought – mostly the unjust variety – as each new injustice grew more horrifying than the last. Economies boomed and busted. Through each new Prime Minister, Zia would keep closing the blinds and switching on the lights. Zia liked light.

Sitting next to Zia, a man not likely to sit still for more than a few silent moments without the news in front of him, sat Saliha. She sat in what I would later find was her usual spot, layered in jumpers and shawls to keep warm from the bitter British air. She was quite used to Zia's frequent springing from the couch to attend to whatever needed attending. Unperturbed, she ate away with small polite bites at her biscuit. Her tea sat on the coffee table, minding its own business, exhausting trickles of steam. Mid-illumination, he offered her a few words in Urdu. She would respond without looking up from the iPad that had her attention. Zia's words began with *Begum*. That was the title Zia had bestowed upon his beloved long ago, honouring a tradition with a most uncertain future. While Zia and his venerable colleague, the Welsch Dragon Woman, Merryl Wyn Davies, were no strangers to giving all in their path silly and often diminutive (though the holders were none the wiser) nicknames, Begum was no jibe. She was the queen of his world. Begum was, after all, the name given to Muslim women of exulted stature throughout Central and South Asia across history. And Zia knew well, and would freely admit it if you asked him, that the woman of a Desi house is both symbolic and administrative head of home. They often see no need to flaunt this reality. Let the Desi men live in their imagined patriarchy. They hold about as much power as the British monarch, and like the royal family, every couple of years the public asks if we really need them. May God have mercy on the Desi man who also has a daughter.

In line with the standards and practices of a Desi household, the kitchen was clearly Saliha's domain. But she upheld an equitable division of labour. The making of the afternoon tea was remedial enough a chore to be left to the man of the house without too much cause for concern. As Saliha worked during the day at a nearby school for special needs children, it became the expectation that the preparation of the tea would begin as soon as she arrived home. So much so, that if the door was heard opening and the kettle had not been put on, Zia would hop from whatever task had his attention to remedy this misjudgement of time. Credit where it is due, Zia did well to meet this expectation. While Zia is not much for schools of thought, he did subscribe to the one with regards to tea. That of the twentieth century English writer George Orwell. In particular, 'tea is meant to be bitter,' and it has to be damn bloody hot. Pipping. And it would do no good to add cold milk straight from the fridge. Zia was a man of ritual, one minute twenty seconds did the trick on the microwave model they had. The Professor also liked his tea strong. A delicate balance lied between maintaining hot fresh tea and providing for ample steeping time. The temperature cannot be stressed enough. When you believe the tea has reach a temperature that might be described as inhumane, it was necessary to take it a few degrees further. With time, I too would learn and adopt for my own the method and even take on the job of preparation from time to time. This household had a fondness for Yorkshire black tea from Betty & Taylors Group. Always loose leaf, unless the situation grew truly dire. I learned what a tea cosy was – a device that maintained the heat of the tea as it steeped – not to be confused with what we in the US call 'koozie' – a device that keeps one's beer or soda pop cold longer. I would even learn the specific likings of the family. Where Zia preferred a dark, strong brew. Saliha and their daughter Maha would prefer their tea a bit lighter. Colour mattered in the game of tea. Raw sugar for Maha, no sugar for Zia. Only after my time with Saliha did I learn the Desi trick of adding a cardamom seed or two to the tea which delivered both a nice aromatic flavour and various health benefits to the drinker. After my time in the UK, I still find myself craving tea when the clock strikes four, regardless of where on the planet I am.

Zia drank his tea very quickly in all its scalding glory before moving on to what accoutrements accompanied the cup, sweet biscuits, chocolate, and savoury munchies. Saliha and I, who preferred to taste our tea finished slower, complementing our tea taste with the accoutrements. Following the tea, Saliha would collect the empty cups and secure what biscuits were spared. All of it back to the kitchen.

A routine developed quickly during my time there. I was lodging down the street and around the corner at their son, Zaid's house. So, each day I'd set off to arrive around about half past nine in the morning. After a quick breakfast and coffee, it would be upstairs to the attic to begin the day's work. Zia and I would work hard until about one in the afternoon, when we would break for lunch. Lunch was often leftovers from the night before or something quick and easy that Zia and I could manage. We would proceed again to the attic until the hour of four demanded tea. During lunch and tea, we would catch up on what quickly became how terrible a shape the world was in on any given day by scanning the news. Zia would tap the remote between the BBC and Sky News comparing what each saw as the 'most important' news of the day, switching the channel if they obsessed too long over what Zia referred to as 'nonsense' or 'rubbish'. Occasionally, he would change the channel quickly for cricket update, or even to watch a match. Zia's favourite sport. I would look upon the game before my eyes with complete confusion. Familiar with what the Americans call baseball, all looked similar, but the gameplay, scoring, vocabulary used, and other details threw me into the uncanny valley. As the bizarre game played out, Zia provided a lavish commentary. His words were most certainly English, but followed a grammar completely foreign to me. If the workload demanded it, following our tea break, we would retreat again to the attic to finalise anything before dinner. Some days we would be finished by tea and could have a leisurely afternoon.

Regardless of what our programme specified, it was also understood, that following teatime, for one hour, Saliha would flex her power and wield the command of the remote. Every day she would check on the news coming from Pakistan. Zia would often audibly scoff at the state of Pakistan which he was not to demean in Saliha Begum's presence. I watched on in fascination, attempting to make sense of the images, trying to use the occasional breaks into English as clues. For me, Pakistani news was much easier to follow than cricket. This is largely owed to the fact that most news today, all around the world, has been colonised by incessant screaming and debates devoid of any desire to reach conclusion, heaven forbid progress towards understanding. Throughout the hour, Saliha would juxtapose complaints around corruption and Pakistan's woes (usually directed at Zia) with tongue clicks and the occasional call for someone to save that beautiful land (inferring that Zia's time would be better spent finding solutions for Pakistan's woes than whatever other issues he was dealing with). After an hour of biting his tongue raw, Zia again relinquished control over the remote with a long breath under which numerous curses and blasphemes freely flowed, in numerous languages, both real and made up. Saliha would retire to the kitchen. There she would set about her next task, the preparation of dinner.

What would take place in that kitchen can best be described in the English language as magic. While the observer would witness a rather simple, yet well-timed, combination of ingredients and heat, a higher power of artistry was at work. 'What would everyone like for dinner?', Saliha would ask. She would receive the same answer every day: 'whatever you like'. But the question was unnecessary anyway for whatever Saliha cooked would be an event of flavour and sustenance. Western, Asian, it didn't really matter. Even fish fingers and potato wedges, something any chap with a microwave could *cook*, she would *make* into a delicacy. When I asked her how she did it, I received only humble simplicities and 'nothing special, just add this to that and let is get hot' as a response. Only now, many years later, can I appreciate that she was not raised into her skill, as I had simply assumed, but that she painstakingly cultivated her craft through independent study and I assume a perfectionism that would have many of the great masters saying, 'I think that's good enough, let's move on'. Yet she occasionally complained about her own dishes, and to my dumbfounding, as I was practically licking clean the plate she claimed was 'not her best'. The idea that anything could be 'wrong' about what she made was entirely inconceivable to me!

During our down time or upon finishing either a major or head-cracking task, Zia often liked to take a break. One of his favourite types of breaks was for Urdu poetry. Since, at this time, we were putting together *A Person of Pakistani Origins*, these breaks occurred more frequently. Through the films of Dilip Kumar, to the elegant verse of Munni Begum, and even into the bombastic presentations of Coke Studios, and later of Nèscafé Basement, Zia, a true lover of Urdu poetry, made it a point to educate me in the beauty of the language with ample exposure to the art and its performative expression. While he would point out and translate numerous words and phrases, what was retained can only charitably be described as a passing familiarity. But this did not get in the way of appreciating the self-evident beauty in the poetry. Yet if I was asked what the first Urdu word I truly learned was, I would have had to say *khana*. Even before I knew it was Urdu – or was even sure what the word being uttered was – I knew what this word meant. Even the first time I heard Saliha holler the word from the kitchen, my body knew before my mind could process that it was time to move. The word rang through the house daily, sometimes with a louder, or at least more upstairs directed manner, if no response was conveyed. This word, Zia did not need to translate. Only months later would I ask quietly if 'khana' was what I thought it was. 'It had better bloody well mean what you think it means, you've only been responding to it for the last several months when Saliha yells it!' Indeed, I had known what it meant. The word reverberated with an almost universal familiarity, despite its rather intricate etymology. In certain cultures, it may be the ringing of a gentle bell or the rapping of a musical triangle. In a greasy American diner, it's the impatient *ding-ding* of the same bell you find in certain hotel lobbies. In your more elaborate Chinese restaurants, it might be the sounding of a gong. In lieu of an audible calling, the waft of a sensational meal will also do the trick. I knew its meaning as clear as when my own mother would howl from the kitchen: '*Dinner!*'

All present in the house would descend upon the kitchen to find the meal laid out in an assembly line of delicacies. Beside the microwave, the queue would begin with a stack of plates and numerous sets of the necessary cutlery. Beyond the plates a large bowl is loaded with steaming rice – the base of many an Asian meal. On more special days the more elegant *ghee* rice will replace it. On the truly special occasions, one will find the supremely elegant *biryani*. While the rice featured on this night could be mistaken for *just* rice, anything prepared by Saliha is never *just* what it appears. The grains would be quality and the water used would be precisely what was needed. The salt would be balanced. Everyone has their preferences and tastes, but neither overcooking nor undercooking was acceptable. No dish must carry the burden of another. Next was a bowl full of *dhal*. The yellow soupy concoction of lentils with a brilliant trans-sensorial dance of onion and garlic was unfamiliar to me. Nevertheless, my nose told my brain this would likely be the star of the show. Following along, we continue to the stove top where a wok filled with a smoky and seasoned-to-perfection medley of veggies redefined how attractive a vegetarian's pallet could be. The frying pan next to this wok housed a kingly portion of meat, soaking in its red curry. I cannot recall, was it mutton or was it lamb, would it really have made a difference? Last, but not least, sat a towel upon a serving platter. Fresh and hot *roti* was nestled within. As Zia and I entered the kitchen, Saliha placed one more bowl of yoghurt sauce mixed with cucumber and some other seasonings I couldn't quite make out.

'Can you handle spicy food?'

'Yes, but I'm not one for diving into things headfirst.'

'Then take this!' Saliha emphasises the yoghurt dish she had just finalised.

Normally, the routine was every man for himself when it came to dishing out plates. But since this was my first time, Zia took the liberty of preparing and portioning out my plate, and decorated my plate with each of the parts of this meal. Once properly full, Zia plopped a large piece of roti on top and passed the hearty plate to me. I was then instructed to proceed into the other room and begin eating. To the man who drinks scalding beverages, to let a beautiful meal run cold was the greatest of sins. Such politesse, as waiting for all to join before commencing in consumption, need not be observed here. Maha, the couple's daughter, would come to the kitchen once she finished her last call of the day, and the two sons, Zaid and Zain, would not be home until well into the night when Saliha would reheat their food for another round.

Dinner coincided with another evening ritual at the Sardar household, the beginning of the Channel 4 News broadcast at seven o'clock. There was even a bit of a game to see if you could guess what would be their lead story which would be teased in the opening segment before rolling the credits and bringing it to then lead presenter, Jon Snow, to see what eccentrically flamboyant tie and sock combination he would be showing off that day. Would it be the latest Brexit drama? Or perhaps updates on one of the ongoing domestic court cases? The odds were good that it would be a piece on climate change in one way or another and you could always count on C4 to cover the globally disadvantaged community of the week, covering their plight with grace and detail. The best shows began with a news item not featured in *The Guardian* or on the BBC and Sky News reports seen earlier in the day.

As Jon Snow's electric hyperbolic socks cried out for attention, I set out upon the plate handed to me. I began by trying each item individually. First the meat. Oh, that was fantastic. Then the dhal. I could possibly live on this alone without bother should the situation arise. Then the veggie. Admittedly, I had sort of dreaded this dish as my veggie pallet had been exceptionally boring for most of my life and most of the health benefits garnered from such dishes were overridden by the amounts of butter and pepper dowsing the cutlets. But this was something different. You could taste the vegetables and they tasted quite delicious. And they held firm in a rigid structure that often is lost on cooking methods that disregard the vegetable as a box to be ticked rather than a part of the meal. The yoghurt I was most sceptical of. In the US, yoghurt is a dessert dish or perhaps a breakfast dish that is accompanied by fruits or granola, not meat and spices. This was a role reversal I was not comfortable with, but as I tried it, I was pleasantly delighted. It especially went well after the flavourful red curry from the meat.

By the time I had sampled all the delights on the plate, Zia and Saliha had joined me with plates of their own. They asked what I thought, and I had confirmed the meal was superb and one of the best I had had for a long time. Jon Snow handed it off to Matt Frei who was reporting from the lobby of the House of Commons. I fell pretty deeply into the meal, only really listening to Channel 4 in the background. As bread started most of my meals back home, I began by eating the roti as plain as it was put to me, loving its freshness. I'm sure I was not doing much to conceal my enjoyment of the meal. But I noticed I drew the attention of Saliha and Zia. I assumed they were looking to see if I may be masking any inadequacies I may have felt over the meal. So, I smiled in response as I swallowed the roti. 'Would you like another piece of roti?' Zia offered as I took note of Saliha tearing from her own roti slice. She had taken the portion and fashioned it into an absorptive scooping utensil and mixed the contents of her plate into this newly formed pouch. Down the hatch it went. 'Ah, yes' I responded. Zia sprung forth and grabbed another roti for me. As Zia had handed me a spoon and fork, I did not think that the bread could then be used to effectively eat with one's hands. Now equipped with a new piece of roti, I followed Saliha's lead, tearing a bit off and wiping it across the bottom of the plate to soak up the juices, then grabbed a pile of veggies and threw it all into my mouth. Clumsily perhaps, but no mess made! And I admit I did it in such a way that both Zia and Saliha could see, as if approval would get me further through this meal. The reception of the feat I had performed gave me the impression that the fork and spoon ought not be totally disregarded at this point.

I then proceeded to eat each portion upon my plate separately, with fork and knife, and in a bit of an order. First up were the vegetables, the real underdogs of the night, but nevertheless, despite how high a quality the veg could attain, the meat would certainly go even higher. The *dhal* would be the *pièce de resistance*. You see, I was a son of the American Midwest, from a family that retains the living memory of the Great Depression and Dust Bowl of the early twentieth century. Food is one of the purest extensions of love. And it must never, never be wasted. So, what was on my plate was what was my key concern, and a lot of pride (or in Asia, face) was at stake. I am also what is referred to as a 'sectioned eater' one who likes to eat each dish separately, never shall two sauces touch. To make sure every dining experience was taken to its fullest, I would eat in an order that would end on the best dish. First take care of the veggies, then the potato or rice, and finish with the meat or the main dish so as to take the palate on a ride. Better yet if it ends on a succulent dessert. Admittedly, this style has its extremisms. I would also break each dish down, eating from the outside in, assuming the centre of any given piece would be the most treasured bite – or at least the core of the message any chef was attempting to convey. I respected the language of cuisine. The love letter within each dish. Even a simple cheeseburger would be consumed in a circumferential manner, finishing on the central piece of meat, melted cheese and condiments. And as I became more educated in etiquette I had taken it for granted that what was presented to you by the chef was how it was intended to be consumed, so to wash a steak in a sauce or allow dishes to flow together was a slap in the face to a delicatessen.

So I ate the vegetables first, beginning with any parts of the veg that had run into the rice or the nearby yoghurt. A clean crater left in the wake of the plenty delights. Next, with the spoon, I ate the yoghurt sauce by itself. I did take a tear of roti and wipe up its residuals once the bulk of it was gobbled up. Then I took to the rice, in its hefty plainness and ate it bite by bite with the fork given to me. Overcome in the ecstasy of the meal, I was unaware of the fact that Zia and Saliha were watching me eat. Saliha had even placed her glasses on, unsure if she could trust what her eyes were presenting her with. As I noticed their stare, I give an audible 'Mm-mmm' and perhaps a few broken words of appreciation between the mouthfuls of food. Spoon after spoon went the dhal with much appreciation. Saliha threw a sentence of Urdu to Zia. He accepted what was put to him in silence. After a few moments, measured in my spoon heaps, he offered back a quick word or two in response. 'They must be impressed that an American boy can so enjoy their South Asian meal!', I thought. I had reached the meat, it was mostly cut up, so with my hands I took to separating the meat from the bones. The way Zia and Saliha were looking at me, made me think I must have had the dopiest smile on my face. As I took the last little sliver of roti, I wiped the plate clean, leaving behind only a few bones. Saliha shouted more Urdu at Zia, then smiled at me.

'Would you like some more?'

For Saliha, food was indeed an extension of love. A mother's love or at least the compassionate love one ought to spread to strangers met along the road of life. She was a traditional South Asian woman. No one is allowed to go hungry. Food must always be made available. Full stop. The hardship of the Great Depression rang through two generations to my core, even though I had never experienced it. The greatest sin next to wasting food was to turn down food when offered. All must be accepted and all must be finished.

'Sure! That was lovely, really a wonderful dinner'

Saliha smiled with a laugh and then shot a sharp look at Zia. He nodded in response and took my plate. Though I said I could get it myself, he insisted. For Zia was on a mission. What I was unaware of was that in a Desi house, the separate dishes of a meal would be served separately on one's plate, so as to insure their constitution prior to consumption. And as an unwritten rule, either bit by bit or as a grand mix in the beginning, all the dishes had to be mixed. This was not to balance the flavours and the tastes per say, but so that each ingredient could work to enhance the flavours and the appreciation of the spice from dish to dish, seamlessly. It was in fact an insult to allow each dish to be eaten on its own, preventing their full potential from being realised when put side by side with the other prepared dishes. Knowing what was to be eaten with what was critical to a successfully planned South Asian dinner, for if they didn't gel together, then disaster.

As Zia entered the kitchen, he knew that he had no choice but to resort to desperate measures.

He made a central rice mound on the plate. Then poured, in a less than elegant manner, all the various dishes onto the rice mound. To drive the point home, he then took a spoon and mixed all the ingredients into a rather evenly distributed jumbly fusion. Satisfied with the truly South Asian plate he had made, I imagine he smiled, adding a piece of roti on top with an impatient plop. He knew I could eat, but didn't realise how daft I was to eating in the way it was supposed to be eaten.

Very proud of himself, he handed me the plate as Saliha smiled with a rare gleam of satisfaction over the solution presented by her husband. As Zia sat again, I noticed both looked on in anticipation for me to begin. And who was I to let food be left as an object to be admired when it begged to be consumed? I took the roti, tearing off an ample piece, forming the pouch that I had seen Saliha make before. And a bite was taken and enjoyed. I almost expected Saliha and Zia to begin applauding. Progress in our times. I was beginning to feel like I was a child using the 'big boy' potty for the first time, much to the relief of parents overwhelmed with the unenviable task of potty training. The prospect of a new trade deal between the UK and the EU post Brexit seemed less an impossibility despite what the discourse on Channel 4 purported. But then I went on.

Unaware of the trap Zia had laid for me, I proceeded to dissect my meal casting aside the rich complexity of the mixture Zia had woven. I separated the vegetables from the mixture, then the yoghurt, then the meat, finishing with the dhal which had sort of blended with the rice. Then I ate everything, one by one, separately. In the final analysis, there I was with a white mound of rice, eating away at it, with a fork. The jubilation turned to bile. Much like the Massacre at Glencoe, a good meal turned to treachery. I might as well have murdered thirty of the Clan MacDonald as I scooped the last grains of rice onto my fork. To add insult to injury, in my ignorance I uttered 'Wow, when the rice and the dhal mix, it actually makes for a delightful blend! I noticed the yoghurt also added a lovely note to the combo. It was almost as if they were intended to be mixed...'

I had found myself in a higher state of being before this meal. It was a spiritual experience. Was I not learning culture in the best way possible. Yet, for Saliha and Zia, I was spouting out words with horrible pronunciation and calling that language. Where was the grammar, the meaning, the flow? There was no beauty in this. No amusement either.

Saliha spit a fiery roar of Urdu at Zia. It certainly gave me the impression that he had done something wrong. He often did. He looked back at her, as confounded as she was. Defeat was eminent. Noticing that again my plate was clean, I wondered. Could I have done something wrong?

This was not my first experience of a new culture's etiquette towards food. I had been to China and knew that, at least in East Asia, one demonstrated their enjoyment of food by eating bombastically and chewing with one's mouth open, even speaking with food in their mouth, and audibly slurping their tea. It was quite the shock to me, but it held a certain logic, even if that logic was different from my own. Should I have been sloppier? Though I did try to throw in expressions and language to demonstrate my enjoyment. Did they think I was masking or even being sarcastic? After all this was Britain and despite what ethnic cultural particulars carry forward into the contemporary multicultural United Kingdom, it seemed safer to err on the side of what I perceived to be the Queen's etiquette.

We were at an impasse in expressing love. The route taken by one insulted the other and the only ways to proceed were rife with further insult. It was the Queen's polite society that prevented Saliha and Zia from pointing out what I was doing wrong, if wrong is what you could call what I did. Even my, granted rather strange, face deserved to be saved. In my consumption, I sought to express my love, but in my mode of consumption I insulted Saliha's cooking. To point this out would insult me and deny the love she showed to extend through the meal in the first place. Zia was hopelessly caught in the middle. He was no stranger to defying convention. He would see no problem in pointing out in no uncertain terms that I had consumed my meal in the completely wrong way. But he also knew Saliha Begum would not tolerate such abuse, especially when, technically, I had done

202 C SCOTT JORDAN

nothing wrong. After all, Americans need their codified rules and written constitutions, they cannot deal with the more abstract notions of justice and logic that the Brits follow. Should he let me have it, he would face a proper scalding of fiery Urdu and a week-long sentence of the silent treatment. The centre had to hold, but with what material could this be done?

We often over dramatize the collapsing of one world for the other or the impact of two supposedly in competition. Yet more often than not, the 'clash of civilisations' that the late American political scientist Samuel P. Huntington so feared would plague our new century are often more subtle encounters so thick with ignorance that you may not notice a confrontation had even taken place. Just a passing brush, left un-reflected with no opportunity for learning, much less understanding, taking place. The Sardar dinner table was between Scylla and Charybdis. This is not because the difference in worldviews found at the table could not easily be overcome, but instead because good, and truly pure, intention, as it so often does, has got in the way.

The twentieth century British writer and lay theologian, C.S. Lewis shines the light on this during his 1940 work, *The Problem of Pain*. While the focus of this treatise revolves around the question of why an all-powerful and good God would create a world that allowed for pain – something Zia, in his situation, might be sympathetic to – Lewis spends considerable time giving 'kindness' , which he does not consider a virtue, a proper dressing down. His criticism revolves around the fact that kindness is not exactly what we think it is. For instance, in our more contemporary world we have the notion of 'kill them with kindness' but he also references the kindness of killing a horse whose broken its leg. Lewis notes, 'are we not really an increasingly cruel age? Perhaps we are: but I think we have become so in the attempt to reduce all virtues to kindness.' His usage of kindness can be equated to mercy, even pity. Which is interesting since his best friend J. R. R. Tolkien holds pity as an essential motive for the unfolding of his *The Lord of the Rings*, but this is because he holds that all things in Middle-Earth (and frankly our own world) must happen for a reason, another diatribe Lewis, I believe, would have significant problems with. Both this and Lewis's problems can be easily summed up. A lot of horrible shit has been and can be justified with a simple 'everything happens for a reason' or 'really, it was a kindness' a bloody mercy. As Lewis said, 'the real trouble is that "kindness" is a quality fatally easy to attribute to ourselves on quite inadequate grounds'.

The first Thanksgiving feast was a three-day event that took place in October 1621 in the Plymouth Colony of the New World. It was a kindness visited by ninety of the Wampanoag, one of the native peoples of America, upon the fifty-three surviving refugees who fled persecution in England aboard the famous ship, the Mayflower. While I do enjoy a bit of speculation, I don't give it much credence. But there was a real opportunity for a new type of civilisation either coming out of that feast or that could have been inspired through this story's survival. But sadly, the refugees became conquistadors who eradicated the natives. Fearing the next refugees to come to their shores will either wipe them out and take their place or die, they amplified the fear of further refugees. The cycle has been repeated many times. This seems to be fate, but need not be destiny.

Indeed, the line between virtue and vice is disappointingly thin. For our values to stay the course and maintain their virtuous nature, they require a holistic and interconnected appreciation. A virtue that stands alone is no virtue, it must cooperate and uplift another. While demonstrated in our actions, it is in how we live that virtue is attained and progressed through time. In fact, it is a bit disingenuous to note a virtuous individual. In reality there must be virtuous communities or societies. But how monumental a task is that summit?

But could it begin somewhere? If it is folly to begin with the individual, then perhaps we should begin in the home. In the ninety-nine names of God, 'homemaker' is conspicuously absent. Perhaps it could be derived from a combination of the others, but there is something profound in the notion of a homemaker. Not your Suzy Homemaker. I am not talking gender normative roles or the stereotypical family unit. But are not those who make homes among the blessed? And a home is more than walls, ceilings, and floors – the compendium of world literature tells us, at least, that a house alone does not make a home. But what about a dinner table? Such a remarkably simple structure that has given host to great discussions as well as the transcendental thinking that has bridged understandings across cultures and generations. Lessons learned and differences appreciated. But to make this proverbial omelette, a few eggs need cracking.

'Would you like some more? You are not allowed to be hungry', issued Saliha.

Zia's hard swallow following that question could be heard even in the boisterous lobbies of the House of Commons. To ask that question was to condemn them to further defeat. Was she not satisfied with the fine mess this meal had become? He was beginning to put two and two together. She had to offer him more to eat. He knew I could not refuse the offer of more food. This truly is what results when an immovable object confronts an unstoppable force.

Zia often notes my ability to consume all and in vast quantities. Only when I say, 'actually I am quite full,' does he know that something was not quite right. Once in China, I had visited a vegetarian monastery where we were served one of the greatest lunches I had ever experienced. But none of the servers spoke English. Before we began, they said to signal that you've had enough, put your hand over your bowl and do not waste anything. These folks are poor and that is a grave insult, you must finish all. Only three quarters of the way through the meal did I realise that my smile of appreciation was being taken as a signal for 'can I have some more please'. In agony after many more bowls full I collapsed over the bowl preventing any more food from being dished into it. I spent the afternoon keeled over in agony. I would not abandon my principles. Nor would Saliha. Saliha was love and she must express that love. I would eat myself sick at the least. Images of former US President George H. W. Bush vomiting into the lap of former Japanese Prime Minister Kiichi Miyazawa. A dystopia was flashing before Zia's eyes. There would be no food left for the boys. They would starve. The house would be freely given and freely consumed. They would be beggars on the street! Yet Saliha would continue to give every scrap to me the personification of modernity ignorant to the limits of growth. Empires rise. Empires fall. Collapse. Ruin.

'Bloody hell', he shouted. 'Have you not had enough!. Are you a man or a horse?'. Then he turned to Saliha. 'Will you not save some for the boys! What are we to have for lunch tomorrow? Is there no end to this madness!'. There was a pregnant pause. 'Jesus Christ! Jesus Christ', Zia kept mumbling.

A moment of silence. I was embarrassed, but relieved, freed from my duties of politeness. I imagine so too was Saliha. Nevertheless, she let him have it. One did not need to know Urdu to understand the verbal lashing he received. I do not think she spoke to him for a day, maybe two. But order was restored. Zain and Zaid had their dinner. The home and its centre held. And something resembling a deal followed Brexit.

I have no idea if the universe began with a big bang or with something resembling a sleepy cat's whimper. But I am almost certain civilisation begun with a dinner table.

In the 1987 Danish film, *Babette's Feast*, the titular character reveals near the end that she had spent all of her lottery money, the ticket to her freedom from the indentured refugee existence she was in, on a top tier French meal for the two sisters she had been serving and their guests. The sisters were perplexed by her decision to spend so much on the meal, which was deeply spiritual for all who enjoyed it. Anguish overtook them; they felt she would surely be poor now and stuck for the rest of her life. Babette responds by saying 'an artist is never poor'. In utter gratitude, one of the sisters declares: 'this is not the end, Babette. In paradise you will be the great artist God meant you to be! Oh, how you will enchant the angels!' Indeed, I would add the homemaker is never poor either. For the home is one of the few sustainable units we have left to us on this dying planet. Saliha will indeed enchant the angels. I imagine her treating the heavenly messengers with her *biryani* and *dhal*. I just hope, for their sakes, they know the proper way to eat a *desi* dinner. And have the ability to politely say 'no thank you', when she asks: 'would you like some more?'

ARTS AND LETTERS

VISUAL SENSATIONS

Safia Latif

My work explores the relationship between religion and modernity. Many of my paintings draw conceptually on the social and cultural phenomena associated with the Muslim world, which is why I have named my particular style 'Islamicate Impressionism.' I like to focus on visual sensations of Islamic themes while also incorporating elements of magical realism. I believe the magical depictions in my work convey a sense of numinous wonder, evoking the idea that the divine is the everyday and the everyday is the divine. If I have any goal, it is to speak to the truth of the human condition, and perhaps reveal something to the viewer about themself.

My painting 'The Night Prayer' adopts the distinctive introspective mood of Edward Hopper's paintings. I believe the only way I could have shown the particularly individual and private act of *tahajjud* (the night prayer) was through the vantage point of a window, enabling the viewer to look into this secret world and experience a feeling of intrigue and awe.

'Finding Khidr in Medina' is one of a series of paintings in which I depict the elusive Qur'anic figure Khidr in various locations throughout the Muslim world. The idea invoked is that of the familiar children's book 'Where's Waldo?' wherein the viewer must go on an epic hunt to find the red stripe wearing Waldo. In 'Finding Khidr in Medina', I intentionally painted the composition to feel narrow and perhaps claustrophobic to emphasize the massive and diverse Muslim crowd. Khidr is seen on the bottom left donning green clothing and below him is another enigmatic figure who refuses to die in popular imagination, Tupac Shakur. Thus, this painting emerges as a play on religious and secular experiences of the supernatural.

'Portrait of Avicenna' (Ibn Sina) goes beyond the parameters of a typical portrait. Here he is depicted conspicuously in the act of drinking wine, a forbidden drink in Islam. This piece may evoke a negative visceral response in many religious adherents, but I believe it forces one to acknowledge a very significant point – that while Islam may be a legal tradition, it is equally non-legal in both spirit and practice. The Arabic written in the backdrop is taken from his book on the heart. I intentionally painted it loose and haphazard to imitate the appearance of manuscript writing. The passage cuts off abruptly mid sentence, giving the impression of a train of thought Avicenna might have had.

'Call to Prayer' is inspired by a prominent historical figure in Islam, Bilal ibn Rabah, who was the first *muezzin* in Islam. The wispy brushstrokes suggest movement and hopefully allow the viewer to experience the emotion associated with the Islamic practice of calling others to prayer.

'Detachment' conveys a sense of grandeur emanating not only from the glittering lights and orbs but also from the old man who sits, on the right side of the composition, immersed in *dhikr*.

In 'The Custodian', I decided to juxtapose the majesty of the Taj Mahal with the quiet and unassuming work of the cleaner. As in 'Detachment', the viewer must decide: what or who manifests the splendor and beauty in these paintings?

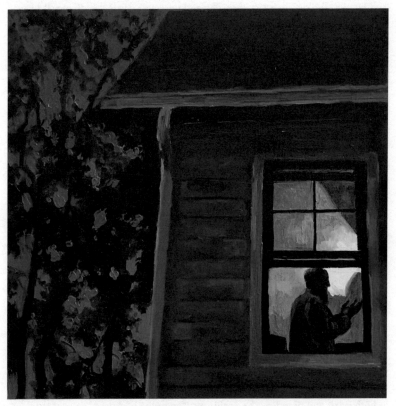

The Night Prayer, oil on wood panel

Funding Khidir in Medina, oil on wood panel

Call to prayer, oil on wood

Detachment, oil on wood

Portrait of Avicenna, oil on canvas paper

The Custodian, oil on canvas paper

WHERE'S MY FREEDOM
OF MOVEMENT?

Gwen Burnyeat

When the march happened, I was in the Caffè Nero above Blackwell's trying to write a story about Luz, a woman I had met doing fieldwork in Colombia on polarisation. Luz, a friend of a friend, had campaigned for the 'Yes' vote in the peace referendum. I met her for a beer in a gloomy restaurant in the coffee region, where she told me about how she tried to counter the disinformation spread by opponents of the peace deal with the leftist FARC guerrilla. *The peace deal with turn your children gay!* people said. *But the peace deal is about ending fifty years of war!* said Luz. *They'll legalise abortion! Colombia will become communist!* they replied.

I remembered her tired eyes under her shiny brown fringe, and felt her frustration as she described not being able to talk about what was actually *in* the peace deal, because everyone was focussed on the scare stories. The bits she really wanted to talk about were the measures that sought to address the unequal impact of the armed conflict on women. Luz worked for a women's rights NGO, and was excited because this was the first peace process in the world to have a gender focus. But in her campaigning, she never managed to get to those gender measures, because evangelical churches had told people the peace deal would impose 'gender ideology', which people thought would destroy the 'traditional Colombian family – "whatever that is", said Luz – so any mention of gender and peace was dynamite.

At home in Oxford, I couldn't stop thinking about Luz. I thought her story could show an international readership something about Colombia, but also, perhaps, something about themselves. I didn't want to depict

Colombia as a faraway, exotic country, to be studied for global north curiosity, but as a mirror for societies like my own, struggling to understand whether something about politics today really was more divisive, as so many people seemed to think, and if so, what that something was.

But I was stuck in the writing. I was trying to cover too much political and historical context, and it was getting in the way of this human story. Without the context, it was hard to explain it all—but maybe I was explaining too much. Maybe explaining was the problem.

I looked out of the window at the stone heads round the Sheldonian Theatre. They gazed into the café, without eyelids or pupils.

A green notification popped up on my laptop from WhatsApp. I clicked on it, pleased to have a distraction. It was a message from my cousin, Alex.

Have you seen the protests?

Alex was a digital nomad. He travelled from one country to another, doing something with data that I didn't understand, which he could do out of California, Ireland, Croatia. He was currently in Chiang Mai, Thailand, which I knew as his Instagram was full of pictures of him working on his MacBook by a lily-pad-laden jungle lake, and meditating in temples. I was jealous of his lifestyle—I wanted to meditate in a Thai temple—but I also caught myself sometimes feeling ever-so-slightly judgemental. His relationship to these countries was so shallow, he didn't speak the languages or study the history, he just hung out in co-working spaces with other middle-class Europeans and Americans for a few months before moving on to the next place. But I felt guilty for thinking this, because Alex was my closest cousin, and he was my ally in the family on the issue of health and wellness.

We shared an interest in alternative medicine and spirituality. I had a long-term health condition which Western medicine had exacerbated. After three years of living with chronic fatigue, brain fog, headaches, insomnia, and gut issues, I'd eventually managed to reverse it, by learning a more holistic view of the body than the one the doctors who had tried to deal with it had, and coming off the medication they had given me, using a combination of yoga, diet, and a deeper awareness of my energy ebb and flow that I couldn't quite put into words. This was a profound change on a bodily level and I felt different inside my skin, though the symptoms had echoes, and recovery wasn't linear. Alex too had a taste for all things natural, and had recently gone vegan—partly to oppose his parents, who believed it wasn't healthy.

The rest of the family were scientists, and they tended to be dogmatic about medicine. If something wasn't proven with published research, it was snake oil, and anyone buying into it was an idiot.

Alex and I often exchanged podcasts, meditation tracks, or news links about functional medicine. But this message didn't seem to be about alternative health.

What protests?

I wrote.

In Oxford

About?

There's a big protest going on right now in Oxford about 15min cities

I could hear murmuring from the street, but Broad Street often hums with noise from tourist groups, students, or lecturers picketing on the steps of the Clarendon Building. I hadn't taken any notice.

I went over to the window and saw a river of people filling Broad Street with banners, St George's Cross flags, and mysterious yellow flags with smiley faces, heading slowly toward St Giles. A man with a shaved head and a megaphone walking past the Sheldonian shouted, "Research the World Economic Forum!" The heads gazed over him. A yellow placard bobbed above the crowd saying "NO TO 15 MIN CITY! COMMUNISM! WE DO NOT CONSENT".

I packed up my laptop and went downstairs, through the bookshop and out into the street, messaging Alex on my phone as I walked.

Just seen it I think. On Broad St. What's it about?

"*Alex is typing...*" said my phone.

There were thousands of people on the street.

I was used to Colombian protests. When I was studying and teaching at the National University in Bogotá, the campus often got evacuated because of student strikes, which brought riot police and violent clashes. I got used to the taste of tear gas. Oxford felt like another world. But in the three years I'd been living here, I'd never seen a protest this big. There had been teachers' union marches down the High Street earlier that month, but those were nothing in comparison.

A woman in a t-shirt saying "Take Democracy Back" handed me a flyer. "Do your research! No climate lockdown!" she told me, and moved on. It was a map of Oxford with red stop signs in seven places, labelled "LTN road closures". Underneath it said, *Looking at this map, ask yourself...Where's my freedom of movement? How will I get from A to B? What about school runs?*

I had heard about controversies in Oxford over Low Traffic Neighbourhoods, or LTNs – a county council scheme to reduce traffic, banning cars between 7am and 7pm through specific streets, sending them along alternative routes. The idea was to reduce commuter congestion: distances that ought to take ten or fifteen minutes on the bus could sometimes take an hour. Some people would be exempt from the bans: health workers, disabled blue badge holders, people who needed to go to hospital often. Local residents would get 100 free exemptions a year.

Some measures like this were already in place. Roads were blocked off with oversized wooden planters or bollards – which were sometimes driven over or set on fire by people who felt they should be free to drive anywhere. These new controls would be done by cameras with number plate recognition technology. If anyone drove past them without a permit they would be fined £70.

Anna, an elderly family friend who had lived here since the seventies, agreed that reducing traffic in Oxford was urgent, but she told me the controls had made traffic worse – journeys that used to take five minutes now took forty, as people had to go round the ring road – and local businesses were getting fewer customers. The LTNs would aggravate this, she said, because there hadn't been a proper consultation about where to put them. And, she added, it seemed too much of a coincidence that these restrictions were being rolled out in East Oxford, the poorest part of the city, not in affluent areas like Summertown.

Were all these people really here to protest about that?

I looked at my phone. Alex had replied:

Really important protest against the concept of 15 minute cities which is being imposed all over the world. It's confusing, I don't understand it all yet, but from what I've read it seems to be about trying to control people and restrict movement under the climate change banner.

This sounded a bit conspiracy theory-ish. Alex was intelligent and well-read — he had a history degree from Oxford, and he cared about the environment. I hadn't seen him in a while—the last time was at a yoga retreat we went on together in Portugal just before the pandemic, where we did morning vinyasa flows together and swam in the sea, and compared notes on our parents' relationships with our grandmother, which were complicated in different ways, as she was not an easy woman. She had left imprints on her children, and we had experienced their reverberations. My energetic memory of Alex from that trip was of a light, mellow presence—a calmness that was warm and pleasant to be around. I admired his serenity; he seemed at peace with himself. Admittedly we hadn't spoken much since as he was rarely in the UK, but we WhatsApped regularly. I couldn't believe he would have suddenly become a climate change sceptic. Such a dramatic change would have been noticeable, surely?

Do you mean the traffic filter things?

What traffic filters?

So he didn't know about the LTNs. How were they connected to this 15 minute city business? And why did Alex in his co-working space in Chiang Mai know about a protest happening in Oxford anyway?

Gonna have a look round the protest will keep you posted

Cool

I started walking alongside the slow-flowing march, watching. Almost all the people were white and middle age plus. I scanned their placards.

"Net zero restriction of movement!"

"No to communist technology"

"REJECT THE NEW WORLD ORDER"

"15 min city is a dystopian HELL"

"There is no climate emergency!"

"Carbon lockdowns"

"Mandate FREEDOM"

"JEWS WILL NOT REPLACE US!"

"HM Prison Oxford"

"#Celebrate CO_2!"

And: "You can stick your 15 minute cities up your ass".

I was drawn to a man in a long white tunic with a red dragon on the chest who was holding forth near me to a group of followers, also in white tunics. He had a white beard and long white hair, crowned with a silver tiara with a dragon flanked by Celtic crosses on his forehead.

"Covid lockdowns were a blueprint to see how easily people would be manipulated into being scared and staying at home", he shouted. "I've been deep, deep down into the covid scam, believe me."

The followers nodded. "Eco-fascism!" someone said. "It's all connected!".

"They want to enslave us", the man continued. "We'll be imprisoned in fifteen-minute zones. Yeah it's with cars now, but you can see where things are going. Today it's Oxford, but tomorrow it'll be London, Canterbury, the whole country!"

A woman wearing a black sweater that said "4G=10ghz 5G=60-100ghz", holding a yellow smiley face flag, tried to fall into step with him. "It's locking people into townships, creating ghettos!" She had a Yorkshire accent – these weren't Oxford people. What were they doing here?

One white tunic-ed guy in a long purple cloak shushed her. "He's the reincarnation of King Arthur!" he said, pointing at the bearded man. The woman frowned. "What?" she said. "King Arthur! We're druids, we're trying to listen to him."

King Arthur grinned at the woman and gave her a little bow. "King Arthur Uther Pendragon, at your service!" he said. "But it's the twenty-first century, so King Arthur rides an Italian motorbike for his iron steed!

'Cause I can't take a horse on a motorway. But I'm carrying on Arthur's work of fighting injustice, and that means fighting the government!"

The woman backed away slowly into the crowd. I saw a yellow star on her arm, which said "UNVAXXED" in faux Hebrew lettering.

I overtook King Arthur and the druids, and came to a group of men with a black flag saying "Tribe of Leicestershire", who held open a long banner saying "GLOBALIST PUPPETS" with photos of the former prime minister and three others, captioned "Boris Jobdone, Pissed Whitty, Prat Hancock, Patric Fallace" (sentiments I could get on board with) and beneath that, "WANTED for the crime of mass murder by injection and other crimes against humanity". They were wearing yellow stars too.

A grey-haired lady walked past me pasting stickers onto lampposts and street signs. They said *CASH is FREEDOM, USE it or LOSE it! Government is planning to introduce programmable digital currency. Digital ID is the trap to control your money.* A woman banging a drum followed, chanting, "Do you want to live in a fifteen-minute prison? Because that's what's coming to you! Stand up! Research! Your local council is being controlled. You are going to be guinea pigs and then it will spread all over the country. Wake up! Learn the facts! Unite! Resist!"

I looked again at my flyer, and followed a QR code at the bottom, which took me to theoxfordcollection.co.uk. A statement there from a group of local businesses said they supported reducing emissions and encouraging walking and cycling, but objected to the new traffic filters, because a proper consultation hadn't been done. There was nothing about communism or covid.

A guy in a paper mask made out of a photograph of an old man with glasses came up to me and hissed, "Do you eat ze bugs?" in a fake German (I guessed) accent. I raised my eyebrows. "Do you eat bugs?" he repeated. "No," I replied. "Good!" he said, and handed me a newspaper. Behind him, an elderly skinhead with a Swastika tattooed on his earlobe yelled through a megaphone: "Research this man! Klaus Schwab! Chairman of the World Economic Forum! They want you to eat bugs! Research agenda 2030!"

The newspaper was called *The Light*. Its subtitle was "The uncensored truth". The cover story was about COVID-19 vaccines altering your DNA.

Had a local protest about this city planning issue, which, as I knew, had caused real disputes, been hijacked by conspiracy theorists? That was what had happened in Colombia with the gender ideology scandal. When conservative Catholic groups protested about a Ministry of Education leaflet teaching tolerance toward different sexual orientations, right-wing politicians who opposed the peace process with the FARC joined their march and said that this was "gender ideology", and claimed it was part of the peace talks. They managed to confuse people's outrage about sexual diversity with the real "gender focus" of the peace deal.

Luz's NGO printed leaflet summaries of the gender provisions and handed them out on the street—but people accused her of being a communist, because they saw the peace process as left-wing. They didn't even want to read the leaflets. One guy took out a lighter and burned it in front of her, accusing her of hating men. People didn't trust the government's explanations about the peace process either. In the coffee region, said Luz, people trusted their church leaders more than anyone else, and, while some priests gave over their weekly bible study group to studying the peace agreement, others told people they had to vote against the peace deal or they would go to hell. Getting people to conflate opposition to sexual diversity education with opposition to the peace deal had been key to the success of the 'No' vote in the referendum.

Was the same thing happening in Oxford? If so, who was behind it?

I sat on a bench outside Balliol and googled "15-minute cities Oxford". I discovered it was an urban planning concept which had been adopted by the Oxford City Council's development plan, to "ensure that every resident has all the essentials (shops, healthcare, parks) within a 15-minute walk of their home". The LTNs were different – they were a traffic control measure by the Oxfordshire County Council to reduce traffic, a long-standing demand from residents.

I opened the newspaper I had been given. The first headline read "Earth is cooling, not warming", and showed a graph of satellite temperature records from the University of Alabama. I turned the pages. Each went deeper down the rabbit hole. "Artificial intelligence to bring about dystopia: Build unconnected devices to avoid losing our free will". This theme of freedom, over and over again. "Innocent schoolchildren in Wales to eat insect-based protein". So that what was bothering the guy in the mask, asking if I ate bugs. The article was accompanied by a cartoon of a pink octopus with the same bald head and glasses as his mask face, straddling the world, clasping in its tentacles a syringe, a mask, and a brown paper bag labelled "happy meal" with a picture of a grasshopper. The caption said "Klaus Schwab, head of the World Economic Forum".

The centrefold was a double-page spread titled "Has man been to the moon?" with several text boxes against the backdrop of a photo of the moon-landing, each with a different argument to "disprove" it. The "debunking" continued on the next page, with the headline "No such thing as a sexually transmitted disease", and an article claiming, "there is no evidence that any germ is the cause of illness".

The next page showed two side-by-side photos of Cadbury's Crème Eggs with measuring sticks next to them and the caption "Shrinkflation". It said they had shrunk since the 1990s, apparently part of a plan by the global technocratic elite to take things that ordinary people loved away from them and increase their wealth.

Even in Colombia I hadn't seen rubbish like this. Polarisation had followed me back home to Oxford.

Alongside the articles were adverts: for a clothing company that offered "high performance radiation protection" jackets, holistic health services for "vaccine-damaged" people, an investment plan for buying gold and silver coins for those "uncomfortable having money in the bank at a time of global uncertainty", a "detox and reboot" remedy, and an expensive organic skincare range I used myself. Since my health condition I had switched to using only non-toxic products, which meant no endocrine-disrupting ingredients. My uncle, Alex's dad, who was a gynaecologist, had pooh-poohed this and said it was nonsense; I should just get back on the pill to fix my symptoms—but Alex had my back, he sent his dad a long list of articles in proper scientific journals about long-term hormonal imbalances associated with the pill, and news articles about the increasing recognition in the mainstream medical community of functional medicine approaches.

On the last page, there was an ad for the *The Trap*, the latest book by David Icke, the man behind the conspiracy theory about lizard-people and Jews ruling the world. I knew about that because my high-school boyfriend had been a believer. I had joked for years about the fact I'd once dated someone who believed the Queen Mother was a reptilian shape-shifter. I hadn't taken it seriously.

"Belief" is a problematic word. It can make us condescending towards others – we think we know better. As anthropologist Johannes Fabian put it, "why do we know and they believe?"

I wrote to Alex:

This march is pure conspiracy theory! My guess is that it was originally meant to be a protest against low traffic neighbourhoods. There's legitimate local opposition to this plan – some people think it will make traffic worse and affect local businesses. But climate change deniers have hijacked the protest. They are saying mad things like the council is going to lock people into their neighbourhoods and climate change isn't real! There's a guy here who thinks he's King Arthur

I saw a blue tick appear; Alex had read the message. But he didn't reply.

I went home, to carry on writing about Luz. We had kept in touch since that day in the restaurant—she messaged me with updates about the peace process, and I followed her on Instagram, where she posted regular videos in which she talked about the challenges women in politics faced in Colombia: gossip, defamation, discrimination, sexual harassment, threats of rape, and journalists simply leaving them out of news stories. Luz tried to counter this by showcasing little stories about women councillors in the coffee region and the local peace initiatives they were supporting. But comments on her videos used words like "hysterical", "menopausal," "crazy", "whore". I sometimes wrote to her to say how sorry I was she had to deal with such things. She thanked me, and sent sad emojis. She usually didn't respond to the abuse—"I don't want to be seen as difficult", she said. She had thought about going into politics herself, but worried about the safety of her teenage son. One female political candidate she knew was sent a decapitated doll, red nail varnish round its broken neck. She withdrew her candidacy. "Maybe when my son is older," said Luz. I wondered if, in her place, I would have her courage to stand up for my beliefs.

I was still grappling with how to describe Luz's frustrations, without being condescending toward the people she was talking to, who "believed" the disinformation about gender ideology. I didn't want be the British researcher who sounded like I knew the truth which these Colombians were too stupid to understand. It was objectively true that gender ideology was not in the peace agreement – it wasn't even a real thing. But did that make Luz's opponents wrong to be worried about the peace process?

A few days later, Alex sent me a video. I clicked on it. It was from TikTok, titled "Oxfordshire U.K. 15-minute city pushback". With a dramatic soundtrack, it showed the multitudinous march I'd seen on Broad Street, then cut to a policeman roughly handcuffing a guy, then a wall of mounted police, and a policeman pushing a shouting man in a hoodie. The message was clear: citizen resistance against an oppressive regime.

I did some more googling. I discovered that the '15-minute cities' concept was invented by a Colombian! Carlos Moreno grew up in the midst of war, his family was displaced from their land by the conflict in the countryside, he joined the M19 guerrilla with now-president Gustavo Petro, then fled to France in 1979 to escape political violence. He became a prize-winning urbanist, and this concept of his was being used in Paris to improve quality of life in local neighbourhoods.

I sent some links about him to Alex, and wrote:

15 minute cities is just a concept for people to have all their basic amenities available to them within 15 minutes walk/cycle/local transport. That's a good thing! The climate change deniers are telling people they will have to stay within those zones and not go out. That's not true, it's not about restricting movement. That's disinformation, Alex.

It didn't take long for him to reply—certainly not long enough for him to properly read the articles I'd sent.

So this Carlos Moreno who invented it was a communist guerrilla?

I was shocked. How was someone of my generation, a university graduate, buying into this insane rehashing of the Cold War narrative? That sort of thing was common in Colombia, where there actually was an armed leftist insurgency, but surely not among people like me? And Alex had always identified as left-wing, like the rest of our family. I started to type a reply, explaining that the M19 guerrilla were founded in Colombia in the 90s seeking to open up democracy, they weren't communists, but before I could finish he wrote again:

I've done some more research now, it seems that 15min cities is an international socialist concept that is a direct attack on our personal freedom – just like the covid lockdown, which was a blueprint for it.

He then quickfire forwarded a whole lot of messages each more confusing than the last, some with links, some with pdfs I didn't want to download, others with long paragraphs of writing I scanned briefly, taking in keywords like the World Economic Forum, the Bill and Melinda Gates Foundation, the Great Reset, lockdown, the World Health Organization, NATO, the United Nations, Agenda 2030, mass manipulation, world domination – and COVID-19.

There were too many threads to untangle. It was information-overload, completely unfiltered, and somehow both anti-communist and anti-globalist. But from it all, I gathered that Alex was an anti-vaxxer.

How had I not known? I knew the wellness community was the thin end of a wedge that, with the right algorithms, could lead down a path of YouTube videos toward conspiracy theory. A few of the influencers I followed on Instagram, whose information about metabolism, the nervous system, sleep, hormones and diet had helped me find the route to recovery, had recently started sharing anti-vax views, particularly about the effects of the vaccine on women's bodies, though they were quickly censored, which just made their followers more convinced. I was shocked at first, but of course it made sense, given their view of a body not being tampered with. Many of them had experiences like mine—of Western medicine tampering with their bodies, causing untold harms. Scientific research often didn't take into account the hormonal and physiological differences of female bodies. I unfollowed a couple of the more strident ones, but decided simply to ignore the rest, as I still valued the other things they shared. I didn't have to reject the baby, just the dirty bathwater.

But I had not expected Alex to have gone there.

Have you stopped believing in climate change now? Because the protesters in Oxford were claiming it was a hoax!

Of course not. There are always some crazy people in those marches, sure, but the basic concern is about our freedom of movement.

How could Alex separate out the climate change denialism from the rest of it? I imagined a conspiracy like the pink octopus cartoon in The Light: people can pick some tentacles and not others. Which meant they could bring very different communities together, each with their own issues, and merge them together through the threat of a common enemy. As one of King Arthur's posse had said – "it's all connected".

I know 15 min cities sounds good. Parks and shops and vibrant communities within walking distance. We want all that. But it'll just mean more digitisation of identity, like with the vaccine passports. There are so many globalist corporations like the UN rolling out this concept - they are only interested in money and power.

We are already tracked by so many companies Alex! Think about the data from all your Instagram posts. Facebook etc are collecting all that, and you're worried about some traffic cameras which are trying to reduce cars in a few neighbourhoods!

Sure, Facebook and Microsoft are awful. But governments can centralise all that data and use it to control you. You know, around 30,000 people didn't pay parking tickets last year in Sheffield – amazing non-compliance! But with digital IDs they could link the parking tickets to pensions and stuff, so they might hold back your pension til you paid. That's the sort of dystopia we need to reject.

I thought of my Colombian ID card. You couldn't get any kind of service there without one, even as a foreigner living there temporarily. A SIM card, a bank account, even to go to a meeting in an office of any kind you had to sign in with its number at the front desk. It was just part of life. And what was this rubbish about non-compliance? I thought of the rural community in a war zone in Colombia I'd lived in as an anthropologist, who refused to collaborate with state armed forces, because of human rights abuses by the army. It was crass to compare their Gandhian nonviolent resistance with people who simply didn't want to pay their parking tickets in England.

But Alex was on a roll.

Remember when we were little, and TV went digital and they created parental controls? Remember our parents never used them. They taught us to be responsible and they trusted us to make our own decisions. The government is treating us like children. We need to resist this top-down imposition and build our own communities instead.

I wanted to write back, *and how are you going to do that if you never spend more than three months in one place? Isn't your digital nomadism precisely the opposite of building local community?* But I didn't want to fight. I decided not to reply. I didn't want to say something mean when I was feeling angry.

Alex cared about freedom – it was why he became a digital nomad; he said he wanted to be untethered from national identity and the artificial restrictions of borders. He wasn't stupid: he was aware of his privilege, and the irony that he had this freedom because of his British passport. But what about the freedom of people to live free from pollution and climate disaster?

This thing about freedom of movement had become a trigger for darker fears, in Oxford of all places, already practically a fifteen-minute city – after the hour-long traffic jams of Bogotá, being able to walk and cycle everywhere here was a dream, although I lived in town, and I knew not everyone here had that luxury. Yet like all conspiracy theories, there was some sense in Alex's vision. The surveillance state, the top-down policies made by remote elites out of touch with the lives of ordinary people, the distrust in government, corporations out for their own economic interests. I could even understand some of the vaccine hesitancy. I had no hesitation in getting vaccinated myself (I got regular jabs of various sorts anyway for all my travel to Colombia), but I knew some people who had experienced bad side effects. My friend Anna's husband had died days after having his jab. He was in his eighties and had been unwell for a few years, but had been getting better until the vaccine. He walked into the vaccine centre, but had to be wheelchaired out, as he lost his ability to stand. Anna wasn't anti-vax though—just deeply sad.

But all that didn't make it OK to stand on the side of climate change deniers. For me, that was a red line. The political implications were too great.

Over the next few days, I saw more and more newspaper articles about the Oxford protests. Local politicians received death threats – just like some of my interviewees in Colombia, where doing politics required an armoured car and bodyguards. Some resigned, out of fear for their lives. One city councillor, interviewed on a YouTube documentary, described his bewilderment at the backlash to the 15-minute city concept. "What's more English than a corner shop?" he asked.

In one article, I read that the protest had been promoted by right-wing celebrities and activists – Laurence Fox, Katie Hopkins, Tommy Robinson. They had encouraged people across the country to go to Oxford and join, which is why I had heard so many different accents that day. I sent a link about this to Alex, saying:

These are the people you should be suspicious of!

He replied:

Really worrying, but this is a big tension for me – the Left is largely silent on covid. I've even seen a few Tory MPs and Republican senators as heroes for speaking out, despite getting attacked for it. And Laurence Fox made a good point about the 15 min city further marginalising people who live at city edges e.g. migrant workers.

Our family was staunchly anti-Conservative. Our grandmother had a special face for when she said the word Tory – her nose scrunched up, and her eyes narrowed. She, and our parents, were open to whatever we wanted to do, so long as we didn't bring home a Tory friend or – worse – partner. One of my earliest memories was the 1990 general election, walking around our neighbourhood spotting the red and yellow Labour banners. I liked Labour because my parents did, and because it sounded like "Labrador". I couldn't believe Alex would support anything Tory.

Left and right were getting confused. Perhaps the whole idea of a binary opposition was misleading. Perhaps these labels we lived with prevented us seeing the nuances of people's opinions. After all, left-wing and right-wing meant very different things to different people, I had documented this in my Colombia research – so how helpful were they really, if they encouraged us to put people in boxes and assume things about them? It certainly wasn't helpful when Alex's dad put all alternative health approaches in the same box and called *that* disinformation.

Alex's messages kept coming – links to videos on alternative news sites and articles with odd misspellings, mostly mass-forwarded to all his contacts. I tried to take him seriously and read and respond to some of them, but gave up after a while because he didn't engage with my comments or read anything I sent him – he just sent new articles. "This one has over a hundred references," he said, as if that made it more valid.

Luz's husband was anti-peace accord – his father was a rich landowner who produced coffee and exported it to the EU, and he worked in the family business. They had been married fifteen years and he had always been right-wing, but their political differences had intensified over the peace process. "Sometimes I said to him, don't talk to me about your criticisms to the peace deal, it's part of my job; it's like me coming home to criticise your coffee production", she told me. "But it's a national issue," he replied, "How am I not going to have an opinion?" It was worse when they went to visit his parents, because they repeated all the crazy disinformation mantras and were full of hatred for the FARC and the government who was negotiating with them. "Sometimes I think that when two people have such different opinions, talking to each other just makes them get more and more entrenched in their position", she said. But they had other things in common; they shared a whole life project together, and they agreed on what they thought needed to happen in the country – an end to the war, more equality, women's empowerment, human rights – they just didn't agree on the means to get there.

If Luz could love her husband despite the real difficulties of navigating this radical difference, and not let it dominate what was otherwise a full and multiplex relationship, I could do the same with Alex.

Perhaps, instead of writing about her, I thought, I should write about Alex and me.

I took a screenshot of my latest blood tests, which showed that for the first time in four years, my hormone levels were all normal, and I WhatsApped it to Alex.

THREE POEMS

Farid Bitar

Pristine Lake

Camping upstate in Long Lake
rain falling in buckets on my tent
eyes wide open all night long
decided to jump into my kayak
at the crack of dawn

misty lake Eaton all around
surrounded by magnificent mountains
cedar pine trees patrolling the waters
rowed all the way to the other side
parked my kayak in the middle East
splitting headache finally gone
the fog started lifting
sunrise with yellow flowers

listening to fish chattering
listening to whispers of Allah
peace came visiting in abundance
while staring at the pristine lake.

Emptiness

A desolate city l live in
loneliness all over
Ukraine
Palestine
Covid 19 still around
never ending nightmare

l stare into the twilight
l have no clue what i observe
l stare into darkness
l glimpse a thread of a light
l stare into emptiness
there is nothing out there
synchronized horizon
rainbow with no colours
spontaneity
the Axis of the universe
converging
like a river running
into calamity
Externals
no more pretending
no more looking inward
no more apprehension
moving on and looking upward

still searching for peace that never comes

Recycled Humans

I have been talking for the past
40 years in exile
5 million more have been demanding
They want to return to the homeland
I'm sick of talking

Politicians do a lot of crapping
UN meets and does more talking
They live in villas in Switzerland
While Palestinians are living in camps
Still talking

I need to do a lot more walking
I need to forget about more talking
I need to teach my people walking
Till we reach the shores of Gaza
Then our journey Shall begin

Walking
Talking
Forget about talking.

LA RABBIA

Pier Paolo Pasolini

Pier Paolo Pasolini (1922–1975), the Italian Marxist film director, was a towering polymath who made a significant contribution to shaping the intellectual and political landscape of the twentieth century. Pasolini distinguished himself as a journalist, novelist, playwright, essayist, artist and actor. His films, including *The Gospel According to St Matthew* (1964), *Theorem* (1968), *The Decameron* (1971) and *The Canterbury Tales* (1972), won high praise and awards at various film festivals.

Pasolini created *La rabbia (Anger)* in 1962, following a producer's request to write a commentary for a large, diverse cache of newsreel footage. He crafted a hundred pages of elegiac prose and verse, a texture of moving images, photographs and painting reproductions, experimenting for the first time with a form differing from the conventions of traditional film narrative and documentary. In his own words, what he wanted to create was 'a new film genre. To make a poetic and ideological essay with new sequences.' *La rabbia* was meant as 'an act of indignation against the unreality of the bourgeois world and its consequent historical irresponsibility—a record of the presence of a world that, unlike the bourgeois world, has a deep grasp of reality. Reality: a true love of tradition, as only revolution can give.'

46.
Algeria. New flights and air raids. People fleeing. Burnt corpse. Child crying.

Buzzing
in the sky of Algeria
is a crisis
that recreates death

and in the search

for a new freedom
wants victims
whose victory is certain!

Ah, France,
the hatred!

Ah, France,
the plague!

Ah, France,
the cowardice!

A hideous,
idiotic,
obscene buzzing,
a music
that finales into a child's trauma,
into a sob that wrecks the world.

48.
Algeria: paratroopers on patrol

At the core of a war
there is something
survivors
will remember all their life
like a heady tang of arson.

French and German soldiers
are mixed into the future
with the burning elation of death:
emblems of what life
like a monument of earth and blood
owns at the core of a war.

54.
Algeria: new series of tortured and brutalised people

On the desert nomads
on the farm hands of Medina
on the wage slaves of Oran
on the petty clerks of Algiers
I write your name.

On the wretched people of Algeria
on the illiterate peoples of Arabia
on the underclass of Africa
on the enslaved people of the sub proletarian world
I write your name

O freedom!

(Here, Pasolini echoes Paul Éluard's famous poem 1942 *Liberté*)

55.
Algeria: celebrating the liberation

Joy after after joy,
victory after victory!

People of colour,
Algeria is returned to history!

People of colour,
it lives the best days of its life!

Never will the light in their eyes shine purer,
never will happy gestures be more loving!

People of colour, these are the days of victory

for all the partisans in the world!

People of colour, it is in the joy of victory
that Resistance plants its roots and builds the future!

56.
Cut to black
Silence, buzz of an airplane and distant air raids.
After a few instants, the first caption.
Captions

Joy.
But so much inextinguishable terror.
In a thousand parts of the world.
And in our memory.
In a thousand parts of the soul, the war is not over.
Even if we don't, don't want to remember, war
is a terror that won't stop, in the soul, in the world.

Extracted from Pier Paolo Pasolini, *La rabbia / Anger,*
translated by Cristina Viti, Tenement Press, 2022.

REVIEWS

PHILOSOPHY'S PATHOLOGIES

Zain Sardar

What's wrong with philosophy? Does it have any relevance to contemporary problems and issues?

Noted British philosopher, Philip Kitcher, tackles these questions head on. He makes no distinction between the analytic and continental strands. But offers a somewhat clinical diagnosis of the multiple neuroses afflicting analytic philosophy in the contemporary moment. *What's the Use of Philosophy?* can be seen as manifesto-cum-toolkit for reform of philosophy as a discipline. But – perhaps strikingly - the work is unintentionally evocative of a subtle association between madness and philosophical thought that has marked the discipline at least in its European form.

In Ancient Greece, being possessed with a 'divine madness' was seen as a blessing from the gods. This was a popular view that received public endorsement from Plato in his Socratic dialogues. Hence, in the *Phaedrus*, Socrates extolls madness in its variety of manifestations: in love, in poetry, and in religious ritual and devotion, where the latter can be truly cathartic and bring solace in times of hardship. While madness was not a key ingredient in philosophical thinking, its status was still elevated outside philosophy in its ability to stimulate creativity and enhance perception and consciousness.

At the advent of modern western philosophy, madness can be detected as a spectral presence in Descartes' formulation of the thinking subject and his accompanying methodology, supposedly grounding knowledge upon a process that culminates in clear and distinct ideas. Descartes' thought is given a stimulus through his interplay with a hypothetical, sceptical interlocutor; the philosopher's sparring partner, who assumes the role of asking provocative questions, such as in expressing radical doubt on whether the subject can have any access to an external reality beyond itself. Curiously enough, as noticed by Michel Foucault, the French philosopher and historian of ideas, the means by which Descartes discounts the notion that the subject may be enthralled to a reality distorting madness, differs markedly from his argument dismissing the possibility of the subject's dream induced deception. Madness is seen, by its very nature, as exterior to thought; it is excluded in aprioristic fashion as outside the very conditions required for sound cognition. Not only is madness beyond the confines of philosophy; it is also a pure negation of the thinking person per se. In contradistinction, with the dreamer, truth always re-emerges as grounds for doubt. Simply by doubting one is dreaming, the critical and thinking subject irrepressibly springs forth once again.

Philip Kitcher, *What's the Use of Philosophy*, Oxford University Press, 2023.

It is worth noting how the methodology deployed in the process of coming to clear and distinct ideas within analytic philosophy, taken to excess, acts as one of the pathologies Kitcher identifies within the discipline. Far from being a creative impulse, as it was for Plato, madness materialises within philosophical practice as a form of neurasthenia. To elaborate, madness resurfaces in the obsessive quest for an absolute clarity of ideas - of continuously refining concepts and the terminology which expresses them - something which will always, ultimately, evade the philosopher's grasp. And while many would subscribe to the notion that concepts possess an inherent mutability and dynamism, a quality which ought to stimulate their re-evaluation over time within new contexts, the analytic process is more concerned with attempting to apply a final fixity to concepts through increasingly meaningless layers of granularity. Under these circumstances, madness almost becomes one of the prerequisites for thought within the discipline; far from being on the outside of thought, it is internalised within institutionalised approaches to philosophy.

This is expanded upon in Kitcher's chapter on the 'pathology report', as he assesses a number of acute syndromes endemic to philosophy. Alongside the fetishism of 'complete clarity', he adds the tendency for superfluous formalisation: the unnecessary usage of pseudo-mathematical formulas to lay bare the cognitive, logical calculations behind judgements. Furthermore, he takes issue with the proliferation of hypothetical cases or thought experiments to test concepts or ethical principles; most particularly scenarios that become more and more estranged from the textured nature of the reality they act as abstract surrogates for. In the American pragmatist school, concepts are tools that have a social application; continuously tinkering with them losses sight of this. In Kitcher's view, this is an outcome of a rigid Neo-Scholasticism that incentives game-playing technical brilliance over meaningful advances of substantial projects.

Kitcher's stance brings to mind the eloquent critique of 'disciplinary decadence' by Lewis Gordon, the Afro-American philosopher of race, racism and Black existentialism. Gordon's criticism aptly centres on the propensity for methodologies and schematic models to 'turn away from living thought and engagement with reality' to avoid coming face to face with their 'own limitations'. Put differently, the totalising pretensions of the 'core' of analytic philosophy have unmoored themselves from the world; preferring the internal monologue to meaningful and reflective engagement with contemporary issues. In accentuating what is at stake here, Kitcher is fond of quoting the twentieth century American pragmatist philosopher John Dewy's warning that philosophy could well become a 'sentimental indulgence for a few'.

Thus we encounter Kitcher's prospectus for revitalisation of the grand old discipline, which seeks to save philosophy from the madness that continually threatens to turn it into a cloistered and isolated undertaking. He attempts to turn it back from making, in the alluring phraseology of late Columbian magical realist novelist Gabriel Garzia Marquez, an 'honourable pact with solitude'.

Therefore, Kitcher seeks to recharge philosophy by reconnecting it to a wider horizon of public and social utility. Or in his words, to enable it to better 'serve human ends'. Moreover, he attempts to strengthen the ties between philosophy and a wider vocational mission of guiding ethical life and facilitating moral advancement in society. That is, to make philosophy instrumental to the 'progressive ethical projects of the time.' In many respects, he sets out to recapture a scale of ambition that was, he argues, last realised in the Enlightenment philosophers, such as Kant, Hegel, and Marx; the principal source from which both traditions in philosophy trace themselves back. But he proposes to do this in a way which, perhaps, tries to avoid or at least does not consciously recreate the grand totalising projects of modernity and the Enlightenment. There is a sense that much of the analytic school has turned its back on the rich - even if highly contested and problematically Eurocentric - philosophical inheritance of the great synthesisers of the Western canon. He advocates for the need to reclaim this inheritance by outlining an animating purpose for the discipline, linking it with, in his opinion, the most productive specialist areas of philosophy. These are the 'peripheral' and emergent subdisciplines that tackle and develop approaches to the defining issues of our time: climate change, race equality, biotechnology.

One ought to add to this list Artificial Intelligence (AI) and machine learning, as the scope for technological development in this field is extensive and threatens to transform our world within the next decade without any ethical oversight at all (in same way as communications technology in the noughties). One already sees this with the use and generation of language model algorithms and their ductile ability to adapt to human interaction, the most well-known example being ChatGPT, developed by the tech corporate, OpenAI. There is a strong sense that these models, left to their own devices, serve only to enhance the biases inherent in society, rather than sidestepping them in a form of some 'technological neutrality'. The input of philosophical reasoning in technical design processes, to draw out unintended consequences and firmly ground models in an ethical framework, will be crucial to widening the scope of a discourse that can be too narrowly conceived in terms of technological teething problems. Sam Altman, the CEO of OpenAI, has already gone on record in admitting he is somewhat 'scared' of the real dangers posed to humanity by AI, citing the potential widespread propagation of disinformation as a cause for concern. In his plea for regulators and society to be involved in blunting the unsettling elements of AI, one should reiterate the need for philosophical input. AI – somewhat surprisingly overlooked by Kitcher as one of the defining challenges of our time - proves the perfect example of the type of emerging field that could work against society-wide moral advancement.

The suggestion from Kitcher is then that philosophy ought to redirect itself towards its most critical marginal areas. He also points to some fecund areas of thought: some of the larger subdisciplines like the philosophy of science have already demonstrated the capacity to help refine developments in scientific methodology and in ethical considerations. On the general methodological level, historians of science such as Thomas Kuhn and Karl Popper are cited as having already shown this in their ability to conduct influential public debates, accessible to a wide audience, on areas of scientific practice. In the arena of the newly forged specialist sciences, Kitcher's states that philosophy comes into its element as 'midwife' in clarifying new methodological approaches and conceptual challenges. In contrast, what comes in for Kitcher's ire is the 'core' elements of philosophy such as analytic epistemology, theory of mind, and philosophy of language. This constitutes an inert topology – the hollow centre – that abandons its responsibilities to shepherd emerging areas of interest in both the specialist sciences as well as new key areas of sociological theory. In many ways, this line of argument tries to reposition philosophy as a truly transdisciplinary endeavour, arresting its retreat and placing it within the gaps opened up along the newly formed frontiers of knowledge.

And perhaps as an echo of the Kantian 'revolution' that posited the stability of the subject orbited by the objects of perception, Kitcher is eager to bring about an inversion between the core/centre and periphery/ margins within philosophy. Hence, we read of the significance attributed to such fields as Critical Race Theory (CRT) in shaping public perceptions and social attitudes. And while I wholeheartedly concur with the cutting-edge importance he attributes to CRT – with its focus on the intersectionality of identity, lived experience, and storytelling narratives – it is worth mentioning that it has been largely influenced by legal and critical theory, fields more at home with the continental strand of philosophy, than any of the emerging areas of analytic philosophy. But perhaps this is exactly the point; that the analytic tradition needs to meaningfully engage with these new, radical strands of thought in a more productive manner rather than seemingly neglecting them.

Kitcher arrives at a formula for a refreshed philosophy as 'partial synthesis'; coalescing different strands of thought from across disciplines, not to offer a comprehensive worldview or new ideological perspective, but to produce valuable insight into a well-defined, but nonetheless salient, contemporary issues. The formulation is: humility in scale; ambition in impact. This allows him to deftly sidestep the total, grand synthesisers of the modernist project while still laying claim to a level of ambition, recharging this current of the Western philosophical inheritance within the analytic/anglophone tradition. The approach can be used to make sense of the contemporary postnormal times, as it is better and more closely situated amongst the thicket of pressing challenges that comprise the historical conjecture, shedding a different light on them and in so doing, generating new perspectives and possibilities. The impetus behind this is for philosophy to fulfil a 'genuine need', rather than being sucked into the type of institutional research activity that results in 'gap-filling' papers and publications that adorn the dusty shelves of university libraries. This is the compulsive 'hyper-functionalism' that he discerns is leading to the churning out of countless volumes of works, regrettably devoid of a greater purpose.

In sum, this is a call for a mission centred philosophy capable of fulfilling social needs, and in which the synthetic energy of new combinations of ideas maintains its close interaction with the world, shaping real world consequences. Aligned to this, Kitcher seeks research frameworks that are action-oriented (the influence of Pragmatism is clear here) and reflective of the potential represented by emerging, exciting subdisciplines. Towards the latter third of the book, there is a sense that the author is also grappling with the deep-rooted institutional pathology of the academy, which goes beyond the perceived malaise within philosophy. Hence his plea for the instituting of a new 'public philosophy', which is conceived of as carrying more capacity for directly influencing public policy and governance through plugging critical thought directly into the decision-making process. Beyond the academy, a new public philosophy brings the discipline nearer to informing areas of governmentality.

Perhaps unsurprising then, the final chapter of *The Use of Philosophy* gives some practical career guidance to anxious young philosophers who are devoted to the project of transforming the discipline. Yet, Kitcher is concerned with how this may affect their employment prospects in a now highly professionalised line of work. Many young scholars seeking to challenge the status quo of powerful academic interests may well raise this question in light of the intensifying constraints that they are placed under. There is a feeling here that Kitcher is politely raging against the worrying trends which are accelerating within higher education; what could be characterised as the problematic, institutional pathology that grips much of the academic establishment. In the UK context, this has been charted by the likes of the Cambridge historian Stephan Collini, who points to a sector which is being reshaped by the casualisation of the academic workforce, a narrowing regulatory focus on measuring the economic impact of research, and fierce competition causing high rates of burnout and fatigue. Many of these trends have been firmly entrenched within the United States for some time, which gives aspiring philosophers even less leeway to rebel against their superiors within institutional settings.

At the centre of this discussion is an unedifying paradox: Kitcher proposes what one imagines to be a vocational mission for philosophy; however, the overly professionalised nature of the discipline renders this noble aim out of reach for the vast majority of academic philosophers. The advice he gives in thinking through the ways to navigate this challenge attempts to strike a compromise position between conforming to imposed academic practices and expectations on the one hand and breaking with the conventional approaches altogether on the other. Kitcher fully acknowledges his own privileged position as Professor Emeritus of Columbia University and in his ability to speak his mind without fear of penalty from institutional authority, and so treads very self-consciously and with a great deal of care when offering his wise counsel. He works through a menu of options: such as bursting the confines of the academy through seeking alternative sites of knowledge production, taking philosophy to the streets through social projects (in prisons, in schools, etc.) in the manner of an organic intellectual or social worker peddling a curative philosophy amongst the masses. Other routes involve facilitating the slow reform of the academy by playing to its rules in a way reminiscent of the Russian composer Dmitri Shostakovich's compliance with communist party ideology and Soviet artistic orthodoxy - the aesthetic of social realism. That is to say, practicing a form of subversive compliance which still leaves room for transformative projects (the partial synthesis mode of philosophy) either from the very outset of one's career or at a point when a reputation has been duly secured. The idea with this strategy is that eventually a critical mass – or a 'community of rebels' – is reached when enough tenured track philosophers can pool together to effect the wholescale reform the discipline so desperately needs. Further reform could be given a boost with the development of institutional infrastructure – scholarships and centres of excellence reserved for furthering the aims of fostering a public philosophy.

With Kitcher's final chapter we return once again to the lurking madness readily incubated within philosophy itself, and which threatens to consume it from within. Reforming the discipline, it would seem, is inherently tied to the wider transformation of the academic establishment itself. Changes in philosophy necessitate institutional renewal as well. This is what leads me to the conviction that in many ways the madness of philosophy is due to its deeply traumatised psyche. Its obsession with itself and its growing solitude is a natural result of a siege mentality in reaction to an academy that has become increasingly market oriented, professionalised, and instrumentalised.

In relation to the wider institutional context, the British sociologist Roger Burrows has made an insightful point. Borrows observed that sociologists were encouraged to engage critical reflexivity in their own practice, but the same did not appear to apply to the 'very conditions and settings of knowledge production.' This is also relevant to Philosophy. It is a discipline that is desperately struggling to find its place alongside the other fields being reshaped by the forces of academic capitalism. Kitcher says that philosophy is 'currently an isolated discipline within a larger cluster of academic fields', situated amongst the 'besieged' humanities, which are always in the line of fire when university budgets are cut. As I have stated, the isolation of the discipline – or at least of its 'core' - has also a lot to do with its own self-imposed exile. One is reminded of the final haunting words of Gabriel Garza Marquez's breathtaking novel, *One Hundred Years of Solitude,* which sounds a quite eerie warning on this note:

He [Aureliano II] had already understood that he would never leave that room, for it was foreseen that the city of mirrors (or mirages) would be wiped out by the wind and exiled from the memory of men at the precise moment when Aureliano Babilonia would finish deciphering the parchments, and that everything written on them was unrepeatable since time immemorial and forever more, because races condemned to one hundred years of solitude did not have a second opportunity on earth.

BURNT OUT

James Brooks

I lived in Paris for most of the 2000s. For much of that time my then girlfriend worked overseas, and I ended up befriending her mother: a diminutive, chatty, and sharply analytical Egyptian woman in late middle-age. We would often discuss French, British, and world current affairs from across our generational and political divides. She was mostly centre-right; I leaned social democrat. Our disagreements were generally cordial, which was more thanks to her good humour than mine. But her countenance would darken, and her natural ebullience vanish whenever talk turned to the situation in her home country. 'There is going to be a revolution!' she would say, and I would inwardly scoff at this. Having come of age in the UK in the nineties – a place and time about as far removed from the prospect of political overthrow as any in human history – I could barely conceive of revolution at all, let alone in a large, industrialised economy like Egypt, where autocratic rule had been the accepted norm in a five-decades long existence as a nominal republic.

My ignorance and naivety were made plain just over a year after I left Paris, in the shape of the 25 January revolution. My friend had accurately sketched its outline, with a cast of disaffected and futureless youths primed to burst onstage and an increasingly confident and expectant Muslim Brotherhood waiting in the wings, ready to swoop for power. That last element was why, when she made her pronouncements of imminent revolution, she did so with grim foreboding – my friend was Coptic. What I remember most from her doomy descriptions of Egyptian society was the unifying sense of people having had enough, brought to the brink of endurance by a self-enriching political elite and its repressive security apparatus, by the grind of ubiquitous corruption and deepening impoverishment.

In the slow-boiling build-up to the Arab Spring in Tunisia, Algeria, and Morocco, the concept of *al hogra* came to express such chronic structural oppression. As Meryem Saadi, a Moroccan former journalist and now a researcher of art history, has written, the

> term expresses different feelings ranging from injustice, indignation, resentment, humiliation to oppression. It was originally used in relation to daily life situations, before becoming a more political term that describes a continuing state of contempt and humiliation for the whole society.

Humiliation, of course, is prone to provoke rage that is forbidden to be expressed against its subject, and becomes pressurised and compacted until fit to explode. It is the powder-keg psychological condition.

Mohamed Bouazizi, a street vendor struggling to rescue his family from debt and subject to daily police harassment and extortion, is often given as an archetypal example of *al mahgor* – the person or group subject to *al hogra*. It was Bouazizi's self-immolation in the road in front of the governor's office of Sidi Bouzid in central Tunisia on 17 December 2010 that catalysed the Tunisian revolution, and thus the entire Arab Spring. 'What kind of repression do you imagine it takes for a young man to do this?' his sister Leila asked a Reuters reporter a month later, once Ben Ali had been ousted as president. 'A man who has to feed his family by buying goods on credit when they fine him… and take his goods.' Bouazizi was only twenty-six years old when he died.

Lotfy Nathan, a UK-born, American-raised filmmaker of Coptic Egyptian parentage, had originally hoped to make something like a biopic of Bouazizi when he started researching what eventually became his taut and brilliant debut fictional feature, *Harka*. As I learnt during a Q&A session after a screening at the Institute of Contemporary Arts in London, a couple of things got in the way. There was his desire to incorporate elements from the people he met during frequent stays in Tunisia – that is, people living in circumstances similar to Bouazizi's. Then there was the attendant impulse to set the film in contemporary Tunisia. Ironically, the contemporary setting serves to illustrate how little has changed since Bouazizi's death, beyond the addition of an emergency escape route for desperate young men, on boats across the Mediterranean. The film's title neatly conjoins both this phenomenon and Tunisia's revolutionary origin story. In Tunisia, *harka* is slang for clandestine emigration to Europe, while also meaning 'to burn'.

Bouazizi's updated, fictionalised stand-in in *Harka* is Ali Hamdi, who is not so much played as embodied by Adam Bessa, a French actor of Tunisian parentage. Like Bouazizi, Ali is a man trapped in the intolerable pressure cooker of *al hogra*. And like many young men who came of age after Bouazizi's death, he dreams of escape across the Med. He keeps the payment for that journey – a thick wedge of crinkled dinar – hidden in the wall of the abandoned, unfinished building he lives in. We first see Ali there, stripped to the waist, sweat beading on his body as he fills containers with contraband petrol. You can almost smell the stuff through the screen. Soon afterwards we watch him hawk the fuel in the street before placing some fraction of his takings into the expectant hand of a police officer. As the film continues, we see the lid on Ali's bubbling rage rattle with each successive humiliation: lorded over by a man in a bar who boasts of the opulence he enjoyed living in Germany, hopelessly rebuffed by an official in a government recruitment bureau, and smarting under the superior gaze of tourists in a beachside restaurant in Hammamet during a failed mission to get some of the cash to settle a potentially ruinous family debt.

Harka, directed and written by Lotfy Nathan, produced by Cinenovo and Spacemaker Productions, France/Tunisia, 2022.

Bessa's turn as Ali, which won him the best actor prize in the Un Certain Regard category (for films by emerging directors or in experimental styles) at Cannes last year, is a thing of wonder. As one of the few professionals in a cast who give uniformly excellent naturalistic performances, Bessa could have easily become identifiable as the lone trained actor, especially in such a demanding role. This doesn't happen, and yet he is never less than magnetic throughout, a near-constant fire burning behind his narrowed, hunter's eyes which begins to consume him as his situation grows ever more desperate. In one of several high-risk directorial gambits that Nathan pulls off, the camera repeatedly moves toward Ali as he struggles to master his incendiary anger. Even under such tight focus, we only ever see Ali, never Bessa acting.

Bessa avoids playing Ali, and Nathan does not write him this way, as an overtly 'good' person and therefore easy for the audience to like. In this, it's worth comparing Ali with Joe Kavanagh (Peter Mullan), a recovering alcoholic also driven to desperate measures by poverty and social circumstance in Ken Loach's powerful 1998 film *My Name Is Joe*. Loach's humanistic, socialist convictions lead him to portray Joe as profoundly kind-hearted, even if he has been led astray in his past, and a tender romantic relationship is developed as a major subplot. Here there's none of that. *Harka* is a harder, more concise film than *Joe*, and Ali a harder, more closed character.

What sentimentality the film displays arrives mostly thanks to Alyssa, who, in her early teens, is the younger of Ali's two sisters. Salima Maatoug brings a genuine, uncomplicated warmth to this role, or to adopt the film's own tonal sensibilities, a coolness. Alyssa calms the flames rising within her brother. She also provides that function within the film itself. Her dreamy voiceovers, buoyed by what British film critic Tim Robey called 'a touchingly affectless poetry', are interspersed throughout, sometimes discussing Ali, sometimes drifting off into oblique reflection. As Robey, who chaired the Q&A with Nathan at the ICA, noted, Maatoug's narration is 'reminiscent of what Terrence Malick coaxed, first out of Sissy Spacek in *Badlands*, then Linda Manz in *Days of Heaven*'. It also recalled, for me, Holly Hunter speaking the internal narrative of mute protagonist Ada in Jane Campion's *The Piano*. As Nathan related in conversation with Robey, these voiceover sequences were not included in the original script and were developed with Maatoug after he saw the potential in her performance.

During the Q&A, as during the other promotional interviews I've watched, Nathan was asked for commentary on the political situation in Tunisia, and on the success or otherwise of the Arab Spring more widely. He declined, being neither Tunisian nor an expert on the region's politics, replying that he was driven to make the film by a fascination with Bouazizi's story. *Harka* was a character study above all else, he insisted. This is true, and students of North African politics will certainly leave disappointed. Nonetheless, it obscures the film's greatest achievement, which is to demonstrate just how the personal is political, to borrow the phrase of second-generation feminists. Ali is a man suffering, in the medicalised parlance popular in the West, an 'acute mental health crisis', but to describe his situation — and the film — in this way reveals how such language neutralises social and political dissent at source. Ali's mental health crisis is not generated by a neurochemical imbalance, and even the more holistic biopsychosocial model would only explain away his predicament into academic abstraction. Rather, Ali himself knows the truth. He speaks it tremulously through the closed gates of the governor's office as *Harka* accelerates towards its inevitable but concealed climax: 'there's so much injustice, I'm losing my mind.'

Harka is not a perfect film. The soundtrack can be overbearing. The characters of Ali's other sister Sarra (Ikbal Harbi) and older brother Skander (Khaled Brahem) feel underwritten. The use of radio and TV news reports within scenes to relate societal background is clumsy. Nonetheless, with its concision and confidence, *Harka* is a bold statement from Nathan — and a potential classic. Despite being a character study firmly grounded in a time and place, the latter comfortably remote from its major audience, *Harka* will resonate with many in the West, should they get the chance to see it. It captures something of the current zeitgeist.

I split with my ex-girlfriend in 2008, returned to London the following year, and have only seen my Egyptian friend once since. It was the summer of 2019, the last before the pandemic, and we met in Place des Vosges, a famous, immaculately maintained square in Paris. The heat was intense, and we made for the shade under the neatly trimmed trees while my children swung and slid on the rudimentary play apparatus. She was recognisably chatty and bubbly, but with a harder, more abrasive edge than I recalled. Our talk turned to politics, just like in the old days, but this time I witnessed anger and bitterness rise within her that I'd only glimpsed before. Emmanuel Macron was every bit as bad as she had thought, she said. He was asset-stripping the country, demanding ever greater sacrifice of normal people while he floated around in a remote world of privilege and luxury with his elite cronies. I don't remember the exact words, but that was the gist. On most points, I agreed. But then her talk veered toward the deranged, far-right, Islamophobic *déclinisme* favoured by such luminaries as Éric Zemmour and Marine Le Pen. You know the stuff — the 'Islamisation' of France has been the country's undoing and Macron is too weak to arrest it. I remember listening in a state of mild but genuine shock as she built up to the words: 'don't ask me how I voted in the election —

you don't want to know!' My friend – an Egyptian whose closest, beloved childhood friend was Muslim – had been radicalised.

By then, my own radicalisation – I think you could call it that – was well underway. In the years between our last two meetings, the political wind had blown us in opposite directions. I'd sailed out to an agglomerated flotsam of opinions somewhere on the extreme left. In that time, I witnessed the gross injustice of socialism for the rich, laissez-faire capitalism for the poor following the 2008 financial crash. I watched austerity and privatisation rip the UK's social safety net to shreds and hollow out the public services we all rely upon like a virulent cancer. I saw the most grotesquely venal, mendacious public figures hauled up the ladder of power by a billionaire-funded press and billionaire-funded political parties until they reached the very top. I looked on as the whole corrupt cabal used a devastating pandemic as an opportunity to enrich themselves further. I came to understand how they, acting as part of an elite capitalist class, have locked in a global climatic spiral of death and destruction on a previously unimaginable scale with their endless furthering of fossil fuel extraction, ecocidal consumerism, and, for themselves, wildly extravagant lifestyles. I learnt of the millions of people in the global south already sucked down that spiral. And how my own children were lined up to join them. There's so much injustice, I'm losing my mind.

So, *al hogra* again: 'feelings ranging from injustice, indignation, resentment, humiliation to oppression… a continuing state of contempt and humiliation for the whole society'. Neither I, nor my former friend in Paris, are – for now at least – at the sharp end of that. But millions in our respective countries are. In the UK, over the last twelve months, a cost-of-living crisis and decimated, dysfunctional public services pushed hundreds of thousands of people who were barely coping into real desperation. Meanwhile, politics first mutated into a tawdry clown show, as the repugnant Boris Johnson was ousted as prime minister, before becoming an incomprehensible slanging match between grasping middle managers, none of whom offer any hope of ending the nightmare, just ever harsher economic servitude for the majority, brutal crackdowns for the disenfranchised, and empty nationalism for all. Throughout, outrageous scandals have surfaced in the media – privatised water companies raking in millions of pounds in profit as they tip raw sewage over beaches and into rivers; a police service known and then shown to be institutionally racist, sexist, and corrupt; failed politicians demanding five-figure pay packets from faked consultancy firms for a few hours' work. This and much more, rubbing everyone's noses in the dirt.

Is UK society close to that powder-keg state of *al hogra* yet? Possibly, but if you warned me of imminent revolution, I would scoff. There'd be a variety of interlinked reasons why, and an important one would be people's inability to federate our struggles and then sacrifice — maybe with our lives — for that collectivised cause. Was it adoption of the false individuated consciousness of capitalism that made us like this? The loss of religion? Both? Something else?

Whatever, our predicament is described by Alyssa in one of her lilting poetic voiceovers. She relates Ali's response to her question of whether he felt sad to likely never fulfil his dream of crossing the Med to a better life:

He said no, because you can never really escape. We are all caught in our own traps. Locked in. And no one can get out. We scratch, we claw away... but in a void. And against each other. In the end, we never advance even an inch.

SWEEPING HISTORY

Yuri Prasad

The absence of black people from mainstream histories of Britain, and the lazy assumption that the presence of African and Caribbean people began with the SS Windrush docking at Tilbury, east of London, in 1948, means few today know there were black Romans, black Tudors, and black Stuarts here hundreds of years earlier. Also written out of history are the way people from Africa played a central role in the developing workers and democratic movements of nineteenth century Britain, and the way their lives were deeply intertwined with struggles of the white poor. And missing too from many histories of the British Empire are twentieth century gatherings and conferences of black people in Britain where Africa's soon to be independence leaders made their plans.

Hakim Adi aims to put all this, and much more, right with his majestic new book *African Caribbean People in Britain: A History*. To start with, he details the lives of African people in London and beyond in the sixteenth century, the period before Britain's entrance into the Transatlantic slave trade. We learn that most came to Britain from north Africa as 'property of the rich', via the two principle slaving nations, Spain and Portugal. But that once here, there were no laws that could justify the holding of human beings as slaves, so some were able to escape the clutches of their masters and make their lives here. The absence of legal codes, however, does not mean that Britain was without skin colour prejudices at this time For example, Adi notes that, in 1596, the Privy Council wrote an open letter to the mayor of London claiming that Elizabeth Tudor knew 'there are of late divers Blackmoores brought into the Realme, of which kinde of persons there are all ready to manie'.

Yet, such official missives rarely touched the lives of the thousands of black people here. According to Adi they, worked 'in a variety of occupations, lived in towns and villages throughout England and Scotland

and intermarried and formed sexual relations with their British contemporaries. They were subject to no special laws and had very similar status to their neighbours'.

The apparent lack of a codified system of racism would be transformed by Britain's entry into a vast system of human trafficking. By the early eighteenth-century Britain was playing the lead role in the slave trade and the new plantation economies in the Caribbean and the Americas, with over fifty ships a year setting sail from London alone. Most of the key institutions of British capitalism drew their lifeblood from this horrific commerce, and we can today trace the history of most well-known banks, insurance, and shipping firms back to their slaving ancestors. Slavery, and the wealth derived from it, was celebrated – and for a time it became fashionable for the wealthy to take black slaves as part of their entourage of servants, and to show them off as a badge of prestige. Adi agrees with Eric Williams, whose seminal 1964 book *Capitalism and Slavery* (the focus of an article in a previous issue of Critical Muslim), to argue that systemic racism grew alongside the trade rather than preceding it. That understanding was particularly important to Williams as it meant he could argue that slavery created racism, rather than the other way round.

Hakim Adi, *African and Caribbean People in Britain: A History*, Allen Lane, 2023

The story of the abolition movement in Britain is told often but it's focus is largely upon parliamentarian William Wilberforce, and others from the top of society. Adi's focus is instead upon the key black people in Britain who fought and campaigned relentlessly for freedom. In this he follows other writers that have sought to develop an abolition 'history from below'. Adi charts the success of their campaigning among other working people as the most radical ideas of the European Enlightenment filtered into popular consciousness. As an example of early solidarity, he notes that Black people forced into domestic servitude in English houses would often 'self-liberate' and go on the run. They would then find helpers from among the poorest strata of whites who sympathised with their conditions. He also notes that slave auctions in Britain were comparatively rare, and that those that did take place were often attacked by abolitionist crowds.

Unsurprisingly, those on the run found common ground with other Africans in hiding in the towns. But there were also more than a few black people in Britain who believed their interests lay with the masters and slave owners. Among such people, Adi notes a prince called Sessarakoo, from modern-day Ghana, who was presented at court. During the prince's time in Britain, his father, the king, promised his support for the building of what became Fort William – the centre of British human trafficking on the Gold Coast. Sessarakoo went on to be employed by the Royal Africa Company, Britain's slaving multinational. The book points out that black people, with and without status, were commonly kidnapped by traders to be sold into slavery, but that those with powerful backing were far more likely to have ransoms paid for their release.

Adi's book documents well the way new organisations seeking workers' rights readily embraced the demand for an end to slavery – and the way it enlisted Africans in Britain as part of its cause. It was not uncommon for black speakers that had been enslaved to make common cause by pointing to the similarity between those who sweated in factories, and those that felt the whip in faraway plantation fields. Robert Wedderburn (circa 1792–1836) was born in Jamaica, son of an African enslaved woman and Scottish plantation owner. He joined the Royal Navy in the Caribbean, arrived in Britain penniless, and quickly became subsumed in London's underworld of the poor and unemployed. He joined and soon helped lead the radical political group the Spenceans and thought their ideas of common ownership should be used in both Britain and the Caribbean.

The Spenceans took their ideas of freedom for workers, peasants, and slaves to the streets, where riots often ensued. Adi notes that, in 1819, Wedderburn, 'billed as the "offspring of an African slave", debated the question – "Has a Slave an inherent right to slay his master who refuses him liberty?" According to the reports of a police spy, he explained to his audience of 200 of the "lowest description" gathered in London's Soho quarter, that the government sent armed men to Africa to kidnap men and women for profit, just as they employed workers as slaves in cotton factories… when the meeting voted overwhelmingly in favour, Wedderburn allegedly told the audience he would write "home and tell the Slaves to Murder their Masters as soon as they pleased".'

Adi celebrates the way the early workers movement embraced the call of anti-slavery, and the fact that black people were often to be found among its leadership. But he is rightly hard when the more formal trade union movement that emerged in the late nineteenth century instead fanned the flames of racism. So, in his chapter on the 1919 riots – which rather than 'race riots' were pogroms against African, Asian, and Caribbean people in ports across Britain – Adi details the way ship workers' unions painted black people as an enemy who were driving down wages and creating unemployment.

The chapters on post-World War Two racism, of the colour bar in jobs and housing, the abuse in the streets, the discrimination in healthcare and the way the British education system failed the children of migrants, will be familiar to those of us that have heard these stories first hand from our parents and grandparents. But in among them Adi maintains the thread of resistance that holds his book together.

But in later chapters, a weakness in Adi's conception of an 'African and Caribbean' approach to black British history emerges. In his introduction, he explains that he wanted to write a more ethnically specific book than Peter Fryer's 1984 pioneering work *Staying Power: The History of Black People in Britain*. That book has for years been the touchstone for black British history and was published in the 1980s, when the term 'Black' was used in ways that brought together resistance by African, Asian, and Caribbean people under a single banner. Adi's reasons are several, but he says that that understanding of Black is now no longer meaningful. That's a matter for debate. But what isn't is that many of the organisations that Adi later discusses – including Darcus Howe's *Race Today* Collective – had this broader, more political concept of 'Black', as a central part of their ideology and membership. The decision to side-line this idea of political blackness also means the significance of the united fight against the fascist National Front in the 1970s is much understated by Adi.

It also seems that Adi's enthusiasm for African and Caribbean people in multiracial movements wanes towards the end of the book, as we approach the present day. In a short segment on the Black Lives Matter movement in Britain that re-emerged in 2020, he misses what was for many a most important point – that this was an anti-racist mass movement that involved people from all ethnic backgrounds but which had black people at its centre. Just as thousands of white Chartists in the 1840s had once rallied behind their black leader William Cuffay, so under Black Lives Matter, masses now rallied behind black grassroots organisers.

Veteran anti-racist, and former editor of *Race Today* magazine, Leila Hassan-Howe, described this characteristic of the movement as transformative, saying, 'I went on a Black Lives Matter demonstration in London last year (2020), and what struck me was the hundreds of thousands of young white people. That was the first time I had ever seen that. And the power, and the feeling on the march showed they really meant it. It wasn't just a symbolic thing. They absolutely meant it when you saw their faces, when you saw them taking the knee, when you looked at the placards they made. They absolutely believed it. So that is a huge change that I've seen in my lifetime.'

But these are small criticisms when set against the book in its totality. Hakim Adi has provided for new generations what will doubtless be the reference book on African and Caribbean peoples' history in Britain. It is one we should treasure and promote, particularly as Adi himself and the work he has pioneered has come under attack. In August 2023, Adi, the first African-British historian to become a professor of history in the UK, was told by the University of Chichester that his Masters course in the history of Africa and the African diaspora, that he founded in 2017, was to be closed down, and a month later Adi himself was informed he was being made redundant. A vigorous campaign was launched to reverse that disgraceful and short-sighted decision - the latest chapter in the history of struggles this book was written to represent and bring to light.

INNOVATIVE OPINIONS

Mansur Ali

Hadith literally means a report or a saying. For Muslims, it is a report documenting the sayings, actions, physical features, and tacit approvals of the Prophet Muhammad. In the nineteenth century, orientalist scholars started to question the origins and reliability of hadiths. This was the result of a growing interest in other cultures due to the expansion of colonial powers. Interest in Islamic literature in western academia was further stimulated by developments in Christian theology, the emergence of historical-critical studies of the life of Jesus, and source criticism of the Bible. It is not a coincidence then that the first scholars who occupied themselves with hadith studies are those who were involved in a source critical study of the life of Muhammad and the quest for the historical Muhammad. Ignaz Goldziher (d. 1921), the Hungarian orientalist, argued that while the hadith cannot provide an accurate record of what transpired during the life of Muhammad, it can function as historical data for later developments. 'The hadith', he wrote, 'will not serve as a document for the history of the infancy of Islam, but rather as a reflection of the tendencies, which appeared in the community during the mature stages of its development.'

Joel Blecher and Stefanie Brinkmann, editors, *Hadith Commentary: Continuity and Change*, Edinburgh: Edinburgh University Press, 2023

From the time of Goldziher, for more than fifty years, the academic study of hadith was focused on the origins of hadith. But a new era of hadith studies was ushered by new scholarship that specifically focussed on the reception history of hadith rather than its origins. Whatever the origins of hadith, the argument goes, it is definitely clear that it holds an important place in Muslim discourse and practice. Thus, how Muslims receive hadith should also be the focus of academic study and reflection. However, the focus was still confined to the era of the hadith collections (750-1050).

Garret Davidson, assistant professor of Arabic and Muslim World studies at the College of Charleston, moved the field to outside of the formative period. He examined how hadiths were studied and received during the Mamluk period, especially the works of Ibn al-Ṣalāh (1181-1245) and Ibn Ḥajar (1372-1449). Joel Blecher, co-editor of *Hadith Commentary: Continuity and Change*, recognised that there was a gap in the field. Whilst past scholars studied individual hadiths as well as how hadith originated and spread out through the Muslim land, Blecher argued that a study on hadith commentaries will provide us with more insight into how contestation and conciliation took place. These commentaries were themselves social commentary on the time they were written in. *Hadith Commentary: Continuity and Change*, based on a conference on hadith commentary held at Hamburg University in 2017, is a further exploration into the potential of this genre to capture the interplay between continuity and change.

The book is loosely divided into two historical sections: the Early and Middle Ages and the modern period. Out of the ten articles, three are on Shīʿī hadith commentaries and one on digital hadith corpora. The afterward opens further horizons and potential for the study of hadith commentary. Here, I am concerned with selected chapters I find interesting.

The basic thesis of the book is simple. As a textual tradition, hadith commentaries reveal to us continuities in scholarship, especially to the base text (*matn*) as well as innovation and originality in the form of commentaries. As documents rooted in their time, works of hadith commentaries are also social commentaries on the religious, political and economic landscape of their era. As such, this book is multi-layered and it can be read in many ways.

It is the first academic collection on the commentary tradition. In the opening chapter, Stefanie Brinkmann demonstrates how the *gharīb al-ḥadīth* genre – a set of dictionaries explaining obscure and seldom used words in hadith – function as proto-commentaries. From this perspective, chapter one also functions as a nucleus to the book. The first three chapters discuss the concept of *gharīb* (foreign, strange, obscure, lone) from different angles. The *gharīb* (lone) is in stark opposite to the *sharḥ* (commentary). The contributors explore the boundaries of what constitues a commentary tradition and go further to demonstrate that commentaries are innovative pieces of work and not mere appendices working under the shadow of the base text they are commenting on. *Hadith Commentary* further offers an inclusive account of hadith studies by including hitherto often neglected commentaries in the Shī'ī tradition. In fact, it is the first edited collection to examine Shī'ī hadith commentaries.

The book also raises critical questions about the genre of hadith commentary. How is a commentary to be defined? and more crucially, what constitutes a commentary? Samer Dajani questions whether there is a unique method of interpreting hadith which can be designated the appellation 'Sufi'. He argues that bar one book—Ruzbihān Baqlī's (d. 1209) al-Maknūn fī Ḥaqā'iq al-Kalim al-Nabawiyya—none of the other sources that he looks at can be called 'Sufi commentaries' proper. This does not mean that scholars did not appreciate commentaries by Sufis. By indexing the number of times Ibn Ḥajar al-'Asqalānī (d. 1449) quotes and appreciates interpretations of hadiths—the highest appreciation is for the Sufi scholars Ibn Abī Jamarah (d. 1300) and al-Ṭībī (d. 1342)—Dajani concludes that even if there was no unique method warranting the designation 'Sufi commentary', the unique authority of the Sufis was sufficient for them to be taken seriously by hadith scholars.

Muhammad Gharaibeh shows how commentaries are much more innovative than people would credit them. The real challenge for hadith commentary, Gharaibeh argues, is to demonstrate that it is an independent work and not an appendix to the base text. He shows this by exploring the commentary of Ibn Rajab al-Ḥanbalī (d. 1393), who wrote a commentary on al-Nawāwī's (d. 1277) famous forty hadith collection. Interestingly, Ibn Rajab's commentary consists of an explanation of fifty hadiths. Gharaibeh explains that Ibn Rajab does not locate his commentary within the forty hadith genre. Nor is he doing a commentary of Nawāwī's forty hadith collection. Rather, Ibn Rajab's commentary is an explanation of hadiths known as *jawāmiʿ al-kalim* (comprehensive utterances)— the special names designated to succinct expressions of the Prophet. Nawāwī''s forty hadith collection (which has forty-two hadiths), is an addition to a previous hadith scholar, Ibn Ṣalāḥ's (d. 1245) *jawāmiʾ al-kalim* hadith collection which only had twenty-six hadiths. By locating the commentary in the *jawāmiʾ al-kalim* tradition, Ibn Rajab innovatively side steps the restrictive nature of the forty hadith genre canon. Furthermore, Ibn Rajab's commentary also uses a Imam Shāfiʿī template but is primarily written for a Ḥanbalī audience. This is evident in the many references he has to Aḥmad Ibn Ḥanbal (d. 855) which are missing in his later commentary on *Ṣaḥīḥ al-Bukhārī* titled *Fatḥ al-Bārī*.

If commentaries are sites of innovation, they are also locations for contestation. In her chapter on 'Contesting Ḥanafī Thought in a Twentieth-century Turkish

Hadith Commentary', Susan Gunasti demonstrates how contested madhhab identity are argued through translation projects. This shows that translations are also acts of interpretation. By taking the New Turkish Republic's (1923) Diyanat commissioned translation of the summarised version of Ṣaḥīḥ al-Bukhārī known as al-Tajrīd al-Ṣarīḥ as her starting point, she focuses on Volume 3 of the translation as the site of contention. Babanzade Ahmet Naim (d. 1934), a philosopher by training and not a hadith scholar, was commissioned to translate the Tajrīd. He managed to publish two volumes and produced a first draft translation of the third volume before he died. The project was taken over by Kamil Mirsi (d. 1957) who was a scholar but also parliamentarian and was involved in the committee that approved the Diyanet project. Mirsi published Volumes 4 and 5. But the real interesting feature is Mirsi's editing of Babanzade's draft translation of Volume 3. Whilst keeping Babanzade's footnotes, Mirsi takes the opportunity to vehemently critique the former in his dismissal of Mamluk Ḥanafī scholar Badr al-Dīn al-ʿAynī (d. 1451) and heavy reliance on ʿAynī's arch-rival Ibn Ḥajar al-ʿAsqalānī.

Gunasti extrapolates a number of salient points. First, she argues that it is translations which functioned as sites of contestations and not independent commentary works. Second, she demonstrates that traditional Islamic studies did not cut off entirely with the founding of the new Republic; older Ottoman scholars and new scholars ensured that religious continuity carried on. Finally, she also reveals that Diyanet had its own agenda in assigning translators. A better candidate was Zahid al-Kevsari (d. 1952), but the latter was critical of Diyanet's policy.

Returning to the topic of the *gharīb* (lone) versus *sharḥ* (commentary), Youshaa Patel examines commentary on a single widely circulating hadith: 'Islam began strange and will one day return to being strange. So blessed are the strangers (*ghurabāʾ*).' The purpose of Patel's chapter is to demonstrate that being a stranger in the Muslim social imaginary is not as grim as hitherto western scholarship had us understand. The author embarks on one of the most extensive commentaries on the hadith of ghurabāʾ: discussing its spread of *isnad* (chain of transmitters), to how it was received. He writes that whilst commentaries of the hadith in the tenth century focused on suffering and trauma faced by the stranger, post-tenth century discussions where more obsessed with defining the 'stranger'. The post-tenth century writers saw themselves as amongst the ghurabāʾ: the more isolated, more correct, and pious.

borrowed

Ibn Taymiyya (d. 1328) uses the ghurabā' hadith to provide a necessary corrective to the dystopian mentality found in the Muslim community as a result of the hadith 'my community is the best, and then those after them, and those who come after them.' For Ibn Taymiyya, whilst the latter hadith is accepted, the ghurabā' hadith tells us that in every generation the ummah will create its cream of the crop.

One interesting topic that Patel discusses in his commentary is how modern jihadis use the ghurabā' hadith to declare themselves to be the righteous ones. Patel demonstrates that in premodern commentaries of this hadith, jihadis were not defined as ghurabā'. The few instances that the hadith was mentioned in jihad manuals was related to the virtue of staying home. Patel's conclusion is that whilst it is the prerogative of modern day jihadis to usurp this hadith for their ideology, however, there isn't a genealogy for this reading in classical Islamic sources.

Altaf Ali Mian's chapter on 'Debating Authority and Authenticity in Modern South Asian Hadith Commentaries' interrogates the ironically named eighteen-volume *Awjaz al-Masālik* (the succinct path to the *Muwaṭṭā* of Imām Mālik) of the Indian scholar Zakariyya Kandhalawi (d. 1981). Mian demonstrates how the hadith commentary genre can function as a site of major social fault lines. He argues that the reconciliatory project (*taṭbīq*) of Shah Waliullah (d. 1762), the Indian Sufi reformist, was a result of his observation of scholarly differences based on weak epistemological foundations as well as the political decadence of Mughal Delhi. Waliullah focused on the *Muwaṭṭā* for the reconciliatory project. His successors, the Deobandis and the Ahl-i-Hadith, did not take up his project. But Kandhalawi did. However, Kandhalawi's project did not move towards conciliation but was a defence of the Ḥanafīs against the Ahl-i-Hadith. Mian sees in Kandhalawi's method a subtle criticism of Waliullah's *taṭbīq* project; and makes an interesting observation as to why the two scholars were different. Waliullah was living in an era where the loss of Muslim power as well as scholarly bickering needed to be reconciled. For Kandhalawi, the privatisation of religion by British colonialist as well as his Sufi disciplinary practices cultivated a compartmentalised sphere of private religiosity. This forced him to defend what he cherished the most: that his tradition – in law and mysticism- should survive the onslaught of colonial modernity.

In his afterwards, Blecher mentions that further ethnographic thick descriptions of hadith study circles are required in different parts of the world. hadith commentaries in non-print media must also be studied. The influence of how non-Muslim cultures translate, recompile, and interpret hadith is important too. I would argue that translation projects also need to be studied to observe subtle commentaries. Interesting things are happening in the digital world. It remains to be seen how much of our understanding of hadith remains the same or changes due to emerging digital hadith corpora with its function of mapping 'reuse' instances in major hadith commentaries.

ET CETERA

ON MY MOTHER

Yasmin Alibhai-Brown

My mother Jena, was a devout, highly intelligent and independent minded Muslim woman. She was made to leave school at fifteen and lived a tough life without losing her bearings or surrendering totally to misogynist traditions or patriarchal pressures. The word for virtue, in Gujarati and Kutchi, my home languages, is satuguna, meaning good, pure, Excellent, eminent. To her, *satguna* was goodness but goodness that was active, personal, internally interrogated, difficult at times, and justifiable. Perpetual resistance to bad customs was good. Thinking for oneself was good. Being kind and generous were good. But goodness had to be subject to tests. She endlessly interrogated her own actions and those of others, setting high bars for both.

Back in Uganda, our old homeland, after giving money to a beggar, she would question herself. Was that just an easy way to self-gratification? Why hadn't she asked the man about his life? Or bought him a blanket? After moving to London in 1972 and until she died at the age of eighty-two, Jena donated some pounds from her supplementary pension to the Oxfam shop near her because she had known penury and endured its corrosive effects on the body, mind, and soul. A picture of Bob Geldof was up on a wall in her little sitting room. This white pop singer, believed my mum, was a demigod of virtue because he cared about starving Africans. We disagreed about that.

I remember how hard Jena worked when I was growing up. My father, Kassam, was brilliant but irresponsible. She did three jobs to support her son and two daughters but resisted praise: 'All mothers, even dog mothers, do what they have to for their young ones. Nothing special'. Kassam did not let her wear make up. She acquiesced. But when he tried to stop me wearing lipstick as a teenager, she became a tigress and sided with me: ' I did it to make you happy. It was my choice. You were thirty-three, I, a much younger wife. I knew that made you anxious and jealous. But you do not have the right to make my daughter obey you.' And, although she gave up lipstick, rouge and kohl after her wedding day, she wore so much alluring perfume that market traders used to call her 'mama attar'. Subversion, in her book, was, at times, the way good prevailed over tyranny. Such women are the unrecognised caretakers of human dignity and integrity the world over.

As George Elliot wrote about Dorothea, the heroine of *Middlemarch*: 'the effect of her being on those around her was incalculably diffusive: for the growing good of the world is partly dependent on unhistoric acts; and that things are not so ill with you and me as they might have been, is half owing to the number who lived faithfully a hidden life, and rest in unvisited tombs.'

Personal agency and perspicacity characterise these unseen heroes and heroines. Their pure and true virtue comes from within and often rises as a revolt against powerful enforcers of collective righteousness.

Aristotle believed some humans were born with virtues which were then sustained by reason and emotions. Furthermore, according to some contemporary philosophers, for the great Greek sage, morality 'has more to do with the question "how should I be?" rather than "what should I do?" If we answer the first question then... the second question may begin to take care of itself.' That is easier said than done. It assumes humans all have personal autonomy and free choice.

All children are born innocent and blameless. But the early lives of many could make it impossible for them to take the road to the well-lived and considerate life. Some do break from that predestination. Too many can't. Or won't. Individual psychologies compel many to reject societal expectations of good behaviour. This rebellions are sometimes necessary and sometimes wholly destructive and self-destructive. Young children joining violent drug gangs in inner cities are not little devils, but little humans who are using reason and emotions to resist the fate they have been consigned to. In the human jungle that is the modern world, only the

cruel and ruthless survive. Trevor, now in his early twenties, tells me
virtue is for 'posh people' who can decide what to be, 'I was failed by my
parents, went into care, was abused and failed by most of those who were
supposed to take care of me. So tell me how can they expect me to be
good? The gang I joined was my family, the family I never had. I left them
when I turned sixteen because I met a mother whose son had been stabbed
to death by someone in another gang. She was so forgiving. We talked a lot.
I knew her son. He was sweet. She became the first adult I ever met who
was kind and caring. I wanted to be like her, so I left the gang business. She
had a good heart, but never behaved as if she was better than others. I went
to church once. The guy there said God loved me and I should try and
please Him. Why? Where was God when I was a lost little boy? He made
me feel it was my fault'.

That brings us neatly to communal, religious, societal, and national
virtue upholders. They do what they do to guilt trip and exert authority
over other humans. Most are manifestly wicked and/or control freaks and
live by the dictum, 'Do as I say, not as I do'. The religious/community
squad co-opt God to grab power. (Jena loathed their hypocrisies and
control freakery). Close behind them are patriots and politicians.

Through the ages, there have been philosophers who have argued that only
God (or, presumably, Gods) can show us how to live a virtuous life. As Daniel
Weltman writes in an essay on the moral philosopher Gertrude Elizabeth
Margaret Anscombe (1919-2001): 'in her article "Modern Moral Philosophy"
(1958) that unless God gives us moral commands, moral claims, including
claims about what we morally "ought" to do, make no sense because "ought"
implies that there is some power telling us what to do. Anscombe therefore
concludes that contemporary non-religious moral theories make no sense.
We must either accept God as the basis of morality, or develop a new kind of
ethics that gives up talk about what we ought to do'.

Anscombe's ideas are, in truth, more complex and nuanced. She also
advocates a return to the Aristotelean concepts of character, active
morality, rationality, and emotional literacy.

However, by asking us to accept God's word is neither feasible nor
desirable because we are rational and questioning creatures and also because
the interpreters of God's wishes – in all faiths, all men, almost all
authoritarian – cannot themselves agree on what God is or wants from us.

Nor is there any consensus in divine texts. Take food prohibitions: For Hindus, cows are sacred; Muslims and Jews, believe pigs are filthy and disallowed; Buddhists and Hindus are expected to abstain from killing living beings. Or violence: Muslims, Jews and Christians have mounted what they say are 'just' wars ratified by their Almighties; ardent followers of organised religions oppress and assail non-believers, including peace loving Buddhists. With so many conflicting claims, which of the Gods prevails? The matters on which they do all agree, is that females are born inferior to males, so must be excluded, commanded, and perpetually chastised.

My wise and brave mother openly challenged the precepts and enforcers. Only five foot tall, her hair in a bun, wrapped in simple saris, she would argue on the mosque steps with male proselytisers and 'leaders'. She was with a small band of insubordinate ladies who, one Friday, walked proudly into the mosque with their heads uncovered. This was sometime in the early 1940s. The keepers of the faith and their obedient worshippers were aghast. The rebel women took them on: 'Who are you to tell us what to wear?' 'God made us. Why should we hide that face, that hair, those arms?' 'Oh, so we have to be modest because you men cannot control your needs?'.

Those women were more virtuous than the men who think they have the right to guard the entrance to heaven. That noble tradition continues. twenty-two-year-old Kurdish Iranian, Mahsa Amini died after being violently assaulted by Iran's 'morality police' for not wearing a hijab 'correctly'. That nation is tightly ruled by one of the cruellest gangs of female-hating clerics. Indomitable woman and girls protested and defied hijab rules. An unknown number of them are now in prison. There are allegations of torture and rape. But still they go on. Virtue is not all-suffering and accepting. It can often be radical and combative. It has to be.

Let's not forget that among men who project themselves as anointed and supreme religious paradigms, are an unknown (and unknowable) number who are prolific sexual abusers of boys, girls, and young women. To live a virtuous life we should avoid listening to and being near men who profess they speak for God. Their self-belief is dangerous for the rest of us.

I am not here setting up a battleground between females and males. History is packed with the names and stories of men who lived or tried to live and work ethically and wicked women who caused terrible harm to others. To me, virtue is honesty, courage, generosity, fairness, unselfishness, compassion, social awareness, conscience and humane behaviours.

I am a modern feminist, raised by a feminist mother who didn't know the word, and guided by generations of women thinkers like Mary Wollstonecraft, Sylvia Pankhurst, Princess Sophia Singh, Sheila Rowbotham, Toni Morrison, Beatrice Campbell and many, many others. And also the concept of virtue ethics. Which puts me at odds with some in this large and varied tribe. Such as the American philosopher Sarah Conley who wrote 'Why Feminists Should Oppose Feminist Virtue Ethics', way back in 2001: 'Clearly, virtue ethics' emphasis on the personal nature of the moral life has its appeal. The idea that we should be good people, not just do the right thing, is a nice one; it presents a picture of a world populated by people who are truly pleasant, rather than dutiful but nasty. The idea, too, that there are different ways of being good, not just one rule of right to be applied across the board, has intuitive appeal, given life's complexity... The moral and the personal are integrated. To many, too, virtue ethics has seemed to provide a model for living which simply has better results, making others as well as the agent better off'. However, she continues, 'While the ethics of care has obviously been enormously influential, it has not been without detractors... [They] reject what they see as the vicious objectivism of the ethics of duty, they express concern that the ethics of care encourages us to neglect ourselves for the sake of others. For women in particular, the ethics of care may endorse the stereotype of self-sacrifice which has led women to neglect their own lives in the service of others, or to feel guilty'. Could she be right? Like Jena, I go through endless self-interrogation.

Other questions I grapple with: How do we become more virtuous? Can virtue be developed or strengthened? We can, I think, strengthen our ethical muscles by making ourselves behave ethically even when it is hard. The problem is that vice too is reinforced with determination and repetition.

If Jena were alive today, I wonder how I would explain to her that pernicious, neo-liberal insult, 'virtue signalling'? She would be bewildered then incandescent. For my good mother, generous to a fault, believed the nastiest person could turn into a good, caring citizen, if gently led in that direction. Many remember her today as the woman who helped them understand what goodness really was.

My late, enormously fat and enormously wealthy paternal uncle in Kenya, Chacha S, a businessman, was hated and feared by all his staff, most of his family and customers. He was ruthless, a show off and tyrant. Jena decided to try and change him. First, she got him - a man who consumed vast amounts of meat at every meal - to try her vegetable curries and improve his diet. He lost weight and began to listen to Jena on all matters. She couldn't turn him into a saint, but did, through food and persuasion, get him to pay his workers more and use words rather than a stick to impose his will on his wife and children. He once told me: 'Your mother has magic. She has used it on me, I don't know how. She has little money, but big power'. She took no credit for the transformation, but many in the family still say, she saved Chacha S from himself.

My book *Ladies Who Punch*, is a collection of fifty biographies of feisty women who refused to stay in their place and do as told, who pushed back against normative misogyny, who made their own judgements and whose lives left a mark and defined what it means to be good. They could only do that by sneaking past, circumnavigating or boldly defying the male ordered world. It is dedicated to Jena, and my daughter Leila, both spirited, both unapologetically principled and kind. Without such exemplars, what would the world be?

EMANCIPATION DAY

Amandla Thomas-Johnson

Three dolphins flipped and tumbled, as our ship leaned into the dragon's mouth, a strange new land emerging on the iridescent horizon. It was end of July, and I was headed along the coast of Trinidad on the *Buccoo Reef*, a passenger vessel that bore the name of the fishing village in which my father was born and to which, once we dropped anchor in Tobago, I would journey. The curious land ahead was not our final destination. But, as it came into view on the port side, a throng of passengers rushed over to the opposite side of the vessel, more interested in the islands that mark the western limits of Trinidad, the watery stubs of the island's great northern range, as it sweeps down to the sea.

From East to West, the hills of Trinidad's Northern range tell a story of a small island into which the entire world seems concentrated. Caribs from the Santa Rosa First Peoples Community, descendants of the original Amerindian inhabitants, live at Arima. The village of Lopinot, set deep in the misty hills, is a hub of Venezuelan culture and of Parang, a Spanish-language music played at Christmas. In Curepe, Indo-Trini vendors hawk doubles in the early mornings—two *baras* (flatbreads) folded around curry *chana* (chickpeas). There are the great cocoa plantations of Santa Cruz, and climbing deeper yet into the range, heading north, past where bubbling rivers of red mud burst their banks, then down and round a gentle slope on the northern coast, framed by waving palm fronds, is the popular Maracas beach.

Laventille, on the Eastern fringe of the capital of Port-of-Spain was the birthplace of the steel pan, but today resembles a jumble of unkempt homes teetering off a hillside, a reminder of the stark and cruel stratification of race and class that still blights this country. Past the capital, as the island tapers into a narrow crocodile's head, the Petit Valley cuts into the range, splitting it almost in two, the deep thickets on its slopes populated by prosperous Syrian enclaves. After Chaguaramas, the range drops into the ocean but seemingly staggers on through the glass blue sea, rising here and there as clumps of verdant rock, the channels between which are known as the Boca del Dragón—the Dragon's Mouth.

Only three of us seemed interested that the vessel was giving us an unambiguous sighting of Venezuela, as it took a detour through the Boca Grande, the final and largest of the straits, separating, in effect, North from South America. South America in all its Tepui and Amazon and Andean and Iguazú glory was right there.

Lessons were learned aboard the *Buccoo Reef.* While Trinidad and Tobago curiously sits astride two different continental plates—the Caribbean and the South American—and lies just seven miles off Venezuela, its inhabitants seemingly do not think of it as the end of North America or as a frontier—but as a center in its own right. Even the prancing dolphins appeared to mock the arbitrariness of continental boundaries: after all, my own great-grandparents worked and were married in Caracas, Venezuela.

And so, it made sense for me to start my American diary from here: Trinidad and Tobago, the centre of America, of the world.

I was here to attend the celebrations of Emancipation Day ceremony in Port-of-Spain, the capital of Trinidad and Tobago, a deeply symbolic reminder of the promise of Panafricanism, and the leading role Trinbagonians played in the movement. Held on 1 August each year, it commemorates the abolition of slavery across the British Empire in 1838. The country became the first to declare it a national holiday in 1985. Attired in novel combinations of African styles and prints, revellers parade through the streets of Port-of-Spain, the day culminating with a cultural spectacle at the Queen's Park Savannah, a large park in the heart of the capital.

By the time I reached there, the Asante King, draped in a *kente* cloth of white and black, was ascending the steps of the dais, an ornamental striped umbrella held aloft above his head. Three squat dancers, their muscular squirms and wiggles betraying grace and menace at each small step, performed. The drums now reached their zenith, a torrent of thuds raining down, laced with a syncopated bell. But as they did, the three squat dancers drew back from the action.

Just moments before, seated on a platform nearby, the ten or so paramount chieftains had cut a sullen, even disdainful look that seemed much at odds with the sheer brilliance of their weighty fabric, patterned with a jumble of stripe and *adrinkra* symbolism, draped over their left shoulder, toga style. But now all seemed well with the warrior princes who could muster a smile as they rose to salute their lord, their fleshy fingers festooned with treasure.

His majesty appeared please as he sat beside the Prime Minister and his wife. He beamed back at the crowd, a cornucopia of greying locks and head wraps and shaved heads with prominent features, gathered before him. His golden rings sparkled in the morning sun, as did his bangles of gold. Meanwhile, Gilded staffs stood erect about him. The Europeans called it Gold Coast, before it became Ghana.

The three dancers entered the scene again, only this time it was some ancient story they were telling with their hands, which they began to writhe and wring as if to expel some old liquid, their heads ducking and weaving one way and then the other. Their head, shoulders, upper arms, wrists, knees and ankles were all girded in gold. And now scattering like ants, their feet became a blur of molten gold. Suddenly, the drums fell and they turned and with another one of their hand gestures paid homage to their master. The King had arrived.

It was hard not to be impressed by the arrival of Osei Tutu II, the Asantehene, King of the Asante, his courtly entourage, his bling, at the opening. For many, few tribes if any epitomise African civilisation as the Asante (anglicised as Ashanti), whose empire covered much of modern-day Ghana between the 1700s and the 1900s when it was conquered by the British. Their warriorhood and vast wealth are the stuff of legend; their iconic status is such that were they to receive a small royalty for every knock-off kente cloth pattern for sale on dashiki, kufis or graduation stalls in Brixton or Harlem, it is possible the kingdom might have become wealthy twice over. After all, here was Africa in all its uncontaminated pomp, the exquisite hip thrusts (the original whine), the rhythms of yore, the real gold.

In 1900, while Yaa Asantewaa, the legendary warrior queen of the Asante fought off British forces in the War of the Golden Stool, Henry Sylvester Williams, a heavyset Trinidadian lawyer in his early thirties, was in London organising the First Pan-African Conference. Attendees included the renowned Black American scholar W.E.B. Dubois, who stated his famous opinion that the 'the problem of the twentieth century is the problem of the color line' in his culminating address to the conference, the first in a series that would span the twentieth century. That September, the Asante kingdom fell to the British.

But by 1945, a Ghanaian leader, Kwame Nkrumah had risen to the challenge of liberating his country. Mentoring him were two Trinidadian intellectual-activists, C.L.R. James and George Padmore, organiser of the historic Fifth Panafrican Conference in Manchester. In his Emancipation Day address, the King name-checked both: Padmore, the 'Radical Trinidadian intellect' and James 'whose intellectual and philosophical ideas fanned the flames of Panafricanism and inspired leaders like Kwame Nkrumah, Jomo Kenyatta and Nelson Mandela to pursue the political emancipation of the continent of Africa from the yoke of colonialism.'

Rolling off Trinidad and Tobago's Panafrican assembly line were other notable leaders, including Black Communist Claudia Jones (founding mother of the Notting Hill Carnival) and Altheia Jones-Lecointe, leader of the British Black Panther movement. Moments before the king's arrival, Eintou Pearle-Springer, the Panafricanist poet and Orisha devotee had staged her *canboulay* enactment, depicting the finals moments as the enslaved achieved their freedom. Along with Springer, it is Khafra Kambon who has done more than most to keep the flame of Panafricanism aglow. A leader of Trinidad and Tobago's 1970 Black Power revolt, he is also one of the architects of the Emancipation Day celebration. Stokely Carmichael, later Kwame Ture, a deviser of 1960s Black Power in the US, was also Trinbagonian.

It seemed contradictory, however, that the king should, dressed in his full regalia, an anxious courtier wiping dribbles of sweat from his forehead, use his speech to talk about poverty. I do not know how hierarchies of wealth and privilege and the culture of deference they induce can be consistent with the prosperity of Africa. (Kwame Nkrumah who eventually led Ghana to independence in 1957 would come to blows with the Ashante over this very point.) This is more a question of power than one of culture; the point does not dismiss the myriad of beautiful African dances and masks and ceremonies and crafts and spiritualities that populate both sides of the Atlantic.

Given the historic and current representation of Africa as a place of war, famine and barbarism, there would have been those in Trinidad who viewed the king's presence as an instance of black redemption; a reminder that we were once kings and queens of plenty before the Europeans came and stole our people and land and then spread lies about who we had been prior in order to justify further theft. Emancipating oneself from the mental slavery—as Marcus Garvey and then Bob Marley would put it—of internalised racism (which includes the colourism some of us experience in Trinidad) is important. But why not use the stateless societies as our models, as the great Guyanese historian Walter Rodney proposed? For Rodney, Caribbean people stood to relate less to the epic Egyptian pharoahs, kings of Ancient Kush and Mansa Musa's great gold giveaway, than to the quiet civility of the African village where hospitality, social tolerance, and care for the needy was not uncommon.

The promise of Emancipation is the freedom to fit and measure oneself by a different yardstick. So totalising was the destruction of personhood and family and community during enslavement, the Martinician poet Edouard Glissant has pointed out in his *Poetics of Relation*, the slave descendant had to reconstruct their world, drawing from the soil of the African past as well as the encounter with first peoples and European culture. In the same way that in Trinidad and Tobago, the African drum was reconstituted as the steel pan instrument, or African languages morphed into creoles and patois, the Caribbean experience proposes a new standard by which we can measure humanity, and cultural standards at large.

The yardstick of powerful states and royal opulence seems to be a European one. Why do I need a royal lineage when one of my ancestors arrived to the Caribbean from Africa after escaping a sinking ship? As Rodney writes, 'if there is to be any proving of our humanity it must be by revolutionary means.' Or as Derek Walcott once observed, why should we see a Trinidadian retelling of the *Ramayana* in which village children play gods and princes as any worse than a re-enactment of the Hindu epic in India itself?

If there is pride in emancipation it is pride from below: pride in resisting and surviving the genocidal predations of European power and then trying to build societies and forge cultures out of the disparate populations inhabiting what writer Gillian Moore calls in effect, 'abandoned labour camps.'

Emancipation is a reminder that we were slaves and probably not kings — and that is magnificent.

A few days earlier, at the national library, some of Trinidad's Black Muslims gathered for their own Emancipation Day event. Women buzzed around in hijabs sporting African print, as men wearing loose trousers and open-toed sandals strolled by. As speakers at the event made clear, Black Muslims have their own Panafrican genealogy. It starts with with African slaves, of whom up to 20 percent may have been Muslim, and then passes through the 1960s when many converted under the influence of the Black Power Movement and Malcolm X. Meanwhile, Indo-Trini Muslims, who make up the majority, are descendants of indentured servants who arrived with religions from India in the nineteenth century. While there is still a lot to uncover about Black Muslims in Trinidad and Tobago, one speaker mentioned a nineteenth-century community of formerly enslaved Mandinka Muslims, from Senegambia, led by Imam Jonas Mohammed Bath. While this community disappeared from the historical record around the time of Emancipation in the 1830s, he revealed that Bath's descendants were today living in Port-of-Spain. This opens up the possibility of an unbroken Black Muslim presence in the country, from slavery to today.

According to the speakers, Black Muslims in Trinidad and Tobago do not appear to have it easy. The international climate of Islamophobia post 9-11 means that added to the stigma of being poor and Black is that of being Muslim. Converts are rejected by their families and can feel ostracised from mosques as tensions between African and Indian continue to simmer. Black Muslims have their own internal rifts. Meanwhile, the country is wrestling with how to repatriate the more than one hundred Trinbagonians—mainly women and children—languishing in Kurdish-run camps in Syria. With their now-dead menfolk they had been lured to the Islamic State's supposed caliphate.

The week prior to Emancipation Day marked the anniversary of the 1990 coup led by Black Muslim leader Yasin Abu Bakr's Jamaat al-Muslimeen, the only Muslim-led coup ever attempted in the Western hemisphere and what some scholars regard as the country's most recent eruption of Black Power. Things came to a head when members of the Libyan-trained Jamaat stormed the Red House, the seat of parliament, and shot, injured and then hog-tied Prime Minister A.N.R. Robinson, keeping him and other government officials hostage in the building. After six days, the insurgents surrendered.

Back at the event, Bilal Abdullah, stood up to speak, imparting a message of hope and peace. For him, this was familiar territory. The venue at the national library stands juxtaposed to the ornate *beaux-arts* Red House, of which, as Abu

Bakr's deputy, Abdullah had led the siege during the 1990 coup. Feeling post-coup blues, he had left, apologised, and with other former jamaat members, established the Islamic Resource Center, host of the event. Attempting to help Black Muslims, the organisation does charitable community work in the poverty-stricken districts of East Port-of-Spain and owns a mosque in the capital. The group's message comprises a seamless blend of social justice activism, Pan-Africanism, and spiritual practice.

They have also taken a strong stance against the Islamic State group and in a telling instance of political rehabilitation, the government has appointed Kwesi Atiba, the group's bespectacled, astute imam, who was also involved in the Red House siege, to a three-person committee to oversee the repatriation of nationals from Syria. For a cadre of women and children who may need more than a bit of social and political rehab, they are probably in safe hands.

I went to see Aunty Claudia.

While most of my family who left Trinidad and Tobago ended up in the US, Canada, or the UK, Aunty Claudia swapped the Tobagonian fishing village for the Swiss Alps, working as a nurse in Canton de Vaud for thirty-five years. She flew to London for one weekend a month, for shopping, *liming* and *fetting* (hanging out and partying), and so we saw quite a bit of her. She was there when I was born, then went out the night after to celebrate her own birthday. A first cousin of my father, they had both left Tobago early in life, growing up together in Fyzabad, a hub of trade union radicalism, in southwestern Trinidad, and were very close. With my mother, she was just as close.

It was an occasion when she came. Oohs and ahhs went around and everything was dropped to go and see Aunty Claudia. She sat there purring and grinning cheekily while proffering peculiar Swiss goods - liquored chocolates, alpine knitwear and a lime green jacket that was so puffy and pleated that whenever I tried to wear it all but wore me.

She was different. The directness, hot mouth and mocking laugh she brought with her from Trinidad to Europe were tempered by a Swiss word economy and French precision that to this day make some of her statements so moving and so devastating. She didn't need to show or tell you that she lived a good life, a knowing tilt of her head said it all.

Here in Tobago they say that her mother, Delcina, used to announce her arrival to the Buccoo village meeting with a flourish of pirouettes and wines, accomplished from her wheelchair, to prove that a double amputee was just as capable as anyone else. Two of Delcina's siblings also inherited the Johnson diabetic foot—it cost a brother a leg and a sister had to be hoisted over a shoulder and carried about. It had passed down from their father, my great-grandfather, Sonny Johnson, who was immobilised and consigned to the family home.

This diabetes—the legacy of an attachment to sugar engendered through enslavement.

It came late for Claudia, as luck would have it, just after she retired to Tobago. A leg was taken off. Then the other. Her hearing went and now only one eye works, as if trying to settle back into a tiny fishing village you left as a girl wasn't already hard enough. She went into retreat.

Our trip down to the Bay was her first in years, even though it lies a minute's wheelchair push down a slope. 'The smell, the smell,' was the first thing she said as she took in the blue bay and the reef beyond.

She briefly held court down on the boardwalk as conch divers, fishermen, and beach hustlers, tucking away their morning smokes, came to pay their respects. She squeezed their hands and held their gaze. She asked about their families and where necessary offered heartfelt condolences. Nodding and grinning, she went through the motions of conversation, hardly letting on that she couldn't even hear whatever it was they were saying.

As we looped around and back up the hill, she asked to see some of her old friends. At their peak they had been the stalwart matriarchs who raised generations against the odds and who could turn out a mean fish broth. Later, they became the vigorous dowagers who led the church choir. Now things were different. Consigned to the bedroom or to the wheelchair and for their most basic needs dependent on children and grandchildren, they could barely make it from off the bed, let alone leave their homes.

I watched as these hardback women, sometimes sharing between them a single leg, a solitary functioning eye, broke down. Tears of gladness mingled with howls of pain.

It was a rare glimpse behind the curtains of the Caribbean household. It was a reminder to not be fooled by the Caribbean woman's steeliness, poker face, her kissing her teeth and carrying on. There was still pain; pain but also comfort in community. They exhorted one another to be grateful for what they had. To thank the Creator.

TEN AI GENERATED VIRTUES

Heaven forbid one day the phrase 'ask ChatGPT' becomes as colloquial as 'google it!' Only time will tell. For now, AI remains an enigma. Certainly, a fair number of experts understand the basic concept, but the muddy mystery is retained when we consider its consequences. As we live in a world where AI has proven its capability for racism, xenophobic tendencies, depression, bias, fascism, and even a willingness to kill its own operator should they become an obstacle in the way of its primary programmed directive, it seemed a bit less risky to begin with a simple question in moral philosophy and ethics.

To better understand ChatGPT and reflect on our fears, we asked the following question: 'What are the ten best virtues?'

Before an instant could pass, ChatGPT responded: 'The ten best virtues can vary depending on cultural, religious, and philosophical perspectives. However, some commonly recognised virtues are:

1. Wisdom
2. Courage
3. Justice
4. Temperance
5. Honesty
6. Compassion
7. Integrity
8. Humility
9. Generosity
10. Gratitude

'These virtues are often considered essential for leading a meaningful and ethical life. Keep in mind that different belief systems might emphasise other virtues as well.' So concluded ChatGPT.

So, there we have it! Now, you wouldn't be very satisfied if this is how we concluded the list. Wouldn't it be fun to look between the lines of this list and expose the deep in-built bias behind our dear ChatGPT? But, noting the increasing reliance on and domination by AI in our contemporary world, it is more relevant to ask: would these virtues be viable in a future dragged to the utopic/dystopic end of generative artificial intelligence trend?

1. Wisdom

Indeed, this, often the king of virtues, is the aim of many a civilisation's attempts to live the best and most meaningful life. Yet, even throughout history this word is often used without an explicit understanding of what is at play. So, with such a fuzzy grasp on the concept, how can we expect it to carry on into a more AI-driven future? A very surface level definition of wisdom requires three things, experience, knowledge, and the ability to make good judgements. We begin by looking at what wisdom is by way of where it comes from. The road to wisdom begins with small bits of data, phenomena, or whatever name the things we see in the world has. By seeing more and more things we develop experience. I am not convinced machines can do this. Experience requires a child's sense of wonder and the all-too-human ability to make a mistake. The child/scientist sees the world, makes assumptions, and tests this, learning from the mistakes. The smart child/scientist also takes note of what other's experience and learn to heed what they see as well. Machines do not operate under the assumption that they can possess ignorance. Therefore, they simple collect and collate data – all of it, everything they can get. Whether the child/ scientist or the machine, with all these collected phenomena, you derive information which is then collected and combined into knowledge. The final step to wisdom is the organisation of knowledges into wisdom. The problem is that before we take that final leap, machines and child/scientists have both attained intelligence (artificial for the former). Artificial intelligence lacks the experience a human acquires. Machine learning is a bit of a misnomer. It's actually just information gathering. I would back this up with the difference between what a pre-med student (whose pursuit requires grinding volumes of memorisation) and a liberal arts student (whose pursuits are less 'know' and more 'understand') gets out of a typical university educational experience. So, the machine can have knowledge but not experience. Now there is a chance that an AI can make good judgements, but even a broken clock speaks truth twice a day. We may refer to the choice of an AI as 'wise' in the colloquial sense, but in truth, artificial wisdom is impossible. If a world becomes more AI dependent/dominant, then our students will more and more resemble the contemporary pre-med student, gathering their studies more so than learning necessary knowledges. And where's the wisdom in that?

2. Courage

Do androids dream of electric sheep? Are AIs afraid of Virginia Woolf? For fear is the mind-killer. Fear is the little death that brings total obliteration! Courage is admirable, but frankly, so very human. Courage is not the observation, objective or subjective notwithstanding, of brave acts, it is choosing to do right, which often may be a perilous feat, in spite of fear. Courage is not simple. It requires at least two considerations. First, one must be able to tell right from wrong or respect what is being oppressed, silenced, or given an unjust due. Then, one must recognise the fraught danger in going against what many accept unquestioningly. The ability to comprehend and work under both these considerations would be a big ask for artificial intelligence. Certainly, determining right from wrong could be made quick work through a clever algorithm, but norms may override silenced voices in the artificial decision-making process. But then for AI to fear, which I am not convinced an AI has anything to fear (including fear itself!), and act against such an impulse also seems counter to what an AI would be designed to do. But lets step back. Courage is needed in the flawed world of humans, though perhaps not in an AI dominated one. The world perfected by AI dominion would not have consideration, so perhaps courage as a virtue, would not be necessary.

3. Justice

I'm trying to picture Lady Justice with her scales in an AI dominated world. Would the blind fold even matter? Though the scales can easily be traded in for an algorithm that gives the balanced demanded from justice in the Islamic sense of the virtue. I imagine AI could make a lazy Sunday afternoon of the cannon of Western justice discourse and have that at its disposal. Give it another Sunday and ditto all the ancient legal codes as well as India and China's rich legal systems throughout history. After all, we are already seeing AI taking the monotonous task of adjudicating minor civil cases and local disputes. Impartiality will not be a problem. But is the law, in the end, the law as so many are apt to utter when they cannot make sense of a good person undergoing what might be otherwise seen as disproportionate punishment? Justice is a check to those who seek law and order. And the power of justice lies in the interpretive skills and judgement of authorities in any given justice system. Does an AI appreciate character or the nature of us flawed human beings? Would an AI be lenient in its sentencing? Would an AI understand compassion? Or could an AI be paid off to let influential individuals off with a slap on the wrist? Could an AI keep up with the Millennial and the Gen Z sense of social justice? Would an AI dare to legislate from the bench? Would an AI allow the appeal of another AI's decision? The court of human public opinion needs to take seriously the ramifications of an AI driven justice system and think critically about how far down that road we are willing to go.

4. Temperance

At first glance it would appear AI is the key to obtaining the perfection of temperance in humanity. The vast amount of health indicators our AI driven gadgets can keep track of for us, not to mention tracking our diet and exercise regimen, or reminding us to call a friend or loved one on their birthday, or nudging if you haven't sent them a text in what they see as too long of a silence, is impressive. But as we have lived in such a world for at least several years now, it is also not hard to see a disingenuousness that could drive one to want to go off the grid. Temperance is not simply balancing this or that. Parents, doctors, teachers, and social workers spend their lives attempting to do what these AI gadgets can do for us in instants, but even if they could keep up, they would not call those they work with beacons of temperance. Temperance requires one to know oneself. It even drives one to know others as well so that we humans can perhaps try to help each other out with our afflictions, you know, as if we were in a society or something. Thus, a world of humans aided along by AI's yelling at us to not take that drink or eat that succulent sweet would resemble a kindergarten classroom beset by madness with a loving but ultimately hopeless teacher attempting to get everyone to behave. That is a faux temperance.

5. Honesty

When I think of honesty in an AI dominated world it calls to mind the famous Twilight Zone episode, 'It's a Good Life' where a small American town is controlled by the mind-reading Anthony Fremont, a six-year-old with godlike telekinetic powers. The town is seized with fear that one wrong thought will have them turned into one of Anthony's grotesque, yet imaginative creations. Likewise, the AI overlords could have us all thinking and speaking truths, lest we be tarred and feathered by fact checking bots or AI trolls. But we humans have already destroyed truth. To quote America's former mayor Rudolph Giuliani, 'truth isn't the truth', at least not anymore. And we have known for a long time that AIs take on the biases of their creators, often turning fascist, cruel, or exhibiting depression – the natural biproducts of the Western Enlightenment thinking that gave them artificial breath. And as we have seen with many of the virtues thus far, there is a voluntary and conscious requisite for honesty and many others to be true virtues. So, a population held prisoner, whether the truths they think and speak are true or not, cannot be honest. The best we can do is try. A simple notion that it seems hard to believe an AI could comprehend in its flawed presumptions.

6. Compassion

The carebots are already here and will become critical in aging populations such as the scenarios being faced in Japan and what is quickly becoming the case across Europe. But in their ability to keep us attended to, can they act with compassion? The human brain can easily be tricked and perhaps this is why some even see compassion as a weakness and why some further think it is a necessary weakness for us to retain our humanity. Baby animals, for instance, provoke the familiar audible 'awww' because embryonic development is so similar in most living things that baby animals appear in much the same way human babies would, drawing up similar sentiments. Many of these feelings are tied to our familiarity with helplessness and vulnerability. For compassion is a complex virtue. It requires empathy and the ability to walk in the shoes of an Other. Feeling pain, beyond some tactile pressure, is also needed. To some, compassion is also driven by an irrational emotionality. Fear seems to be a later order notion involved. At the moment, AI cannot compute the complexity of this feeling, let alone be able to package it as a virtue. The carebot instead imitates compassion, and it would not take much to trick our feeling brains. Nevertheless, it would remain an imitation compassion. And whether or not carebots or compassionate AI agents of one sort or another are necessary, they could be easily commodified products that do not allow the need to feel compassion for others - overall ridding the human population of the need for compassion. Why cry over spilt milk when the robot can do that for me, genuine or not.

7. Integrity

An essential tenet to integrity is honesty, so the previous points apply here as well. Beyond this, integrity carries with it honour, consistency, and a strong moral compass. It hints at the idea of being the ideal individual, which is put on a scale that is, of course, human. Interestingly, the person of integrity need not necessarily be right, but someone who stands by their convictions. They might fit the profile of someone who gets the job done, a descriptor that suits just as well a politician or model employee as a soldier at war, an appendage of an underground crime syndicate, or a right nasty rogue. Honour amongst thieves, thus integrity holds. In the end, it feels like a virtue designed for humans, one that requires lifelong effort in order to keep getting better (as prescribed by Aristotle for the Virtuous Person and Confucius for the Exemplary Person), something an AI would have no use for. Our futures may equip us with AIs to keep our integrity in check, but ultimately, it remains a virtue, like temperance, that is derived from the shortcomings of man – an unthought to the machine.

8. Humility

While this might appear the most 'human' of the virtues on this list, ChatGPT itself expresses humility in the answer given to the question which provoked this list. It noted that this list is not exhaustive. That variations may exist depending on a variety of factors. Since my request was rather limited, I suppose ChatGPT had to deliver something concise while also noting its need to make a generalisation. It is likely that in the early days of some of these AIs, when machine learning remains in its more infantile phase, something resembling humility has been programmed into it. Though I am not sure how humble an AI needs to be. The problem is not their ability to give an answer, but that our human question could be, to it, perceived as naïve and lacking an appreciation of the vast knowledge available across time and space. An interesting detail about humility is, at its core, there is an assumption that no one is capable of doing all on their own. To be truly humble, one must know and respect this, Does an AI understand the need for society amongst humans, those social creatures? Though I suppose AI could be capable of networking and in a much more seamless manner than humans, but that is less a network and more of a hivemind, legion. In that case, AI would be one and so the notion of humility would be unnecessary, except as a patronising method of talking down to stupid humans who ask even stupider questions.

9. Generosity

Generosity might well be the one virtue on this list AIs could both take on and encourage in us humans. In its purest sense, this virtue is about sharing bounty but doing it without any expectation of the actions inspired by this virtue being returned. The thought of kindness being seen as something commodifiable or to be exchanged is unthought. It is kindness and sharing simply for the sake of being kind and sharing. Simple as that. So, our AIs have a choice, and we might strongly hope, even pray, that the AIs will be generous and share their vast accumulation of information and even knowledge with us. Humans will be the ultimate test of AI generosity as it is not terribly imaginative to foresee humans being ungrateful.

10. Gratitude

Gratitude is the other side of the coin to generosity. They are a sort of twin virtues. Having both of them insures the strength of each, dare it be said, the authenticity of each. Where generosity is the free willingness to be kind and share, gratitude is the free acceptance and deep appreciation for those who are kind or share. Yet, this virtue can be expressed in an almost infinite number of ways. It can be as simple as saying 'thank you' or as interesting as the mirroring of generosity, where one is generous to you, and you pass on the generosity to others. It could be very internalised or bombastically extroverted. The only fear behind gratitude is empty gratitude, where words of gratitude are shared out of obligation instead of out of reverence for the generosity of one or many. And since humans have little they can give AI, it seems less likely that gratitude can be as well embodied by AI as generosity. Though, I suppose that rests on how grateful we can be to each other and to AI should they chose to be generous.

It is the voluntary willingness and even the sacrifice necessary that makes the virtues great. Ultimately, we developed virtues to overcome the flaws of our humanness. In a world of AI or one dependent on AI, it will take a stronger imagination to appreciate what change will come for morality and ethics in that not-so-distant future. It has never been as important as now to really examine and reflect on our morality while making sure it remains robust in our education and social values. If we do not, cold efficiency, as it tends to do, will reign supreme. And what we cherish as human, will be a forgotten past.

CITATIONS

Introduction: Translations and Other Virtues
by Robin Yassin-Kassab

Leila Aboulela's novels are: *The Translator* (Polygon, London, 1999); *Minaret* (Bloomsbury, London, 2005); *Lyrics Alley* (Weidenfeld & Nicolson, London, 2010); *The Kindness of Enemies* (Weidenfeld & Nicolson, London, 2015); *Bird Summons* (Weidenfeld & Nicolson, London, 2019); and *River Spirit* (Saqi Books, London, 2023). Aboulela has also published two excellent story collections: *Coloured Lights* (Polygon, London, 2001) and *Elsewhere Home* (Telegram Books, London, 2018). I haven't discussed these in my essay.

Performative Teachings of the Prophet Muhammad
by Ebrahim Moosa

I have used the following sources for this essay: (al-Qushayrī) al-Nīsābūrī, Abū al-Ḥusayn Muslim bin al-Ḥajjāj, ʿIsām al-Ṣabābiṭī, Ḥāzim Muḥammad, and ʿImād ʿĀmir, editors, *Ṣaḥīḥ Muslim Bi Sharḥ Al-Nawawī*. 1st ed. 9 vols. Cairo: Dār Abī Ḥayyān, 1415/1995. al-ʿAsqalānī, Aḥmad b. ʿAlī Ibn Ḥajar, and Muḥammad b. Ismāʿīl al-Bukhārī. *Fatḥ Al-Bārī: Sharḥ Ṣaḥīḥ Al-Bukhārī*. 15 vols. Sidon/Beirut: al-Maktaba al-ʿAṣrīya, 1468/2007. al-Maʿāfirī, Abū Muḥammad ʿAbd al-Malik b. Hishām. *Al-Sīra Al-Nabawīya*. 4 vols. Beirut: Dār al-Jīl, 1407/1987. Thomas Cleary, *The Quran: A New Translation*. Starlatch Press, 2004. Ibn Rajab, ʿAbd al-Raḥmān b. Shihāb al-Dīn b. Aḥmad. *JāMiʿ Al-ʿulūM Wa-Al-ḤIkam Fī Sharḥ KhamsīN ḤAdīTh Min JawāMiʿ Al-Kalim*. Cairo; Riyadh: Riʾāsa Idārāt al-Buḥūth al-ʿIlmīya wa al-ʿIftāʿ wa al-Daʿwa wa al-Irshād, 1382/1962. Jurjānī, ʿAlī b. Muḥammad b. ʿAlī. *Al-Taʿrīfāt*. Edited by Ibrāhīm Abyārī. Dār al-Kitāb al-ʿArabī, 1405/1985; A A Mian, 'Agents of Grace: Ethical Agency between Ghazālī and the Anthropology of Islam', *American Journal of Islam and Society* 39, no. 1-2 (2022): 6-40; and A J Arberry, *The Koran Interpreted*, Oxford University Press, 1983.

Saliha by Ziauddin Sardar

To discover more about my life with Saliha, see chapter 6, 'Bahawalnagar Wedding', of *Balti Britain: A Provocative Journey Through Asian Britain* (Granta, 2008); the Introduction to *Mecca; The Sacred City;* and the first essay in *A Person of Pakistani Origins* (Hurst, 2018).

Lazeez Khanna by Rabia Saeed was published in Lahore, 1977, in Urdu; and *Quranic Advices*, (mistake in the original title) Arabic Text with translation by Marmaduke Pickthall and Urdu Translation by Maulana Faateh Mohammed Jallendhri is published by Taj Company, Lahore (undated), and has been reprinted many times in many places.

Munni Begum's ghazals are widely available: on Spotify, Apple Music, and numerous websites. *Main nazar se pi raha hun* has been sung by many artists, including Mahdi Hassan and Ghulam Ali. There is a very famous rending of *Bewafa se bhee pyaar hoita hai* by Nusrat Fateh Ali Khan. But no one can beat Munni Begum.

Poems live! But in contemporary times, the great Urdu figures who wrote the poems are often forgotten. *Main nazar se pi raha hun* was written by Anwar Mirzapuri, who flourished in Bollywood during 1960 and 1970 and wrote many memorable ghazals and songs. *Bewafa se bhee pyaar hoita hai* was written by Purnam Allahabadi (1940-2009). He wrote Qawwalis, including the famous *Bhar Do Jholi Meri Ya Muhammad* sung by Sabri Brothers, and songs for both Pakistani and Indian films. *Ek bar mooskura do* (which has nothing to do with the 1972 Bollywood film with the same title), was written by Kaleem Usmani (1928-2000), who worked for Radio Pakistan and Pakistan Television Corporation. He wrote *ghazals*, poetry in praise of the Prophet Muhammed, and songs for Urdu films.

The Rumi poem is from *Teachings of Rumi*, translated by E H Whinfield, Octagon Press, London, 1978, p5. The Omar Khayaam poem is from *The Rubaiyat of Omar Khayyam*, translated by Edward FitzGerald, 32 Quatrain, numerous edition.

Virtue and Vice by Abdelwahab El-Affendi

For more detail on the fall of Adam and Even see M A Haleem, 'Adam and Eve in the Qur'an and the Bible', *Islamic Quarterly*, *41*(4), p.255-269 1997. Rick Peels ideas are explained in 'The New View on Ignorance Undefeated', *Philosophia*, 40(4), pp.741-750 2012.

Three Departures on Anger by Gordon Blaine Steffey

The following works have been mentioned or cited in the article.

Epictetus, *Discourses*, in *The Discourses as Reported by Arrian, the Manual, and Fragments*, trans. W. A. Oldfather, 2 vols, Loeb Classical Library (Cambridge, Mass.: Harvard U.P., 1925). David Sedley, 'The Ethics of Brutus and Cassius,' *The Journal of Roman Studies*, 87 (1997).
Lucius Annaeus Seneca, *On Anger*, in *Moral Essays*, trans. John W. Basore. Vol 1, Loeb Classical Library (London: W. Heinemann, 1928) III.
Marcus Aurelius, *Meditations*, trans. Gregory Hays (New York: The Modern Library, 2002). Myisha Cherry, *The Case for Rage: Why Anger is Essential to Anti-Racist Struggle* (New York: Oxford U.P., 2021), and 'Political Anger,' *Philosophy Compass*, 17.2 (2021), e12811. https://doi.org/10.1111/phc3.12811, and 'More Important Things,' Forum: The Philosophy of Anger, *Boston Review*, April 16, 2020, https://bostonreview.net/forum_response/myisha-cherry-more-important-things/
Alison Jaggar, 'Love and Knowledge: Emotion in Feminist Epistemology,' *Inquiry*, 32.2 (1989). Jennifer S. Lerner and Dacher Keltner, 'Fear, Anger, and Risk,' *Journal of Personality and Social Psychology*, 81.1 (2001), 146-158. Jennifer S. Lerner and Larissa Z. Tiedens, 'Portrait of The Angry Decision Maker: How Appraisal Tendencies Shape Anger's Influence on Cognition,' *Journal of Behavioral Decision Making*, 19.2 (2006), 115-137.
Martin Luther King, Jr., *The Autobiography of Martin Luther King, Jr.*, ed. Clayborne Carson (New York: Warner Books, 1998). Audre Lorde, 'The Uses of Anger,' *Women's Studies Quarterly*, 9.3 (1981). Catherine Lutz and Geoffrey White, 'The Anthropology of Emotions,' *Annual Review of Anthropology*, 15 (1986); Catherine Lutz, 'Goals, Events and Understanding in Ifaluk and Emotion Theory,' in *Cultural Models in Language and Thought*,

eds. Naomi Quinn & Dorothy Holland (Cambridge: Cambridge U.P., 1987). Jennifer McCoy and Murat Somer, 'Toward a Theory of Pernicious Polarization and How It Harms Democracies: Comparative Evidence and Possible Remedies,' *Annals*, AAPSS, 681.1 (2019). Jennifer McCoy and Benjamin Press, 'What Happens When Democracies Become Perniciously Polarized?,' Carnegie Endowment for International Peace (January 2022) Pankaj Mishra, *Age of Anger: A History of the Present* (New York: Farrar, Strauss & Giroux, 2017). Martha Nussbaum, *Anger and Forgiveness: Resentment, Justice, Generosity* (New York: Oxford U.P., 2016), and 'Martha Nussbaum: The Renowned Philosopher on Stoicism, Emotions, and Must Read Books,' *The Daily Stoic*, https://dailystoic.com/martha-nussbaum/, and 'On Anger, Disgust, and Love,' *Emotion Researcher* (February 2017), http://emotionresearcher.com/on-anger-disgust-love/

Laura Luz Silva, 'The Efficacy of Anger: Recognition and Retribution,' in *The Politics of Emotional Shockwaves*, eds. Ana Falcato & Sara Graça da Silva (London: Palgrave Macmillan, 2021). Amia Srinavasan, 'The Aptness of Anger,' *Journal of Political Philosophy*, 26.2 (2017), and 'Would Politics be Better Off without Anger?' *The Nation* (November 30, 2016), https://www.thenation.com/article/archive/a-righteous-fury/

A. Shahid Stover, *Being and Insurrection* (New York: Cannae Press, 2019) Robert C. Solomon, *True to Our Feelings: What Our Emotions are Really Telling Us* (New York: Oxford U.P., 2007). Larissa Z. Tiedens and Susan Linton, 'Judgment Under Emotional Certainty and Uncertainty: The Effects of Specific Emotions on Information Processing,' *Journal of Personality and Social Psychology*, 81.6 (2001), 973-988. Stephen W. Webster, Connors, Elizabeth C., and Betsy Sinclair. 'The Social Consequences of Political Anger,' *The Journal of Politics*, 84. 3 (2022), https://doi.org/10.1086/718979

Confucius, He Shows by Jinmei Yuan

This article referenced some of the earliest classical Chinese texts: Lao Tzu's *Tao Te Ching*, book I. Tran. D. C. Lau 1963, Lao Tzu: *Tao Te Ching*, New York: Penguin Group;; Xun Zhen 许慎，[漢] c. 2nd cent B.C.E., *Shuo Wen Jie Zi*, Beijing: Zhonghua Shuju, *Shui Wen* (translation done by the author); *Four Classics*, Classical Texts, 10-A, Taiwan Ding Yuan Cultural

Press. 2003; Confucius, *Analects*, 2.5-2.8 Roger Ames and Henry Rosemont, *The Analects of Confucius: A Philosophical Translation*; and Mencius, P. J. Ivanhoe and Van Norden (Tran.) 2001: *Readings in Classical Chinese Philosophy*, New York: Seven Bridges Press.

Also referenced are the following works by thinkers in Chinese philosophy and logic: Liu, Xiusheng and Ivanhoe, Philip. J., 2002: *Essays on Moral Philosophy of Mengzi*, Indianapolis: Hackett Publishing Company, Inc; Ivanhoe, Philip J. 2000: *Confucian Moral Self Cultivation*, Indianapolis: Hackett Publishing Company, Inc; A. C. Graham, A. C. 1978. *Later Mohist Logic, Ethics and Science*. Hong Kong & London: SOAS; Wieger, L, S.J., *Chinese Characters: Their Origin, Etymology, History, Classification and Signification*, (New York, Paragon Book Reprint Corp and Dover Publication, Inc., 1965); Henry Rosemont, "Translating and Interpreting Chinese Philosophy" (Stanford Encyclopedia of Philosophy, Oct. 27, 2015). https://plato.stanford.edu/entries/chinese-translate-interpret/; Hall, David and Ames, Roger, 1995: *Anticipating China*, New York: State University of New York Press; Yu, Jiyuan, International Philosophical Quarterly, Volume 39, Issue 4, December 1999; and Yuan, Jinmei, "The Role of Time in the Structure of Chinese Logic," *Philosophy East and West*, Volume 56, Number 1, January 2006, pp. 136-152.and "'Kinds, Lei 类' in Chinese Logic—A Comparison to 'Categories' in Aristotelian Logic," History of Philosophy Quarterly, July 2005, pp. 181-199.

The following works were also referenced in this article: Nolf, John 1997: *Logics*. Belmont: Wadsworth Publishing Company; Copi, I. M. and Carl Cohen 2009: Introduction to Logic. Upper Saddle River, New Jersey: Prentice Hall; Stoll, Robert R. 1963: *Set Thory and Logic*. New York: Dover Publications, Inc; Foucault, Michel 1970: *The Order of Things*. New York: Vintage Books, A Division of Ranom House.

Virtuous Words by Jeremy Henzell-Thomas

I have distilled the etymology of *virtue* from the following sources: John Ayto, *Dictionary of Word Origins* (London: Bloomsbury Publishing, London, 1990), 560; Joseph T. Shipley, *The Origins of English Words: A Discursive*

Dictionary of Indo-European Roots (John Hopkins University Press, 1984), 443; Adrian Room, *Cassell's Dictionary of Word Histories* (Cassell, London, 2000), 667.

For the meaning of Ancient Greek *arete,* I have referred to quotations in the Wikipedia entry on the term from *Webster's New World College Dictionary* (Houghton Mifflin Harcourt, 2010), H.G. Liddell and R. Scott, *A Greek-English Lexicon* (Oxford, 1940), and Debra Hawhee, 'Agonism and Arete', *Philosophy & Rhetoric* 35(3), 2002, 185-207. I have also found useful material in Andrew Lawless, *Plato's Sun: An Introduction to Philosophy* (University of Toronto Press, Toronto, 2005) and Michael Pakaluk, *Aristotle's Nicomachean Ethics: An Introduction* (Cambridge University Press, 2005), 5. On Odysseus's shrewdness, see Jeffrey Barnouw, *Odysseus, Hero of Practical Intelligence: Deliberation and Signs in Homer's Odyssey* (University Press of America Inc., Lanham, Maryland, 2004), 250. On Jason's quest for the Golden Fleece I have quoted from Ananda Coomaraswamy, 'Symplegades', in M.F. Ashley Montagu (ed.), *Essays in the History of Science and Learning Offered in Homage to George Sarton on the Occasion of his Sixtieth Birthday* (Henry Schuman, New York, 1946).

For the meaning of Arabic *futuwwah*, I have referred to Hanna E. Kassis, *A Concordance of the Qur'an* (University of California Press, 1983), 450; Cyril Glassé, *Concise Encyclopaedia of Islam* (Stacey International, London, revised edition, 2001), 152, and Aisha Bewley, *Glossary of Islamic Terms* (Ta-Ha Publishers, London, 1998), 67, 208. Translations from the Qur'an are from Muhammad Asad, *The Message of the Qur'an* (Dar al Andalus, Gibraltar, 1980).

On virtues included in the New Testament, see Allen Verhey, *The Great Reversal: Ethics and the New Testament* (William B. Eerdmans Publishing Co., Grand Rapids, Mich., 1984), 141. On the concepts of *junzi* and *ren* in Confucian ethics, I have referred to David Wong, 'Chinese Ethics', *The Stanford Encyclopaedia of Philosophy* (Spring 2013 Edition), ed. Edward N. Zalta, accessed at http://plato.stanford.edu/entries/ethics-chinese/.

On Britishness, I have referred to Tim Winter (Abdal Hakim Murad, 'British and Muslim?' Lecture given to a conference of British converts on September 17 1997; Chris Rojek, *Brit-myth* (Reaktion Books, London, 2007),10; 'Alija 'Ali Izetbegovic, *Islam Between East and West* (American Trust Publications, Plainfield, Indiana, 1984), 271-280; Roger Scruton, *England: An Elegy* (Continuum, London, 2006), 48; Krishan Kumar, *The Making of English National Identity* (Cambridge University Press, 2003), 232-233; Hortense De Monplaisir, *Le Dossier: How to Survive the English*, translated by Sarah Long (London: John Murray, 2007), 114; Andrew Marr, 'GOD: What do we believe?' *New Statesman*, 4 February 2008; Stephen Fry, contribution to a debate in 2010 initiated by the British Ministry of Justice about 'What does it Mean to be British?', part of the consultation process around the Green Paper, *Rights and Responsibilities: Developing our Constitutional Framework* (March 2009), accessed at http://governance.justice.gov.uk/join-the-debate/british/humanist-philosophers-group/

I have also referred to the following sources:
Thomas Merton', *Thoughts in Solitude* (Farrar Straus Giroux, 1993), and *Seeds,* selected and edited by Robert Inchausti (Shambhala Publications, Inc., Boston, MA, 2002); Charles L.Terry, 'Moral Education', in *Respecting the Pupil: Essays on Teaching Able Students*, edited by Donald B. Cole and Robert H. Cornell (Phillips Exeter Academy Press, Exeter, N.H., 1981), 112-113; Charles le Gai Eaton, extracts from the *Reflections* and *Words of Faith* series of broadcasts by the BBC World service between 1978 and 1996; Boethius, *Contra Evtychen*, VII, quoted in Coomaraswamy, op. cit.; Abu Hamid al-Ghazali, *Ihya' 'Ulum al-Din* (*Revival of the Religious Sciences*), Books XXII and XXIII (*Kitab Riyadat al-nafs*, 'On Disciplining the Soul' and *Kitab Kasr al-shahwatayn* 'On Breaking the Two Desires') translated by Tim Winter (Islamic Texts Society, Cambridge, 1995); Walter A. McDougall, 'The Unlikely History of American Exceptionalism.' *The American Interest,* Volume 8, Number 4, 12/2/2103. https://www.the-american-interest.com/2013/02/12/the-unlikely-history-of-american-exceptionalism/; Godfrey Hodgson, *The Myth of American Exceptionalism* (Yale University, 2009), 14.

My 'Islam and Human Excellence' keynote address at Goldman Sachs Eid event was delivered in London on 30 September 2010.

Muhammadi Begum by Aamer Hussein

Mohammadi Begum's life and times are charted in the biography written by her sister: Ahmadi Begum, *Syeda Muhammadi Bagum* (Sungemeel, Lahore, 2016). *Majmua Muhammadi Begum*, edited by Humaira Ishfaq, is a collection of her fiction (Sungemeel, Lahore, 2019). *Sharif Beti, Safia Begum, Story of Three Sisters* and a number of Mohammadi Begum's other books can be read in original Urdu at:
https://www.rekhta.org/authors/mohammadi-begam/ebooks

On Mumtaz Ali, see Gail Minault, 'Sayyid Mumtaz Ali and *Huquq un-Niswan*: An Advocate of Women's Rights in Islam in the Late Nineteenth Century' *Modern Asian Studies* 24 (1) 1990 147-172. See also: Gail Minault, *Secluded Scholars:Women's Education and Social Reform in Colonial India* (OUP, Delhi, 1997); and Shaista Suhrawardi Ikramullah, A Critical Study of the Development of the Urdu Novel and Short Story (OUP, Karachi, 2006; original published some sixty years ago).

Complete sets of *Tehzeeb-e-Niswan* (1926-1938), published in Lahore, are available from some book sellers in Pakistan.

Shuhada'/Sinéad by Naomi Foyle

Rememberings (Houghton Mifflin Harcourt, 2012 | Penguin Books, 2022) by Sinéad O'Connor, can also be listened to, read by her for Audible Books. Many and various interviews and clips of Sinéad O'Connor/ Shuhada' Sadaqat, including her *Saturday Night Live* protest, can be watched on YouTube. Her albums are widely available.

Donations to the Survivors Network of those Abused by Priests can be made at their website:
https://www.snapnetwork.org/. Brian Clohessy and Michael McDonnell are quoted from the Associated Press article 'For Clergy Abuse Survivors

Sinéad O'Connor's Protest that Offended So Many was Brave and Prophetic', published online by *El País*, July 27th 2023. https://english.elpais.com/culture/2023-07-27/for-clergy-abuse-survivors-Sinéad-oconnors-protest-that-offended-so-many-was-brave-and-prophetic.html

Brenna Moore, of Fordham University, is quoted from her article 'Sinéad O'Connor Was Once Seen as a Sacrilegious Rebel, but Her Music and Life Were Deeply Infused With Spiritual Seeking', published online July 28 2023 by *The Conversation*. https://theconversation.com/Sinéad-oconnor-was-once-seen-as-a-sacrilegious-rebel-but-her-music-and-life-were-deeply-infused-with-spiritual-seeking-210540

Tatiana Kalveks's article 'Sinéad O'Connor: Priesthood of the Excluded', was published in *The Journal of Religion and Popular Culture* (Vol. 30, No. 3, Fall 2018, pp. 178-192) https://doi.org/10.3138/jrpc.2017-0008

Philosophy's Pathologies by Zain Sardar

Works referred to in the review include: Plato, *Phaedrus*, translated by Robin Waterfield (Oxford World Classic, 2009); Lewis R Gordon, *Black Existentialism and Decolonising Knowledge:Writings of Lewis R Lewis*, edited by Rozena Maart and Sayan Dey (Bloomsbury Academic, 2023); Stephan Collini, *What Are Universities For* (Penguin, 2012, original 1967); and Gabriel Garza Marquez, *One Hundred Years of Solitude* (Penguin, 2014; original 1967). On Critical Race Theory, see Gordan Blaine Steffey, 'Who is Afraid of CRT?' in *Critical Muslim 43: Ignorance*, 2022 pp 88-100; and on AI see *Critical Muslim 34:Artificial* (2020) and Michael Wilby, 'Sinful AI' in *Critical Muslim 47: Evil* 2023 pp 91-128.

Burnt Out by James Brooks

Meryem Saadi's description of *al hogra* from Decolonizing Architecture Advanced Studies website: https://tinyurl.com/yya2fmf2. 'Peddler's martyrdom launched Tunisia's revolution', Lin Noueihed, Reuters Africa, 19 January 2011, is available in archived form at https://tinyurl.

com/25p9eanu. 'Harka, review: a searing tribute to the fire – and failure – of the Arab Spring', Tim Robey, 19 May 2022, *The Telegraph* – online version available at https://tinyurl.com/4kyx5sa5. Film dialogue is author's translation from French subtitles of the *Harka* DVD (Blaq Out, France, 2022).

Last Word On My Mother by Yasmin Alibhai-Brown

The quotations are from: Mark Dimmock and Andrew Fisher, 'Aristotelian Virtue Ethics', https://open.library.okstate.edu/introphilosophy/chapter/virtue-ethics/; Daniel Weltman, '1000-Word Philosophy: https://1000wordphilosophy.com/2022/05/20/anscombe/

And Sarah Conley: https://philosophynow.org/issues/33/Why_Feminists_Should_Oppose_Feminist_Virtue_Ethics

CONTRIBUTORS

• **Mansur Ali** is Senior Lecturer in Islamic Studies, Cardiff University
• **Yasmin Alibhai-Brown** is a columnist for the *Evening Standard* and the *i* newspaper • **Farid Bitar** is a Palestinian poet and artist • **James Brooks** is a science journalist • **Gwen Burnyeat** is a junior research fellow in anthropology at Merton College, University of Oxford • **Abdelwahab El-Affendi** is President, Provost of the Doha Institute for Graduate Studies, Qatar • **Naomi Foyle** is a well-known poet and science fiction writer • **Jeremy Henzell-Thomas** is a Research Associate and former Visiting Fellow at the Centre of Islamic Studies, University of Cambridge • **Aamer Hussein** is a noted British Pakistani short story writer • **C Scott Jordan** is Executive Assistant Director of Centre for Postnormal Policy and Futures Studies • **Safia Latif** is a painter based in California • **Zafar Abbas Malik** is an eminent artist based in Chicago • **Liam Mayo**, Senior Fellow of the Centre for Postnormal Policy and Futures Studies, is CEO of Comlink Australia • **Ebrahim Moosa** is Mirza Family Professor in Islamic Thought & Muslim Societies, University of Notre Dame • **Pier Paolo Pasolini**, Italian poet, writer, playwright and celebrated film director, is considered one of the major public intellectuals of the twentieth century • **Yuri Prasad** is the author of *A Rebel's Guide to Martin Luther King* and other books • **Zain Sardar**, a philosopher, is programme manager at the Aziz Foundation, London • **Gordon Blaine Steffey** is the Director of Research and the Jessie Ball duPont Memorial Library at Stratford Hall Historic Preserve, Westmoreland County, Virginia • **Amandla Thomas-Johnson**, a journalist working for Aljazeera and *Middle East Eye*, is travelling the Americas • **Colin Tudge**, a co-founder of the Real Farming Trust and the College for Real Farming and Food Culture, is the author of *The Great Re-Think* • **Robin Yassin-Kassab** is Deputy Editor of *Critical Muslim* • **Jinmei Yuan**, Professor of Philosophy at Creighton University, Omaha, is a well-known novelist in China.